GIRLHOOD IN THE B

NATION OF NATIONS:
IMMIGRANT HISTORY AS AMERICAN HISTORY
General Editor: Matthew Jacobson
Founding Editors: Matthew Jacobson and Werner Sollors

Girlhood in the Borderlands

Mexican Teens Caught in the
Crossroads of Migration

Lilia Soto

NEW YORK UNIVERSITY PRESS
New York

NEW YORK UNIVERSITY PRESS
New York
www.nyupress.org

References to Internet websites (URLs) were accurate at the time of writing. Neither the author nor New York University Press is responsible for URLs that may have expired or changed since the manuscript was prepared.

Library of Congress Cataloging-in-Publication Data
Names: Soto, Lilia, author.
Title: Girlhood in the borderlands : Mexican teens caught
in the crossroads of migration / Lilia Soto.
Description: New York : New York University Press, [2018] |
Includes bibliographical references and index.
Identifiers: LCCN 2017045036 | ISBN 9781479838400 (cl : alk. paper) |
ISBN 9781479862016 (pb : alk. paper)
Subjects: LCSH: Teenage girls—Mexico. | Teenage immigrants—United States. |
Transnationalism. | Mexico—Emigration and immigration—Social aspects. | United
States—Emigration and immigration—Social aspects.
Classification: LCC HQ799.M6 S68 2018 | DDC 305.235/20972—dc23
LC record available at https://lccn.loc.gov/2017045036

New York University Press books are printed on acid-free paper, and their binding materials are chosen for strength and durability. We strive to use environmentally responsible suppliers and materials to the greatest extent possible in publishing our books.

Manufactured in the United States of America

10 9 8 7 6 5 4 3 2 1

Also available as an ebook

To my parents, Matias and Maria Elena Soto,
gracias por todo. Soy por ustedes.

To my sisters—las chiquillas—Lupe, Olivia, Silvia, Martha and
Lorena, thank you for being with me.

To my nephew Jiulian, I welcome you back.

To my niece Sofia, thank you for being so lovely.

To my nephew Eztli, my chiquilinguis,
I love you to the moon and back.

To my sobrino-nieto Jay, thank you for brightening our lives.

CONTENTS

Introduction

I have moved this project forward by looking backwards.[1] I began this research in the early 2000s looking back on my childhood experiences of migrating to the United States in the 1980s. I decided to conduct a multi-site research project in the U.S. and Mexico focused on young im/migrant women to see if contemporary migrant girls had the same aspirations, anxieties, expectations, and experiences that I had had. My father had made repeated trips back and forth between Zinapécuaro, Michoacán, and Napa, California, before he settled in the United States permanently. My mother and siblings remained in Mexico where we anticipated moving north someday. Fragmentation and transnationalism defined our family life. It was fragmented by moves to the U.S. and back to Mexico, and then to the U.S. once again, and by visits, phone calls, letters, and other efforts to share affection and intimacy with family members living in two different countries. We did not simply move from our country of origin to our country of arrival, but lived physically and psychically inside and across national borders, simultaneously and sequentially.

I was born in Napa and raised in Zinapécuaro until the fourth grade. After living in a transnational family for ten years, my mother, five sisters, and I reunited with my father. I know Zinapécuaro and Napa very well, and have witnessed how migration, globalization, and the flow of transnational products have altered both locations. In this study, my insider's perspective allows me to have an intimate and personal understanding of girls' lives and place in which they live, yet my training as a researcher enables an analytic and impersonal understanding of social structures and social forces. I can view my objects of research both from close up and from far away. Over the years, I have witnessed how the city of Napa has grown to cater to its tourist industry and wine economy, while my annual trips back to Zinapécuaro allowed me to trace the changes in the town that were due to the national and transnational dimensions of its diaspora caused by new international trade policies and neoliberal restricting of the social wage. Having lived in the U.S. since 1986, I am no longer considered an immigrant, which removes me from the immediate immigrant experience. Still, I am able to ask interviewees about details I may have otherwise missed if I were a complete outsider, such as the importance of schooling, afterschool activities, and family life. Unlike most of the girls I interviewed, I was privileged enough to have been born in the U.S., allowing me to move legally within and across transnational social fields. Such privilege and mobility places me as a member outside of the immediate migrant community. I try to make the best of my contradictory and ambiguous identities—to negotiate my positionality—by listening to the girls, by not interrupting them or inserting myself in their interviews. Once I pressed the stop button to cease recording, the girls invariably asked me questions about me and my relationship to migration. During these moments, I usually revealed my story and shared why this project matters, why their stories need to be heard.

I began this research by interviewing nineteen Mexican immigrant girls between the ages of fourteen and seventeen who had arrived in Napa between 1998 and 2006.[2] Their testimony made me look backwards again, to wonder what their lives would have been like if they had never migrated. I returned to Zinapécuaro to conduct interviews with girls who had not migrated. My purpose was to explore how migration and transnational family life can shape a young girl's sense of time and place. Before migration, girls inhabit a time of waiting, of preparation for a departure on an unknown date. Those who do not migrate nonetheless must anticipate departures of many of their acquaintances. After migration and arrival in a new country, girls experience a sense of fragmented and disrupted temporality shaped by lost years of schooling in Mexico and a feeling of being behind other students in the United States. In the Napa area, unpredictable and irregular —yet chronically long—working hours in the vineyards and tourist venues produce additional experiences of fragmentation and anticipation: waiting to be hired, waiting to be called to report for work, waiting for the work shift and the school day to end, waiting for parents to arrive home from work and enable the girls to move from household and childcare chores to homework. On Sundays, Mexican migrants in Napa wait for the start of the Spanish-language mass in church, and afterwards they wait for the English-language church services to start and the Anglophone diners to clear the eating establishments to attend them, so that they can occupy the very tables they usually wait on at restaurants.

This study focuses on collecting testimonies about migration from teenage girls raised in transnational families. The majority of my interviewees came from households where the father was the initial migrant, followed by the rest of the family later.[3] These father-centered families appear to be heteronormative nuclear units, immersed in traditional practices of companionate marriage and child-rearing. Yet the disruption and fragmentation attendant to migration inflects them with new qualities. Living with an absent father creates new responsibilities, opportunities, and relations among mothers, daughters, sons, members of extended families, neighbors, and co-workers. At different times, family members may live in differently organized households. Girls who grew up with their fathers never or rarely at home do not so much experience family reunification in the country of arrival as a new kind of family formation. Seemingly heteronormative families become queer, not in the sense of being organized around same-sex relationships (although that does happen, too), but in the sense of improvising fundamentally new ways of being and knowing in the face of the inadequacy or inapplicability of traditional forms of association, affiliation, and affection.

Relying on their own memories, the girls time and again described their pre-migration lives as marked by anticipation, by waiting for fathers' visits, waiting for their documents to be approved, waiting for a car to arrive in the middle of the night to take them on a long journey to a clandestine border crossing spot, or waiting for their parents to decide which members of the family would move and when. Many doubted that their new lives would ever really begin, fearing that they would be caught forever in a state of suspended animation. All of this waiting provoked tremendous uncertainty and ambiguity about their past, present, and future. Three brief narratives illustrate the ways in which migration causes girls to inhabit a variety of temporalities:

1) Seventeen-year-old Silvia grew up in Michoacán in a household with a stay-at-home mother and a father who lived and worked in the United States. Her father had commuted back and forth

between countries, engaging in cyclical migration since he was a teenager.[4] Silvia grew up knowing her own journey north was simply a matter of time, so she lived in anticipation of her own migration. Her father filed paperwork so that Silvia, her mother, and her younger brother could legally join him in Napa. Because migration loomed, Silvia's schooling was cut short as she awaited the approval of her *papeles* (legal papers). By the time she migrated to Napa, she had missed four years of school.

2) Sixteen-year-old Elena had waited eagerly every year for thirteen years for her father's annual visits in April, July, and December. On those occasions when he did not show, she recalled the ache she felt as she awaited his next visit. During his visits, relatives always asked Elena's father when he would take his family to Napa. He usually responded with a discussion of the dangers of raising children—especially girls—in a liberal and non-traditional country, which he considered a major deterrent. Finally, when she turned ten years old, she noted a shift in her family's discussions and a movement towards her own journey north. It took three years for Elena, her two younger brothers, and her mother to join her father in Napa, the place where he had lived since he was sixteen years old.

3) Dulce, also sixteen, described waiting years for her father to finally make the decision to send for her. Although she had desired migration to the U.S. eagerly from a young age, the choice was never hers to make. It was her father's decision when to take Dulce to Napa, the place he had lived in since his late teens.

In all three accounts, the girls' fathers had engaged in cyclical migration since they themselves were teenagers. They commuted between nations, traveling to Napa for work but regularly returning to Mexico. Once the fathers felt they could provide for a family in the U.S., they could go back to Mexico, get married, and continue their cyclical migratory journey, forming the fragmented transnational families into which the girls were born.[5] For the girls, it seemed like simply a matter of time before they embarked on their own migratory journey. The testimonies by Silvia, Elena, and Dulce also point to a conflation of present and future tied to their fathers' commutes. These girls grew up feeling caught between their fathers' comings and goings. While waiting, the girls developed desires to travel to El Norte, desires that produced much uncertainty, ambiguity, and anxiety as they looked for signs or clues about their own possible journey.

Perhaps less obvious is how the decision to migrate was not theirs to make. It was influenced, as this book will examine, by the girls' age, gender, sex, and sexuality, but also by structural changes in the economic and political orders on both sides of the border. As children, the girls experienced migration through the frames of interpersonal family ties, yet the forces driving their parents' movements originated far away. They were born of trade agreements between nations, new patterns of investment and ownership on both sides of the border, and practices of immigration regulation designed to open up opportunities for U.S. investors in Mexico and to secure an easily exploitable, low-wage labor force in the U.S. Such workers' uncertain legal status made them unable to bargain freely over wages and working conditions. Seeing things from close up, the girls in my interviews conceived of the family as the principle site where decisions about their lives were made. Their anxieties, antagonisms, desires, and resentments focused on the family as the key social institution in their lives. But seeing things from the outside, it becomes clear that the family is not the major force promoting or regulating migration but rather the final factor restraining or allowing it, timing and shaping it. Just as international investors and financial institutions outsource production to low-wage regions and dump toxic waste in areas inhabited by relatively powerless people, they likewise outsource the emotional and psychic costs of dispossession to the households of migrant families struggling for subsistence and dignity. Even within these families, there is a hierarchy of agency. Migration by fathers imposes new demands on mothers who then need to pass along new responsibilities to their children. Immigrant daughters inherit particular burdens in this context, doing housework and caring for siblings so that mothers can work outside the home to make up for the temporary and sometimes permanent loss of support from migrant fathers. Girls who have migrated and girls about to migrate can come to resent what they perceive to be the power of their families to constrain their desires and choices without realizing that it is the relative powerlessness of those families in the global economy that shape the decisions they make.

The girls' vivid and emotional testimonies narrated to me in Napa led me back to my family's home terrain in Zinapécuaro, a *municipio* in the state of Michoacán, Mexico.[6] In 2010, I traveled there to conduct interviews with forty girls between the ages of thirteen and nineteen living in transnational families where, in the majority of cases, the father was the migrant. I wondered how the experiences of Mexican teenage girls living in families embedded in transnational migratory practices were similar and different from those of the girls I interviewed in Napa in 2006. I assumed I would find a similar group of girls saddened by a father's absence and living in a liminal state in Mexico, where time appeared to stand still while waiting persisted. Instead, I found a group of cheerful girls with complex and contradictory views about life in Mexico, the United States and their familial arrangements. On both sides of the border, I encountered young women with lives filled with what Avery F. Gordon (1997) defines as complex personhood.[7] But I was struck especially powerfully by the active imaginations and self-active sense of agency that girls in Mexico had developed in the midst of migratory practices surrounding them.[8] Three examples illustrate the point:

1) Eighteen-year-old Jessica is eager to return to the U.S. Her family moved back to Zinapécuaro from Chicago two months after she was born. As a U.S. citizen raised in Mexico, she has been persistent in trying to figure out how to get her passport so that she can return legally to the country where she was born. Her eyes glow with excitement when she speaks of her present life in Mexico and her possible future in the U.S.[9]

2) Camila is seventeen years old. She lives with her parents, while eight of her nine siblings are dispersed throughout Utah and California. Her brothers' remittances allow her to stay in school and, if accepted, she will attend the Escuela Médico Militar (Military Medical School) in Mexico City. She is very adamant about not wanting to move to the U.S. because she has witnessed what she describes as the materialistic and selfish behavior her brothers have developed there that has strained their relationships with their parents.[10]

3) Thirteen-year-old Toñita is the daughter of a once U.S. resident who has become a citizen, yet still commutes between Mexico and the U.S. She describes her understanding and acceptance of

the reasons behind her father's commutes. Now in her second year of middle school, she hopes one day to migrate to the U.S. to study engineering in college. She feels a degree from a U.S. university will open doors for employment. Her father, however, has refused to take her to the U.S. According to Toñita, he argues that, in El Norte, girls are exposed to dangers he could not protect her from.[11]

These three examples illustrate varied stances toward migration and transnational family life. Jessica and Toñita long to migrate so that they can pursue their desires for a brighter future, while Camila believes her well-being depends on *not* migrating. The familial arrangements the girls describe reveal a complex variety of transnational family forms and a wide range of feelings, fears, and aspirations.

Unlike the girls interviewed in Napa, the girls in Zinapécuaro did not seem continually saddened by their fathers' absences.[12] Rather, they seem to understand the reasons behind migration. They live in familiar circumstances, immersed in the everyday concerns typical of Mexican teenage girls. Their worries seem to revolve around dating, school, family life, and after-school activities. Although part of a transnational family, their own sense of self does not seem to be marked significantly by the shadows of migration—unlike girls interviewed in Napa. Yet, for those who do express a desire to migrate like Toñita, their present and future seem uncertain and ambiguous. They are waiting for a future they cannot count on arriving. Moreover, like the girls interviewed in Napa, this crucial decision is not theirs to make. Fathers like Toñita's thwart daughters' desires for migration because they are young and because they are girls, which highlights the power of patriarchal relations within the home. Despite their lack of power in the decision-making process, these girls developed strong desires for migration and envisioned an idealized future in the U.S. Like the girls in Napa, their consciousness is inflected by their age, gender, sex, and sexuality, and their future seems tied to decisions made by their fathers. However, as this book will illustrate, even when fathers deny migration to their daughters, the prospect of moving is always looming. Different migratory forms and patterns of migration mark girls' lives precisely because they are growing up in transnational families and within transnational social fields.

The interviews that I conducted in 2010 in Zinapécuaro and in 2006 in Napa reveal two different kinds of stories told by two different groups of girls who have grown up in similar transnational families. The first group consists of forty girls between the ages of thirteen and nineteen interviewed in Zinapécuaro, Michoacán, most of whom have not yet experienced a physical migration to the U.S. Some of the girls are part of families wherein the father is living and working in the U.S. while others live with both parents. For all of these girls, Zinapécuaro often seems to be a transitory place, particularly for those who express a desire for migration; a transitory place where one waits for the time to migrate. In the process, as will be examined, it provides them with a unique perception of time. As such, the town and the life of its transnational families are part of a transnational social field that Peggy Levitt and Nina Glick Schiller (2004) define as "a set of multiple interlocking networks of social relationships through which ideas, practices, and resources are unequally exchanged, organized, and transformed."[13] All of these aspects of a transnational social field shape the lives of the Mexican teenage girls interviewed in Zinapécuaro.

The second group consists of girls interviewed in Napa, California, who lived in transnational families before migration similar to those interviewed in Zinapécuaro, and who have since migrated to join their father or other family members, bringing with them experiences of being raised in a transnational family and within a transnational social field where they are used to seeing themselves as members of multiple communities and familial arrangements. They, too, see daily life as a series of temporary moments. Their transnational experience then allows them to develop a unique perception of place and time. These girls understand the world as transitory, constantly comparing "here with there" and developing what Patricia Zavella (2011) defines as "peripheral vision" as members of multiple communities.[14]

Both groups point to shared experiences as girls whose lives are shaped by migration, a migration that often begins long before they are born when their fathers first migrated to the U.S. for work, and then developed through the constant movement of people, products, ideas, aspirations, communications, and culture across the U.S.-Mexico border. Their desires for migration are influenced by what they see, hear, and imagine. Such experiences generate a knowledge that is peculiarly both intimate and distant. At an intimate level, Mexican teenage girls experience migration via their fathers' departure, the migration of family members, and, for some, their own desires for migration. At a more distanced and seemingly impersonal level, their lives are shaped by the forces that have led to their transnational family structure—globalization, U.S. immigration policies, lack of jobs, and reduced government support due to neoliberal economic policies adopted in the 1980s in Mexico—and a desire for social mobility that motivated their fathers to leave for *el otro lado* (the other side).

Their accounts also point to an oftentimes assumed inevitability of migration. Douglas Massey (1999) describes this seeming inevitability as part of a culture of migration emanating from a cumulative causation through which each subsequent journey of migration becomes easier.[15] In other words, migration facilitates further migration. This is another way in which they inhabit a distinct temporality in which the patterns of the past shape both possibility and peril in the present. The social networks and social capital that are developed become accessible to family and community members for pre- and post-migration use. Migration then becomes so embedded in certain communities that it becomes difficult to avoid as an option or as a solution to economic hardships. As Leisy J. Abrego (2014) has found, however, the importance of social networks post-migration varies depending on the immigration status of individuals.[16] In this book, I examine how the seeming inevitability of migration impacts girls in conflicting and contradictory ways. First, a father's transnational migration places daughters on a migrant path. Not all girls will migrate or wish to migrate. Yet, regardless of their own personal wishes, they have already been drawn into migratory practices and transnational living. Second, those who express desires for migration lack access on their own to the social networks and social capital needed for migration. Husbands and fathers do not always want wives and daughters to follow them.[17] For Mexican teenage girls, having to depend on adults leads to uncertainties, ambiguities, and anxieties about migration that produce moments of endless waiting. Some will wait until they are old enough to reach adulthood and develop their own networks through family and social networks or marriage, causing lengthier feelings of uncertainty, ambiguity, and anxiety.[18] But this unease can also be productive. It creates what Alicia Schmidt Camacho

(2008) terms "migrant imaginaries" or ways of envisioning and enacting different futures that give the girls assets as well as liabilities that produce achievements in the face of injuries.[19] Anne Line Dalsgård and Marin Demant Frederiksen (2014) describe an imaginary as "an open field of possibilities [where t]he mere fact that it has not happened yet makes it fertile ground for the imagination."[20] It is in what they imagine that agency is located, regardless of whether or not physical migration unfolds.

In my research, I explore the migrant imaginaries of teenage girls in Mexico and in the U.S. As Noel Salazar (2010) states, "[m]igration is as much about . . . imaginaries as it is about the actual physical movement from locality and back."[21] Schmidt Camacho defines the imaginary as "a symbolic field in which people come to understand and describe their social being."[22] Girls do not have to physically migrate to experience migratory movements or migration, as it begins in their home and in many cases long before they are born. They grow up seeing and experiencing multiple patterns of migration. Their imaginaries are possible precisely because of someone else's migration and continuous movement within and outside of their home. Salazar describes these as "mobility imaginaries" defined as "socially shared schemas of cultural interpretations about migratory movements that mediate reality and help form identifications of Self and Other."[23] Using this concept of mobility imaginaries, I examine how a father's departure simultaneously places daughters on the migrant path and, as migrants in waiting, shapes how they imagine and idealize their own present and future. In Zinapécuaro, a mobility imaginary permeates the ways girls envision an uncertain present and future either in Mexico or the United States. They imagine that a transformation of their lives is possible. Some girls begin to self-identify as potential migrants expecting a better future on the other side of the border. For those already in Napa, the mobility imaginary can take the form of a longing to return to the Mexico they left behind. It influences the ways they recreate their childhood memories and romanticize their possible future back in Mexico. Yet, while looking backward, they live their lives moving forward inside the public spheres they inhabit after their arrival in Napa.

For the girls in my study, transnational living takes place within three modalities that create distinct temporal and spatial imaginaries. The modalities of a desire to remain in Mexico, a desire for migration, and an actual physical migration encompass three distinct experiences and frames of mind, but they all generate migrant imaginaries. Even girls who have not migrated grow up in and around the possibility and likelihood of moving. Those who wish to move sometimes cannot because of their fathers' ideas about the dangers of life in the U.S. For those who do move, migration does not end conclusively upon arrival in a new country, but rather continues to shape immediate realities and long range plans in an existence haunted by instability and insecurity, by displacement, deportability, and disposability. While victimized by forces beyond their culture, however, these girls are not victims. They work with the tools they have in the arenas that are open to them to envision and enact new imaginaries, temporalities, and spatialities from which new ways of being women can emerge. Transnational migration entails fragmentation, but that fragmentation can become the basis for an imagination that does not require wholeness and closure, that makes an art out of living in multiple times and places, that teaches girls and women how to feel "at home" everywhere and nowhere, that creates affective practices and imaginaries that constitute a "home" from which one can never be evicted.

Growing up in a transnational family surrounded by movement of bodies, ideas, and cultural practices allows Mexican teenage girls to accumulate knowledge that becomes part of who they are and of their subjective understanding of themselves as migrants in waiting able to imaginatively map *El Norte, el otro lado*, the United States. Schmidt Camacho explains Mexican migrants' agency as a fragile one, as they are in motion, unbound to a nation.[24] But, insofar as they "narrate a condition of alterity to, or exclusion from, the nation," migrants "also enunciate a collective desire for a different order of space and belonging across the boundary."[25] This is fragile agency, but with insights about how power works, how lives are destroyed, and how society might be reorganized so that it could potentially be valuable to everyone. Their collective desire for a different life filled with opportunities and options, for a better future, rebukes the political and cultural hierarchies of both Mexico and the United States. They know that, at present, life in Mexico cannot provide them and their families the opportunities available in the U.S., but living as raced and gendered "others" inside U.S. society, they recognize that subordination and exploitation moves even more freely across borders than they can. Line Dalsgård and Demant Frederiksen argue that, when youth imagine their futures, what matters is not the outcome but the imagined possibilities. As they state, "it may turn out in one way or another, but the important thing is the openendedness of the situation."[26] The role of the imagination, then, is to transform the contradictions, conflicts, uncertainties, ambiguities, and anxieties of migrant life into powerful tools for Mexican teenage girls to critique, understand, oppose, and embrace a very personal and intimate understanding of migration and its place in the world.

Migrant imaginaries are spatial as well as temporal. Borders divide nations and imbue them with sharply different legal, political, economic, and cultural realities that can seem incommensurable, but for border-crossers it is necessary to negotiate both national contexts as one. Fathers, mothers, sons, daughters, extended family members, co-workers, and neighbors become separated and divided across national political borders.[27] Family members can spend months or years working in another country to support a family "back home" that survives wage cuts and the termination of price supports in Mexico largely thanks to these remittances. Girls growing up in Zinapécuaro are keenly aware of everyday life in the U.S., while the daily round in Napa for Mexican migrant girls involves past memories and present connections to what is happening in the U.S. Yet spatial distance is often experienced temporally, as a time lag.

The time lag is a key modality that Mexican teenage girls inhabit as they are forced to wait for a promised but abstract future life, as they wait for their fathers to visit them or to send for them, as they endure interruptions, anxieties, uncertainties, and ambiguities in their young lives. The time lag emanates from the workings of distant structural forces: U.S. immigration policy; the racialization, exploitation, and vulnerability of Mexican migrants in the U.S.; the labor control strategies of business and the state in the U.S. and Mexico; and the segmentation of the labor market in the U.S. that channels most Mexican migrants to minimum wage jobs there. These factors shape the experiences of time—the length of time workers remain in the U.S., the length of time girls wait for migration, and the chronological time of major life course events such as school attendance and graduation, entry into the paid labor force, dating and romance, family formation, and career trajectories.

In her research on the historical production of migrant illegality, Mae Ngai (2005) emphasizes how undocumented migrants know that their so-called "unlawful entry" makes them constantly vulnerable to apprehension (in both senses of the word) and deportation.[28] Ngai is concerned with the suspension of time attendant to the uncertainties and ambiguities felt by migrants between the moment of crossing and the possibility of deportation. Even documented migration entails temporal instability. A girl witnessing her father's departure to the U.S. constantly anticipates her migration. Life becomes a series of interruptions that do not allow for long-term planning and mark every present moment with an aura of "not yet."

For girls in Napa who have already migrated, the waiting, anxiety, uncertainty, and ambiguity they experience before migration becomes part of a detailed retrospective assessment of their lives in Mexico. They look back to moments when they waited for migration and recall their lack of power in the decision-making process. They tell stories of interrupted lives on the brink of migration. In Napa, Mexican teenage girls experience a different time lag as they become caught between identities, no longer temporary but not yet permanent, no longer completely Mexican but not completely integrated into the U.S., no longer Mexican but not yet Chicana/o-Latina/o. They do not know if they will become circular migrants like their fathers. They cannot be sure that their migration is permanent.[29] They feel ambiguity in their new places of residence as they did in Mexico, because as teenage girls they generally still lack any significant decision-making power in their new home. The temporal and spatial dimensions of migrant imaginaries in the stories of Mexican teenage girls provide a new perspective on the well-documented migratory journey.

As I listened to the interviewees' narratives about migration and fragmentation, loss and longing, desire and disappointment, I discerned a powerful nexus of affect that corresponded with what Raymond Williams (2001) terms a "structure of feeling."[30] More than a subjective personal perception, yet not quite an autonomous "social structure," a structure of feeling emerges in the culture of a period. It expresses what John Storey

(2006) describes as the "shared values of a particular group, class, or society" at a particular moment.[31] Lisa Lowe (2002) sees "structure" of feeling as registers of the "quality of life at a particular place in time," while Ruth Wilson Gilmore (2016) explains them as response to structures that every age in every single generation shares.[32] In relation to migration, Zavella uses the concept of the "structure of feeling" to capture a "betwixt and between" reality, neither fully "here" nor "there."[33] In this study, the girls' pre- and post-migrant lives point to a particular experience of growing up in transnational families, within transnational social fields, imagining a better life in the U.S., and of being migrants in waiting. These are experiences, which all girls share, that shape how they think of themselves and others, about their past, their present, and their future.

The Zinapécuaro interviews provide insights into a particular "structure of feeling." Mexican teenage girls experience a Mexico they are told is yearning for modernity while dealing with its indigenous past and present. It is influenced by the constant movement of the part of its population that spends most of the year abroad and returns only during certain months of the year.[34] The incessant flow of ideas and material goods across borders gives the Zinapecuarenses an intimate and tangible relation to the U.S. through both the image of the U.S. held out to them and the consumption of products associated with it. They inhabit what Arjun Appadurai (1996) refers to as a diasporic public sphere, a space produced through movement and mass media, which allows the diaspora to consume home from abroad and consume the abroad from home.[35] What is the "structure of feeling" among these Mexican teenage girls that captures a transnational experience in Mexico? How do their fathers' departures to the U.S. mark their lives in Mexico as they either wait for their own migration or re-direct their energies in imagining a future there? I examine the unique and typical ways they carry themselves that speak to their lived experiences of being teenagers growing up in Mexico, albeit living in a family with a father who commutes to the U.S. for work.

In Napa, Mexican teenage girls couple their feelings and emotions of migration with the reality adjustment to a place saturated with racialized, gendered, and classed hierarchies. How do their worlds unfold in the U.S. after their own migrations? What lasting effects does this "structure of feeling" have on the girls' subjectivities? This book examines how growing up in a transnational household and within transnational social fields produces new imaginaries emanating from alterations in the girls' senses of time and place.

Transnational Migration: An Approach

Transnational migration and the formation of transnational families are not new phenomena. As early as the 1860s, men from northern Mexico commuted to California for work.[36] It was not until the 1990s, though, that the concept of transnationalism became a prominent theoretical framework raising challenges to the theories of linear assimilation that previously dominated migration scholarship.[37] It became difficult to make binary distinctions between countries of origin and of arrival in an age where people, products, investments, and images move back and forth rapidly, where living in one country routinely entails awareness of and association with activity in another. Studies of transnational migration emphasize the intricate ways in which migrants continue to remain connected to the homeland despite the distance. They note that immigration patterns reflect previous histories of imperial domination and colonization as well as present policies about investments. Differential systems of production and legal regulation make it advantageous for migrants to return to their countries of origin with wages earned elsewhere, to move back and forth seasonally in response to cycles of agricultural production and service sector employment, and to create networks in and across several different nations of arrival.

These forms of return migration, circular migration, and secondary migration are not new; they have long shaped and reflected migrant imaginaries. They are more prevalent today because of new technologies, new patterns of investment and trade, and new practices of labor control. Yet they have been learned and legitimated over centuries. As Schmidt Camacho reminds us, those "who traverse the boundary between Mexico and the United States have rarely conformed to the usual trajectory of immigration, leaving behind one national polity to assume a settled existence as citizens of another."[38] As a framework, transnationalism opened a space to examine this history and its enduring presence in the present through exploration of plural and diverse conceptions of nation, home, identity, place, placelessness, and belonging.

Nina Glick Schiller, Linda Basch, and Christina Szanton-Blanc (1992) helped launch a new and generative scholarly conversation by defining transnationalism as "the process by which immigrants build social fields that link together their country of origin and their country of settlement."[39] This definition underscores the reproduction of customs and traditions via social fields and the flow of images and cultures on both sides of the border. Peggy Levitt (2001), Lynn Stephen (2007), Gina Perez (2004) and Zavella have produced exemplary studies that demonstrate the utility of thinking beyond single national contexts.[40] Levitt and Glick Schiller succinctly state that scholarship in the U.S. examines various aspects of transnational formations that include transnational identities, networks, and typologies "to capture the variations in the dimensions of transnational migration."[41] Similarly, Takeyuki Tsuda (2012) argues that at the core of transnationalism is the element of simultaneity that allows transnational migrants to "affect and influence both the sending and receiving countries."[42] These arguments have highlighted migrant temporalities that do not follow a trajectory of linear assimilation.[43] Tsuda argues that the ties transnational migrants develop produce long-distance nationalism, a type of nationalism that grows out of exile influenced by migration, movement, and capitalism.[44] Scholars highlight a new spatial imaginary within transnationalism that "binds together migrants, their descendants, dispersed minority populations, and people who continue to live within the territory claimed as the homeland into a single trans-border citizenry."[45] Levitt and Glick Schiller argue that transnationalism requires a fused methodology of ethnographies, participant observation, and surveys to examine the networks of affiliation and engagement created by those who have migrated with those who remain behind, and those who move back and forth.[46]

Critiques of transnationalism come from scholars who have argued that highlighting the primacy of circular movement overlooks the permanency of migration and assumes migrants are always in transition, never becoming permanent residents of the U.S.[47] Migration, however, is *both* permanent and volatile, national and transnational. One framework does not need to replace the other. Critiques also come from scholars who opt to use other concepts to describe migrants, such as trans-border migrants as opposed to transnational migrants to highlight that there are various borders migrants cross and negotiate that the concept of transnationalism may be unable to capture.[48] For Roger Waldinger and David Fitzgerald (2004), transnationalism should be viewed as a social process tied to others that are "inextricably intertwined."[49] Finally, transnationalism sometimes seems to allude to borderless nations where the power within a bounded territory is somewhat weakened. This reflects how the rapid mobility of capital and the rules issued on its behalf by the World Bank, the International Monetary Fund, and international treaties make it difficult for nation-states to trap and tax capital to benefit the social welfare of the populace. Yet migrants know that the nation-state remains powerful in other ways, that it plays a crucial role in establishing and enforcing migration quotas, incarcerating unauthorized border crossers, racially profiling targeted populations, providing subsidies for overseas investments, and forgiving corporate debts. The militarization of the border is just one example, but a powerful one in the quotidian experiences of migrants.

Despite its potential flaws, the framework of transnationalism seems the most fitting to analyze the experiences of the Mexican teenage girls in this study. They are raised in transnational families and inhabit a transnational social field produced by transnational migration and diasporic communities. In this book, I use the concept of the diaspora to describe Mexican transnational migrants. Jolle Demmers (2002) cautions against the interchangeable use of diaspora and transnational migrants as the latter may not necessarily be a community in exile.[50] Central to diasporic communities is the element of exile, of not being able to return home. Yet all migration, whether transnational, temporary, or permanent is a one-way trip, as Stuart Hall (1987) states, since there is often no original home to which to return.[51] Migration changes countries of departure as well as countries of arrival. Migrants, whether they engage in permanent or transnational migratory practices, are never able to return to the time of the past, to the home they left behind. I certainly do not mean to conflate exile with migration, but I do want to highlight the instability of the ideal of the home under present conditions. In this sense, the concept of the diaspora is useful in capturing the feeling of longing for a home that ceased to be. The latter chapters examine how Mexican teenage girls who did migrate to the U.S. became part of the Mexican diaspora. Regardless of their legal status, many longed to return to an imagined home, to the home they left when they departed Mexico.

I examine transnationalism and the formation of transnational families as products of twentieth-century U.S. immigration policy and economic shifts in both countries, and expand on two critical elements. First, Mexican teenage girls in this study inhabit a Mexico shaped by a past and present that defines who they are and influences their shared experiences. They are embedded in daily practices common among teenagers in Mexico who have yet to experience migration. Yet they also live within transnational social fields that shape their embodied sensations and desires, and allow them to imagine that better things await somewhere else.[52] They inhabit national and local spheres alongside the transnational. Moreover, transnational migration as a framework produces elements of waiting among those who remain behind that vary depending on their age, gender, sex, and sexuality. I question the concept of simultaneity as a central component to transnational migration, and ask: where do waiting and the unequal experiences within families, transnational families, and social fields fit within transnational migration? What happens when we bring a temporal analysis to the study of transnational migration, social fields, and the formation of transnational families?

The National within the Transnational

Mexican teenage girls inhabit a contemporary Mexico that has local, national, and transnational dimensions. It is the larger Mexico that Guillermo Bonfil Batalla (1996) defines as an imaginary opposed to the ideal of *México profundo,* and which Néstor García Canclini (2005) perceives as embodying "hybrid cultures."[53] According to Bonfil Batalla, the imaginary Mexico is always moving forward, desiring to be part of the West, of achieving (what scholars used to refer to as) "First World" status. It is a modern Mexico looking to govern its citizens democratically, an imaginary Mexico that embraces western hegemonic cultural forms, including music, aesthetics, films, and television shows, some of which are brought back to the nation by the diaspora upon their return. As Bonfil Batalla describes, it is an imaginary Mexico that aims to obliterate the *profundo,* the world of the indigenous that presumably stands in the way of progress and modernity. The temporality of modernity presumes its universality and inevitability. Those who do not participate in, or succeed within, it are imagined to be rationally and ontologically deficient because of their inadequate modernity. Discourses of modernity in politics, law, and business have their corollary in scholarship through what Johannes Fabian calls (1983) the "denial of coevalness," which examines how anthropologists construct the Other.[54] Anthropologists, according to Fabian, imagine they are studying a culture trapped in a previous static frame and cannot place the Other in the same temporal space as themselves, lest their analyses fall in the face of the obvious similarities between so-called primitive and western behaviors.[55] Thus they distance the Others by locating them in a time frame distant from their own.[56] García Canclini proposes a recognition of Latin America, including Mexico, as embodying "hybrid cultures" that make it possible for the "presence of indigenous crafts and vanguard catalogues on the same coffee table,"[57] while Ana Amuchástegui Herrera (1998) heralds the existence of a "heterogeneous but unequal co-existence of tradition and modernities" within Mexico.[58] This larger Mexico shapes the lives and daily practices of Mexican teenage girls.

Along with living within a transnational social field, Mexican teenage girls also inhabit a Mexico influenced by the diaspora that contributes to the flow of transnational products they perceive as emblems of modern life such as cars, clothing, music, digital cameras, iPhones, iPads, and laptops. Their social fields include constant arrivals and departures from the diaspora that produce a type of space saturated with notions of migration, the U.S., and general difference. In fact, any rural town in any given season may be inundated with cars with U.S. license plates that tell multiple narratives of each town's diasporic communities— communities located in traditional receiving states such as California, Texas, and Arizona, and non-traditional receiving states, such as Iowa, Utah, and South Dakota. Rural towns also have other signs and symbols that reflect transnational influences, such as: *casas de cambio* or *cambio de dólares*, English music blasting from cars driving down the street, or even clever names on shops such as Papelería de Sonia's, instead of Sonia's Papelería—which, albeit grammatically incorrect, reflect migrants' influence.[59] These quotidian signs tell a narrative of a transnational social space where the influences of residents abroad bring a different dimension to what otherwise might be perceived as an isolated and premodern town.

Girls in Mexico are then exposed constantly to what they imagine to be the modern life awaiting them in the U.S. Their consciousness is framed by what Appadurai defines as the embodied sensations of modernity reflected in material culture, in television shows, in Hollywood films, in music by American pop stars, and by copies and imitations of those influences by Mexican entrepreneurs and artists.[60] Such embodied sensations of modernity allow Mexican teenage girls to dream of what they perceive as "better." It is within this idea of "better" that mobility imaginaries unfold and where agency is located.

Temporality and Transnationalism

Within studies of transnational migration, Levitt and Glick Schiller posit that simultaneity rather than sequential progression now defines the migrant experience. The phone call, the text message, the online posting, and the satellite transmission of news and entertainment rely on a simultaneity that blurs the borders that demarcate nations. They produce discursive spaces that transcend the borders of physical places and bounded territories. Within transnational migration, the concept of simultaneity pervades intimate and personal events and experiences: a celebration, the birth of a child, a school graduation, and other emotional occurrences and occasions that allow families separated by borders to participate in the same event. Yet, Helga Nowotny (1994) questions the very concept of simultaneity, arguing that it "does not automatically become translatable to equality."[61] Differently positioned people receiving the same message remain differently situated. In this book, I look at the unequal aspect of simultaneity by incorporating the temporal and spatial imaginaries of Mexican teenage girls to the study of the migrant experience.

Youth Studies, Girlhood Studies, and the Temporalities of Youth

In the course of my discoveries about the central role played by waiting in the lives of migrant girls, I came to realize that I had to reckon with the fact that migrant girls are both migrants *and* girls. This allows me to bring migration to Youth Studies, which may allow us to view the stage of adolescence as a migratory stage. Migration imposes relentless regimes of waiting, but adolescence is already a time of waiting for migrants and non-migrants alike. When migration and adolescence intersect for the girls in my study, waiting takes on a particularly powerful meaning.

Within Youth Studies and, more specifically, Girlhood Studies, youth is defined as that stage of becoming between childhood and adulthood.[62] There is a betwixt and between quality to adolescence. Yet contemporary scholarly research on youth emphasizes that this duality takes on a new meaning within the context of the failed promises of the neoliberal era and modernity in general. The transition into adulthood has become longer, forcing us to rethink the meaning of youth and adolescence in particular. The benefits and rewards associated with adulthood have diminished. In some communities, environmental pollution, inadequate health care, criminal violence, and police violence portend premature death for significant numbers of young people. Rather than the triumphant modernity promised by Mexican nationalists and social scientists alike, the girls in this study confront what Zygmunt Bauman (2003) calls a liquid modernity suffused with instability and uncertainty. Young people can come to expect wasted rather than fulfilled lives.[63]

In the age of faith in a believable modernity, it was assumed that if youth only applied themselves, they would be rewarded. As Michael G. Flaherty (2014) argues, however, the current inaccessibility of higher education and good jobs leads "to impoverishment and thwarted desires for a better future promised by modernity."[64] Such promises include a stable job, a home, and a better life than their parents. Extending these promises means that temporality and maturation become intricately connected, which under current conditions are severed. Alcinda Honwana (2012) argues that adolescence in general is now a time of waiting, a waiting that "represents the contradictions of modernity, in which young peoples' opportunities and expectations are simultaneously broadened and constrained."[65] The ideal of "better" appears more possible than ever, yet access to it is limited and constrained, so youth have to wait.

Jennifer Cole and Deborah Durham (2008) found that what youth do as they wait for their future is imagine that it "will be better than the past."[66] How far away that future seems and what youth do while they wait differ greatly according to socioeconomic status, though. Constance Flanagan (2008) conducted a study in which the youth sampled would generally respond in one of two ways: either they adhere to the idea of meritocracy and apply themselves in school, believing that adulthood and a bright future are within reach, or else they make "public and political the private anxieties they share, challenging the world organized on market principles and seeking a fuller sense of character than jobs alone can furnish."[67] Given their complex circumstances, migrant girls may find themselves situated uneasily betwixt and between these seemingly clear and opposite options.

In another study that examines the educated middle class of India, unable to find work despite completing several university degrees, Craig Jeffrey (2010) describes the process of waiting to enter adulthood and the labor force as "the permanent state of not now, not yet,"[68] lost in time and space. One of the consequences of the temporalities of youth today is this general sense of being stuck, of waiting—often for a job that may provide entrance to a middle class lifestyle.[69] In the study, this limbo state causes tremendous uncertainties for men who earn two or more degrees in hopes for a better chance at a job.

These studies make no distinctions between male youth and female youth or between migrants and non-migrants. In the present study, I examine the distinct temporalities experienced by Mexican teenage girls through the lens of concepts and theories honed and refined within Girlhood Studies. Following the tradition and legacy of U.S. feminists of color who apply an intersectional analysis, I examine how the critical categories of age, gender, sex, and sexuality shape the shared experiences of Mexican teenage girls growing up in transnational families and within transnational social fields. Alys Eve Weinbaum et al. (2008) deliberately use the seemingly demeaning term "girl" because to them (as for me) "it signifies the contested status of young women, no longer children, and their sometimes subversive relationships to social norms relating to heterosexuality, marriage, and motherhood."[70] Their definition of a girl resonates with similar definitions of migrants in terms of betwixt and between. In this book, the concept of girlhood allows for a focus of that in-between stage of not quite being children or adults, but also of the in-between stages of their identities that emanate from the categories of age, citizenship and social membership, class, race, and gender. The in-betweeness of Mexican teenage girls in the U.S. has been well documented in relation to education, class, gender, race, sexuality, and identity.[71] But girls' experiences as migrants, as people in the making, in the process, in the transition from arrival to local agency, has yet to be fully documented, particularly the multiple ways in which age, gender, sex, and sexuality shape migratory practices.[72]

There are other ways in which distinctions around childhood and youth need to be made. Stories of immigrant girls often get entangled with those of adults and other children. For example, when adults are asked to provide reasons for their own migration, the answer tends to be for their children to have an education, therefore a better chance at life in Mexico or in the U.S.[73] Rubén Martínez (2001) notes that, in the families he studied, parents pinned their hopes on the value of an American education for their children.[74] Yen Le Espiritu (2003) found a similar response among Filipino immigrant parents who told her that "we did it for the children."[75] In most cases, children become the stated reason for adults' migratory practices. As children, girls' experiences are also lumped with boys with the underlying assumption of a shared experience disavowing the critical differences marked by age, gender, sex, and sexuality.[76] These gestures seem to place girls at the center of the migrant process, but their personal experience and subjective perceptions indicate otherwise. The stories used to include them wind up erasing the specificity of what they have experienced, what they know, and what they want.

At any moment, age, gender, sex, and sexuality are central to processes of migration, yet gender and most recently sex and sexuality have been examined more thoroughly than age. Within migration, gender is defined as a "set of social relations that organize migration patterns" that can facilitate migration.[77] For men, gender often clearly facilitates their migration as it is considered a rite of passage into male adulthood.[78] Networks are at their disposal whenever they feel ready to embark on the journey. Such an invitation also extends to boys. Accounts of women's journeys of migration with gender as a central component were somewhat limited until the 1990s. During the 1970s and 1980s, for example, scholars produced "add and stir" or "women only" portraits that addressed the experiences of women and migration with migration tangentially and tokenistically.[79] But, by the 1980s and 1990s, migration scholars began to examine gendered patterns and practices of both men and women.[80] Today, gender is recognized as "a key constitutive element of migration . . . that permeates a variety of practices, identities, and institutions implicated in migration."[81] Research on adult women's migration to or across the U.S.-Mexico border has since become quite extensive.[82] This is not the case with teenage girls.

In terms of sexuality, scholars such as Lionel Cantú (2009), Hector Carillo (2004), and Gloria González-López (2005) have examined intersecting categories of sex and sexuality in processes of migration.[83] Earlier studies pointed to sexuality as a push-factor for migration for some groups, as it was assumed for example that Mexico's repressive practices in relation to sexuality pushed the LGBT community to a free and modern U.S. and its liberal laws and policies on sexuality and sexual practices. Ana Minian (2012) found that this argument no longer holds as gay Mexican men, for example, no longer view the U.S. as a safe haven.[84] Changes in Mexico's same-sex marriage laws and intersecting categories of sexuality and race in the U.S. that racialize immigrants of color are two of the reasons that have influenced this shift in attitude. As with gender, sex and sexuality remain adult-centered. My research incorporates age as an analytical and intersecting category with gender, sex, and sexuality with the goal of pointing to nuances and the troubles of lumping boys and girls together in a way that obscures critical differences.

With very few exceptions, age has not been recognized as critical to processes of migration. Yet, as Barrie Thorne (2004) argues, age, "like and in conjunction with the study of gender, racial ethnicity, sexuality, social class, religion, disability status, nationality . . . crosses levels of analysis."[85] When age is accounted for as an intersecting category with gender, sex, and sexuality, the persistence and pervasiveness of gendered and sexist practices within migration come forward. For girls in this study, age limits their access to the decision-making process of migration and to social networks. It has a bearing on their possibilities for migration. Because they are girls, they are conditioned to depend on adults—not on their networks—who often deny them the opportunity of migration and access to networks. Moreover, alleged patriarchal protection of female "innocence" works relentlessly to objectify and disempower girls. In the families I studied, fathers are still largely the ones who make migratory decisions. They tell their daughters explicitly that they will not fix their documents because, once they are adults, they will become the responsibility of another man. Although I am unaware of the sexual preference of the girls interviewed, their fathers seem to universally assume their heterosexuality. Therefore, the likelihood of another man benefiting from his social capital seems like a strong possibility and reason to deny their daughters access to his own networks. Women are possessions traded between men for advantage in competition for resources, status, prestige, and power. For girls, there is no rite of passage into adulthood or access to social networks similar to the ones men enjoy until they become adults. They are taught to depend fully on someone else for their future, until they are old enough to have another man decide it for them.

The girls I interviewed related to me their struggles to develop agency in challenging sexist and patriarchal practices at home by not acquiescing to fathers' beliefs and by imagining a different future in the U.S. This is what Flaherty defines as temporal agency.[86] Their free will to imagine, to hope for a different future, is a space where we can witness agency. This agency, however, takes place within discourses and practices structured in dominance, inside the persistence of gendered and sexist practices. To assume boys and girls share a similar experience is to ignore the intricacies within migratory practices that are linked to heteronormativity and patriarchy. Girls experience waiting differently from boys who knowingly await migration as a rite of passage. Their waiting is also different from the waiting of adolescent girls and boys living lives that are not immersed in migration practices.

By focusing on girls, I do not aim to construct a "type" of girl but rather to understand a set of complex experiences related to transnational migration. Echoing Weinbaum et al., to construct a type runs the risk of generalizing, which ignores the wide range of lived realities and complex personhoods girls embody. To move away from typologies, Weinbaum et al. propose what they refer to as a connective comparison method, which, "avoids recourse to abstract types and instead focuses on how specific local processes condition each other."[87] Instead of constructing a type of girl, I examine a type of "structure of feeling," of shared values, in a particular place in time of growing up in a transnational family and within a transnational social field. That specific context is shaped by growing up with an absent father, with migration always looming, with living in what may feel like a transitory existence, and with the various ways they imagine life in the U.S. For those who cross over to the U.S., a different shared experience unfolds within a different context, and a different "structure of feeling."

The Study

As a multi-sited ethnography, this study takes its own unexpected pathways and trajectories in tracing the experiences of Mexican teenage girls raised within processes of migration.[88] I aim to capture the "busy intersection" in which they live.[89] I move backwards by starting with my 2010 and 2012 interviews in Zinapécuaro, then turning to my 2006 interviews in Napa to highlight what happens among girls who have already migrated to Napa and continue to live transnational lives. I situate both groups' stories within these locations and time periods to grasp the "structure of feeling," of shared values, at a particular place in time.

Each time I introduce a girl, I describe her aesthetic—clothing and hairstyle—to point to signs that U.S. mainstream consumer stylistics are also in force in the girls pre- and post-migration. These, as Appadurai states and as I mention earlier, are examples of embodied sensations of modernity.

Zinapécuaro, Michoacán, 2010 and 2012

When I did my first interviews in Zinapécuaro in 2010, Mexico was celebrating both the centennial of the Mexican revolution—a moment in history when the landless stood up to the landowners and to the dictatorship of Porfirio Díaz—and the bicentennial or Bicentenario of Mexico's independence from the Spanish empire. Along with a massive celebration in Mexico City's Zócalo on September 15, these two historical moments included the minting of commemorative one-hundred peso bills adorned with iconic images of the Mexican revolution—*campesinos* (peasants) and railroads—and two-hundred peso bills with representative images of Mexican independence—Father Hidalgo and the Angel of Independence. These celebrations also included television ads produced and aired by one of Mexico's main television channels, Televisa's El Canal de las Estrellas. Known as *Las Estrellas del Bicentenario*, these commercials ranged from thirty seconds to three minutes, airing daily in between *telenovelas* (soap operas). They displayed beautiful landscapes of Mexican states including Veracruz, Chiapas, and Sonora.[90] Three young women who were selected from over fifty thousand who auditioned for the coveted role were featured.[91] I further discuss the significance of this celebratory backdrop in chapter 3.

I returned to Mexico in 2012 to conduct follow-up interviews with eleven of the forty girls I interviewed in 2010. The 2012 presidential elections featuring debates among candidates Josefina Vázquez Mota (PAN), Andres Manuel López Obrador (PRD), Enrique Peña Nieto (PRI), and Gabriel Quadri de la Torre (PANAL) were difficult to avoid, as were protests by students in Mexico City that began at the Universidad Iberoamericana and evolved into the nationwide Yo Soy 132 movement, sometimes referred to as the Mexican Spring.[92] A government effort to force teachers to take the mandatory exam known as Educación de Calidad Universal, or universal quality education, prompted strikes from teachers who opposed it in many states throughout Mexico, especially in the states of Oaxaca and Michoacán.[93] Closer to home, the student takeover of the Universidad Michoacana de San Nicolas de Hidalgo, or La Michoacana as it is popularly known, shut down the university facilities for weeks.[94] All this influenced the girls' worlds. Though perhaps not active participants in formal politics or student movements, this context allowed and encouraged the girls to form an opinion of the place and time period in which they live.

Forty interviews were conducted with Mexican teenage girls between the ages of thirteen and nineteen raised in transnational families and living within transnational social fields. Though a nineteen year-old may have a much wider range of emotions or understanding about her life than a thirteen year-old, I was interested in varied experiences of transnational living. This allowed me to follow Weinbaum et al.'s connective comparison method where I honed in on the specificities of transnational living among girls of different ages. I discerned four familial arrangements in the testimonies I elicited. I list them here to emphasize the broad range of transnational familial arrangements that exist and to illuminate their changing nature. I am not positing that family form is decisive in shaping consciousness, or that the family is the only or even the most important institution shaping migrant imaginaries. The family does emerge, however, from the words of the girls as the central force in their lives, as the terrain upon which their lives are shaped.

First, I examine girls raised in father-away transnational families with limited contact with fathers. I refer to these fathers as having a ghost-like presence in their daughters' lives. Like ghosts, these fathers make rare apparitions. Their uncanny presence alters their daughter's lives and sense of selves. The second arrangement includes girls in father-away transnational families where the father commutes regularly to the U.S. Girls raised in this familial arrangement see their father more consistently as he remains a present figure in their lives. The third group consists of girls who were once raised in transnational families and no longer live in a separated family. Lastly, there are girls who live in heteronormative families where no immediate member has ever lived in the U.S., but whose extended family do. By heteronormative I mean here a traditional familial arrangement entailing a father, a mother, and children living under one roof. As mentioned earlier, heteronormative then means the opposite of queering. Yet here I am also queering transnational families that are then assumed to not be "normal." Regardless of their familial arrangement, all girls are still *hijas de familia*, or family centered girls, who fully depend on their parents—especially their fathers—for any decision-making, whether it involves dating, where to go to school, or which career to pick.[95] Being *hijas de familia* can mean endless support or limits for their future plans in Mexico or the U.S. These girls of course have vital, valuable, and varied relations with other women, with their mothers, grandmothers, aunts, sisters, cousins, friends and neighbors. There are men important to their lives other than their fathers, too, including their grandfathers, brothers, uncles, cousins, friends, and neighbors. Yet they perceive their families to be father-centered and they describe their father's experiences and beliefs as the key factors shaping their relations to migration.

When I returned in 2012, I was able to track twenty-six of the forty girls interviewed in 2010. Of the twenty-six, one had moved to the U.S., twelve had dropped out of school after having completed either middle school or high school, four were pregnant, and four ran away with their boyfriends, with two of those eventually marrying. Five of the girls were attending college in the state capital of Morelia. Though I tracked over half of the girls from the original sample, I was only able to conduct follow-up interviews with eleven of them. In some cases, the partner of those who were married did not allow their young wives to be interviewed.

The interviews in Zinapécuaro were semi-structured and include basic information such as age, schooling practices, and familial arrangements. Central to the interviews were girls' ties to the U.S., including family members who first migrated, and any desires they themselves may have had or continue to have of moving north. Girls were also asked about embodied sensations of modernity—for example, the images and imaginaries they have about life in the U.S., especially the music, films, and television shows they watch and listen to that provide them with an idea of what they perceive modern life to be. All of the interviews were conducted in Spanish and lasted an average of forty-five minutes. I recorded and transcribed each verbatim. To protect the identity of girls, all of the names were changed.

The interviews were conducted in April of 2010 as I was about to complete my second year of appointment as a University of California President's Postdoctoral Fellow at the University of California, Los Angeles. The almost daily articles of "Mexico under siege" in the *Los Angeles Times*[96] and the war on organized crime declared by then President Felipe Calderón in 2006 forced me to choose a town I was familiar with to conduct the interviews. My parents' hometown of Zinapécuaro is approximately thirty minutes northeast of Morelia, the state capital of Michoacán. Though I was not born in that town, I lived there for ten years. Familiar with the town—its people, the *plaza*, the streets, and the church where each night at seven thirty in the evening bells serenade and bless the Catholic town—it seemed a safe place to conduct interviews. Upon my arrival, I heard the story of Poli, a nineteen-year-old woman who had gone missing since September of 2009. Poli, who did not come from a family of migrants, decided to leave for the U.S. to improve her and her single mother's economic status and relieve the incurred debt they had acquired. She and her mother hired a *coyote* (smuggler) to help her cross into the U.S. Because they lacked direct access to migration and social networks—a rare case in Zinapécuaro—they were not too familiar with the *coyote* they hired. Since her departure, no one has heard of Poli. The *coyote*, presumably responsible for her disappearance, fled town. A town that initially felt safe immediately became suspicious of me, as the researcher, asking questions and wanting to interview young teenage girls.

The context of my arrival forced me to develop a homegrown project and rely on trusted members of the community for recruitment purposes. Inevitably, the recruiters were related to me. My cousin, a devout Catholic who teaches catechism and is a trusted member of the community, assisted me in recruiting the first sixteen girls. These interviews were conducted at my cousin's home, which was a place that was considered neutral for the girls being interviewed as well as for myself. My mother recruited seven girls from her local neighborhood. These interviews took place at my mother's home at the dining room table. One of my aunts recruited three girls from her neighborhood. These were the only interviews that were conducted at the girls' homes, which allowed for a glimpse into their lives and private spaces. Finally, the last fourteen interviews were conducted at the Centro de Bachillerato Tecnológico Industrial y Servicios, or El CBTIS for short, a technical high school that offers diplomas for nursing, business administration, computer science, or electronics, after which graduates can immediately work if they so choose or else attend college. With the principal's approval, my cousin—a teacher at El CBTIS—allowed me to recruit the rest of the girls who were interviewed between lunch break or after school.

The study then is based on a convenience sample, as I was introduced by known parties to all of the girls who seemed eager to chat about their lives, dreams, the Mexican diaspora, and the U.S. Their stories guide chapters 2 through 4 of the book. The girls expressed a bit of confusion in terms of the purpose of the study. I was asked a few times if I was a psychologist. Though this may seem like an unusual form of recruitment, trust in these towns is of extreme importance, and it became even more so after Poli's disappearance. My "in" into the community was through family members who were trusted by the community. One of my aunts, who has since passed, kept track of all the girls who came to her house to be interviewed. Each time I completed one interview, she reminded me how many I had done and still needed to complete. In the eyes of my family, I was a student doing "homework" who needed help and they were willing to help me. I not only welcomed their assistance but embraced it as well.

Napa, California, in 2006

The first set of interviews were conducted in 2006 in Napa, California, a time when the country witnessed massive immigration protests against what was popularly known as the Sensenbrenner Bill, or the Border Protection, Antiterrorism, and Illegal Immigration Control Act of 2005 (H.R. 4437). From March to May of 2006, immigrant rights supporters marched in New York, Chicago, and Los Angeles, among other cities, to express disdain for the bill. The Spanish language media, especially on radio, advertised marches in support of the plight of immigrants and was a key factor in promoting opposition to the bill and assuring that masses of people would turn out for the marches.[97] Smaller demonstrations took place in Napa where high school students participated, including some of the girls interviewed in this study. Many of the girls in Napa also partook in the "Great American Boycott"[98] of May 1, 2006, the name given to the boycott of businesses, marching, or wearing the color white to school to show solidarity with the movement. The protests and the anti-immigrant sentiment that caused them affected the recruitment process, limiting the number of girls willing to participate as parents were suspicious of who I was and what I would do with the information gathered.

Nineteen girls were interviewed from a public high school in the heart of Napa. I selected this high school for three reasons. First, it has the largest student population of English Language Development (ELD) students. In the 2006–2007 academic year, the school had a forty-percent Latino student population. Of those, twenty-one percent were ELD learners.[99] By 2015–2016, the Latino population in this high school was well over fifty percent.[100] Second, I visited other high schools and met with principals for recruitment purposes but was unable to recruit any girls due to lack of parental consent. Lastly, I am an alumna of this high school, and was familiar with the principal and the administrators. I felt my history would give me an "in" into the school.

All the interviews, then, were conducted at the same high school with the assistance of the principal, the senior counselor, and the facilitator of an after-school program for Latinas. The principal first took me to ELD classrooms and allowed me to make an announcement, pass out slips to request permission from parents to let me first contact them at home and inquire into the possibility of interviewing their daughter. Six girls returned the next day with permission slips and, after receiving parental consent, the first interviews took place. Word spread among ELD classrooms that someone was writing a book about Mexican immigrant girls at their high school. These six girls introduced me to some of their friends who did not want to be left out. The senior counselor followed a similar approach as the principal and contacted some students who fit the profile I was seeking. We handed out permission slips, waited for them to ask for parental consent, and finally began the next round of interviews. Lastly, the facilitator of an after-school program for Latinas allowed me to sit in at their weekly meetings and, within a few weeks, pursue the same process resulting in the rest of the interviews.

I recruited a total of nineteen girls who had arrived in Napa within the previous seven years. Their memories of growing up in a transnational family were relatively recent. Most of the interviews took place at the girls' homes or on school premises. One interview was conducted outside the Napa City County Library. Seventeen interviews were conducted in Spanish and two in English. The girls migrated from various locations, although most came from the traditional sending states of Michoacán, Zacatecas, Jalisco, and Guanajuato—all points of origin for the laborers who were recruited to work in Napa during the first half of the twentieth century.[101] Nine girls were in twelfth grade, four in eleventh, one in tenth, and five in ninth. They ranged in age from fourteen to seventeen years. All of them migrated to join one or more family members in Napa: fourteen girls joined their fathers, one joined her mother, two joined a sibling, one joined both parents, and one joined her grandparents. I recorded and transcribed each interview verbatim. The interviews were divided into four sections: basic information; life in Mexico, including ties to the U.S.; migratory transitions; and life in Napa after migration. To protect the identity of the girls, all names were changed. Their stories guide the end of the book.

Unlike the interviews conducted in Zinapécuaro in 2010, the Napa interviews are not a totally home-grown project. They began as a convenience sample as I relied on school administrators for recruitment purposes. Given the sensitive anti-immigrant sentiment in Napa and the rest of the U.S. during this time, this felt necessary. Once the girls were interviewed, it snowballed into a larger sample as they began to introduce me to their friends.

Structure of the Book

I begin the body of this book in the next chapter by presenting an overarching examination of the "why" behind transnational familial formations. I argue that transnational families, particularly wherein the father is the migrant, are products of twentieth-century U.S. immigration policies, global restructuring from the 1970s onward, Mexico's economic crises of the 1980s and 1990s, and its transitions from a nationalist economy to a neoliberal one of free trade and open markets. Having migrated to the U.S. for work since the 1980s—and as products of much earlier movements—the fathers of the girls I interviewed had developed strong social networks and secured social capital. They, however, were not always willing to share what they had with their daughters.

The first half of the book is based on the interviews conducted in the town of Zinapécuaro in the state of Michoacán, Mexico. Chapter 2 examines girls' familial arrangements in the town of Zinapécuaro as well as their responses to their upbringing. Chapter 3 situates the girls' daily lives and practices at home, school, and after school to understand that part of their world. I look at the penetration of U.S. modernities as "embodied sensations" that fuel girls' imaginations and desires for migration.[102] Using Salazar's concept of "mobility imaginaries," I examine more carefully how girls envision a different present and future in the U.S., whether or not actual migration takes place.[103] In chapter 4, I situate the national and local alongside the transnational that Mexican teenage girls inhabit, and provide a temporal analysis to transnational migratory practices that surround them. Girls who express desires for migration often have to wait for migration. In this chapter, I argue that the intersections of age, gender, sex, and sexuality elongate the temporality of the girls' desires and possible journeys to the U.S.

The second half of the book—chapters 5 and 6—documents the lives of girls who migrated to California's Napa Valley. Using interviews and ethnographic work conducted in 2006, chapter 5 traces girls' transitions from migrants in waiting to actual migrants—the moment when the imaginary becomes the real. It captures the moment they are told of their migration, highlighting the preparation, fear, doubt, and uncertainty the girls felt. Chapter 6 examines the girls' arrivals to Napa, a tourist destination and place they had imagined ever since they were little.

It is a place they have always known, yet they discover there that they have already been written out of the dominant Napa Valley narrative. They are present in the schools, businesses, and neighborhoods, but feel invisible to many.

I provide a concluding chapter wherein I propose new areas of study. I argue that girls' stories of migration are produced and created by external forces. They do not simply happen or unfold. As Nicholas De Genova (2002) states, furthering Saskia Sassen's (1998) arguments, migrations "are not self-generating and random; they are produced and patterned."[104] For girls, their lives become a product of, or an unintended consequence of, someone else's migration. Their lives are a constellation of different forms of migration—a result of U.S. immigration laws, immigration policy, and globalization—all of which girls can articulate in their own way that allows them to have both an objective and intimate understanding of migration, and to develop temporal and spatial imaginaries.

1

The Why of Transnational Familial Formations

la suerte viene, la suerte se va por la frontera, la suerte viene,
la suerte se va,
el hambre viene, el hombre se va, sin más razón, el hambre
viene, el hombre se va,
cuando volvera,
por la carretera, por la carretera, por la carretera

[luck comes, luck goes through the border, luck comes, luck
goes,
hunger comes, man leaves without a doubt, hunger comes,
man leaves,
when will he return,
on the road, on the road, on the road]
—Manu Chao, "El Viento" *Clandestino* (Paris: Virgin Records, 1998)

El hielo anda suelto por esas calles
Nunca se sabe cuando nos va a tocar
Lloran, los niños lloran a la salida
Lloran al ver que no llegará mamá
Uno se queda aquí
Otro se queda alla
Eso pasa por salir a trabajar.

[ICE is on the loose out on the streets
You never know when your number's up
Cry, children cry when they get out
They cry when mom's not coming to pick them up
Some of us stay here
Others stay there
That happens for going out to find work."
—La Santa Cecilia, "Ice el Hielo" *Treinta Dias* (Universal Latino, 2013)

Seventeen-year-old Marbe and her sisters—fifteen-year-old Emilia and thirteen-year-old Toñita—live in the town of Zinapécuaro in the state of Michoacán, Mexico. Since birth, they have lived in a father-away transnational family. Their father Sixto also grew up in a transnational family. As a son of a former bracero, he came to understand migration as cyclical and family life as something stretched across international borders. Sixto began helping his family through hard labor at the age of eleven, having only completed the sixth grade. According to Emilia, her father is a brilliant man. While in elementary school, his hard work was rewarded with high grades in math and penmanship. Grammar and spelling were also strengths of his, which makes Marbe, the oldest, feel self-conscious whenever she shares her writing with him. He is the motivation behind Emilia and her sisters' success in school. "Had he had the opportunity to go to school," said Toñita, "he would have done great things, but poverty pushed him to drop out." When he was younger, his family used to produce and sell the ceramic items they made in their backyard kilns. As the family grew, space was needed to build extra rooms, so the kilns were demolished. This forced the family to purchase the merchandise they once produced to make ends meet.

Sixto's father, a U.S. resident, assisted him in getting his *papeles*. Following in his father's footsteps, Sixto began his commutes to the U.S. in the 1980s. These continued after his marriage to Poncia and the birth of his six children—four daughters and two boys. As a legal resident turned citizen, Sixto spends six months of the year in the U.S., usually in Chicago, Portland, or Alaska, and the rest of the year in Zinapécuaro. With six children, one en route to college, ailing parents, and a sister under his care, money is always in short supply. He has plenty of contacts that inform him which city he should try on his next trip to the U.S. Sixto leaves in June, after Holy Week and Saint John the Baptist's Day (June 24), and returns by November just in time for the Christmas holidays.

Seventeen year-old Elena arrived in Napa in 2002 at the age of thirteen to live with her father Silvio. Like Sixto, Silvio began commuting to Napa for work as a young man. Once he married, his cyclical commutes continued until 2002. Living in Oaxaca, Elena always knew her father lived in Napa. Events such as Father's Day or school-related activities provided painful reminders of her father's absence, of his geographic location and distance from family and home. Because her father always returned in April, July, and December of each year, Elena always knew when to expect him. As a U.S. resident, his commutes were regular and relatively easy as the border did not serve as deterrent. When he was away, he called every week. Elena's household did not have a phone then, so each Sunday, wearing their Sunday best, they walked to the phone booth down the street to await his call. During his visits, outings to fairs, restaurants, and belated birthday celebrations were common. For Elena, his departures meant feeling empty and lonely. She recalled one particular departure: "On one occasion, my mom and dad told me that, when my dad was about to leave [back to Napa], he told us he was leaving, but—I was little, I don't know, I must have been four, I don't know, I think, I'm not sure, and my mom says that—I grabbed my lunch box and I went to get a bag of chips and some *frutsis* (Mexican juice drinks) and when my dad was about to leave, I grabbed his hand and told him 'all right, let's go!'" Elena became emotional as she shared this particular story, but insists she never felt abandoned by her father. At home, her mother always made his presence felt by speaking about him and consulting with him on any decisions she made about the children's schooling and household matters. Her extended family, including grandparents, also lived nearby. They cared for and looked after Elena and the family. She found comfort in knowing her father cared for her and loved her very much.

The stories of the three sisters and of Elena represent two examples of transnational families. The first concerns girls still living in this familial arrangement while the second is an example of a family that once lived transnationally but later experienced what Zavella describes as family reunification.[1] Reunification may be a kind of misnomer since, for some families, it may actually mean unification for the first time, as some children may grow up without ever living with their father or mother. When they dwell in the same household in the U.S. or Mexico, it may be the first time that all members of the family live together. In both examples, the girls were raised in a transnational family from birth with a migrant father whose commutes to the U.S. began in the 1980s.

The majority of girls that I interviewed in Zinapécuaro and in Napa came from this transnational familial arrangement. Sixto and Silvio left their families for work in the U.S. in order to provide them with better living conditions and opportunities. Sixto's ability to provide for his family from the U.S. is reflected in Marbe, Emilia, and Toñita's enrollments in school. In 2012, Marbe was in her third year as a nursing student at La Michoacana; Emilia was completing her last year of high school and preparing to take the entrance exam to enroll in La Normal, with hopes of earning a degree in childhood education; and Toñita's high marks in high school were being rewarded with scholarships.[2] The family owns their home and manages to get by economically. Similarly, while Elena lived in Mexico, her father Silvio was able to pay tuition for her and her brothers at a private Catholic school—a luxury in rural towns. Silvio also sent enough money in remittances for his family to enable them to own their own home and a couple of businesses: a minimart and a bakery. For these girls, their fathers' departures materially improved their lives. Silvio decided to bring Elena, her mother, and her siblings to Napa while Sixto has emphatically refused to take his family to Chicago, Alaska, or Portland.

There is something seemingly traditional in these girls' stories that revolve around a man leaving to the U.S. in search of a better future for his family. As Rhacel Salazar Parreñas (2005) explains, for many families in migrants' countries of origin, a father's departure is expected and celebrated—it becomes a logical part extension of his role as the breadwinner.[3] This chapter examines the formation of transnational families with a focus on father-away families. This familial formation is the product of twentieth-century U.S. immigration policy, of failed neoliberal economic policies in Mexico, and of the global restructuring witnessed from the late 1970s onward that has placed men and women on the migrant path.

The Production of Transnational Families: An Overview

When I began to conduct interviews in Napa in 2006 and subsequently in Zinapécuaro in 2010, I noted a pattern. Most of the girls were born into an already existing father-away transnational family. Their fathers began migrating to the U.S. during the 1980s and 1990s. This period saw devaluation of the Mexican peso and an end to government subsidies guaranteeing low prices for food and fuel, creating an economic crisis. The resulting increase in migration to the U.S. led to the passage of the Immigration Reform and Control Act (IRCA) of 1986 by the U.S. Congress, which in turn led to the militarization of the border on the U.S. side. These seemingly distant events registered themselves indirectly in the lives of the girls I interviewed, in the form of migration and family fragmentation.

A long prior history of labor control and recruitment paved the way for the creation of transnational families in the 1980s and 1990s. They followed a pattern of movement north from Mexico established by U.S. employers over decades seeking cheap and willing labor.[4] This labor recruitment was shaped by draconian U.S. immigration policies that excluded and restricted entry by racialized and ethnic groups deemed unassimilable. During the first half of the twentieth century, nativists claimed racialized and ethnic groups were a threat to the racial composition of the nation and, thus, to its very being. While U.S. law and custom resisted granting citizenship and full social membership to Mexican immigrants, U.S. employers welcomed the profits made from the exploitation of low wage immigrant labor. Immigration control functioned as labor control, not reducing the number of immigrants arriving in the U.S. but making sure that their legal vulnerabilities prevented them from bargaining freely over wages and working conditions. Three immigration acts in particular—in 1917, 1921, and 1924—were passed to control entrance into the U.S. and preclude future generations of citizens. Mexicans were exempted from the restrictionist policies directed at other immigrants, not because they were deemed assimilable within the nation, but because of the cheap and disposable labor they could provide.[5] During the second half of the twentieth century, the militarization of the U.S.-Mexico border disguised labor exploitation as border defense.

Following DeGenova's arguments about how migration produces subordinate inclusion for Mexican migrant workers, the section below provides an overview of the production of transnational families.[6] Central to this chapter is how and why fathers left for the U.S. and the varied ways in which their daughters' lives became entangled within these migratory practices.

Immigration Policies in the Twentieth-Century U.S.

Transnational families where the father is the migrant emerged in concert with twentieth-century U.S. immigration policy and labor recruitment. During the nineteenth century, between the end of the Mexican-American War and the 1900s, estimates indicate that fewer than 50,000 migrants arrived in the U.S. from Mexico.[7] By the 1860s, however, men from northern Mexico were already commuting to California for work.[8] Though small in numbers, cohorts of Mexican men migrated to the U.S. and formed transnational families.[9]

Mexican migration and the formation of transnational families continued into the early years of the twenty-first century. Although there has been a recent decrease in U.S.-bound Mexican migration that should not be overlooked, processes of migration are so rooted in Mexican families—such as the ones in this study—that a complete cessation seems unlikely.[10] When debates over immigration arise in the U.S., proposals for visas for low-skilled workers continue to be one of the solutions. These proposals are reminiscent of previous guest worker programs such as those during the bracero years that targeted mostly single men to labor in low-skilled jobs, and the laws governing special agricultural workers (SAW) under IRCA that continue to address the demand for cheap labor to sustain agricultural production and the service sector in the U.S. economy.[11]

Drawing on the generative scholarship of Sassen, DeGenova argues that migration is produced and patterned systemically.[12] In the case of Mexico, this production began in the early 1900s, during a time of heavy recruitment of Mexican workers known as the era of the Enganche (1900–1929). Enganchadores would travel into Mexico to hire men as railroad laborers and bring them to the U.S.[13] The Immigration Acts of 1917, 1921, and 1924 had practically eliminated all other sources of cheap labor as the U.S. practiced a closed-door immigration policy. These acts targeted Asian migrants not included in the Chinese Exclusion Act of 1882 or the Gentlemen's Agreement of 1907, as well as Southern and Eastern European migrants who possessed allegedly undesirable religious and political views purported to threaten the ontology of the U.S. nation. The Immigration Act of 1917 enforced literacy tests, but exempted Mexicans. The Immigration Act of 1921 barred the "Asiatic zone that ran from Afghanistan to the Pacific."[14] The architects of this 1921 act also "restricted immigration to 355,000 a year" and "set a quota for each European country at 3 percent of the number of foreign-born of that nationality residing in the United States in 1910," targeting Southern and Eastern Europeans deemed to be the "wrong kind of migrants."[15] By 1924, the new immigration act had perfected and reduced the quota system to a two percent numerical restriction based on the 1890 census, significantly decreasing Southern and Eastern European migration. Mexican workers were partially exempted from these acts, but they were not welcomed or incorporated into U.S. society. Deportation practices mostly based on racial assumptions began along the U.S.-Mexico border, and as Kelly Lytle-Hernández (2010) found, coincided with the creation of the border patrol in 1924, which mostly targeted undocumented dark-skinned Mexicans.[16]

Heavy recruitment continued, pausing only during the Depression years. In the 1930s, over 400,000 Mexicans—many of them U.S. citizens—were repatriated to Mexico as the U.S. continued its closed-door immigration policy.[17] Mexicans were scapegoated as being responsible for the economic disaster. They were denied the unemployment benefits, poverty relief, and employment on public works projects that cushioned the blows of the Great Depression for other workers. Yet, anti-Mexican worker policies proved to be short-lived as the need for labor during the war years resulted in an agreement between Mexico and the U.S. to import workers in the early 1940s.[18] Known as the bracero program, this labor recruitment sought mostly men to work in states in need of cheap labor, including California, Texas, Arkansas, and another twenty-three states.[19] The idea was to hire men who were already heads of household so that they would return home after their contracts expired. Thus, family fragmentation became official state policy. The hope was that family ties would discourage Mexican men from settling permanently in the U.S.[20] Such recruitment accelerated the production of transnational families and normalized the departures of fathers from their homes.

By the Civil Rights Movement, the rhetoric in the U.S. had changed, particularly under the aegis of Lyndon B. Johnson's Great Society. The Immigration and Nationality Act of 1965 dissolved the racist quotas inscribed in earlier laws and allowed for family reunification. The bracero program came to an end.[21] Routes and destinations, however, had already caused undulations among communities in Mexico. For those communities, the U.S. became the place that would relieve families from economic hardship. People came to imagine the U.S. as a place that could provide wages high enough to produce a better future. With the end of the bracero program, the period of undocumented migration began. The northward movement of men continued the cyclical and temporary practice of migration of the bracero era and before, solidifying the formation of transnational families.[22] Douglas Massey et al. (2002) found that, between 1965 and 1986, the number of undocumented migrants entering and leaving the U.S. remained relatively at the same level. These patterns were altered with the passage of IRCA and its employer sanctions, which proclaimed to protect the border from excessive migrant mobility. This immigration reform placed the numbers of legally permissible Mexican immigrants far below the numbers needed by employers and the numbers that routinely migrated as part of an organic regional economy. This effectively created migrant illegality by criminalizing the survival strategies of Mexican families. At the same time, stricter border control made it more difficult for workers to move back and forth, increasing the numbers of undocumented workers who remained in the U.S. Moreover, structural adjustment policies orchestrated by the U.S., the International Monetary Fund, and the World Bank sharply reduced the social wage in Mexico, while free trade agreements devastated agriculture in southern and central Mexico, producing a new wave of migrants seeking work.

U.S. immigration policy thus contributed to the formation of transnational families. Today, men continue to migrate, normalizing transnational households in areas where the frequency of migration is high. The expectation for a migrating father is tied to his gender-based familial role and is considered an extension of his duty to provide for the family.[23] Within the family, his departure is expected, normalized, and celebrated.

The production of transnational families orchestrated by U.S. immigration policy led to varied familial formations and consequences. Pierrette Hondagneu-Sotelo (1994) describes three types of familial arrangements and migratory practices that were produced: a permanent transnational familial formation, a temporary transnational familial formation, and one where the migrant—usually a single family member—leaves to the U.S. for work of their own accord. Despite the consequences that transnational family living had on those who remained behind—particularly the wives of braceros—prior to the 1970s, studies highlighting this historic production focused on the lives of men.[24] Studies after the 1970s, including Hondagneu-Sotelo's, began to document the consequences of this familial arrangement on adult women who stayed behind. These studies revealed that, even though it was assumed that men were usually the ones who migrated, women, too, were always migrating, often following a husband or father but also on their own.

In recent years, a new generation of scholars has shifted the focus from men to women in examining periods of significant migration, including the bracero era. Having a father living and working in the U.S. meant wives and mothers had to play several new roles in their country of origin. In *Abrazando El Espiritu*, Ana Rosas (2014) found that, during the bracero era, most women remained in Mexico. This was partly due to the program's enforcement of limited communication between fathers, husbands, or brothers, and their daughters, wives, or sisters. Women who stayed behind took care of the children, younger siblings, and the household. They often pursued higher education, with some becoming teachers to supplement their income. Some women migrated to bracero program centers near the U.S.-Mexico border to be closer to their husbands, while others crossed into the U.S. to follow their spouses.

In revisiting the 1960s and 1970s, Hondagneu-Sotelo found that, when a husband left, women became the head of the household and in charge of making financial decisions for the family. They looked after any family-related matters—land, business, debt—that would have fallen on the husband if he'd been present. As Stephen discovered, some women experienced a sense of freedom in their new roles. Those who wanted to join their fathers, siblings, or husbands in the U.S. usually had to develop their own networks, which often took years. Men, who saw their stay in the U.S. as temporary, had little desire to bring their families with them, as that usually led to permanent settlement. González-López found this pattern and attitude persisted well into the 1990s.[25] In other cases, González-López found that, if women wanted to migrate to join their husbands in the U.S., they simply showed up on the doorsteps of their husband's house. Regardless of the amount of time that a husband was away, studies consistently find that women became the heads of household, altering traditional gender roles in Mexico.[26]

The 1970s and 1980s also witnessed an increase in adult female migration to the U.S. In her study of Mixtec and Zapotec migrants in Oregon and California, Stephen links the worldwide economic restructuring—globalization—to the need for migrant labor, particularly women's labor.[27] U.S. middle-class families and their need for dual income households meant hiring laboring hands within the home to perform the reproductive labor that facilitated that middle class lifestyle. Domestic workers, nannies, and gardeners were needed for the middle class to function, to "pick up pre-washed and precut salad mixes, cut and washed fruits, and more".[28] Stephen notes that, "as American women entered the paid labor force in greater numbers, their demand for domestic service and for easy-to-prepare foods increased."[29] Women's migration, in particular, is due in part to the entrance of American women into the labor force, which led to the demand for domestic workers.[30] These domestic workers' migration facilitated the lives of the American middle class. It ensured their ability to function.

Unlike men, women's departure and how it is viewed depends on the context. Ethnographic studies on transnational mothers, for example, present varied forms of understanding the decisions mothers have to make.[31] Parreñas argues that when women began migrating, their departure was viewed differently than men's, particularly if children are left behind.[32] Her departure is not celebrated as an extension of her role as a mother. Instead, she is viewed as having abandoned her children. Abrego found that, by the time a Salvadoran mother decides to leave El Salvador and look for work in the U.S., she most likely has already previously left her children at least once.[33] Salvadoran mothers first try to look for work away from home within El Salvador leaving children under the care of a relative. This means that children have already experienced separation from their mothers. International migration, in some cases, becomes the next step.

U.S. immigration policies, then, has produced and accelerated the formation of transnational families. Even if families are able to (re-)unite in the U.S., deportation is always looming. The scholarly focus on these familial arrangements has changed from men to women, but children, particularly daughters, are still rarely the focus. In this study, Mexican teenage girls born into families with historic ties to migration practices are placed front and center.

Immigration Reform and Control Act and Border Control

U.S. immigration policies and border control go hand in hand. The two thousand miles that mark the division between Mexico and the U.S. was first drawn on February 2, 1848, and altered in 1853.[34] By 1924, the policing began to deter the undesired and fueled the American imagination. Those who cross the border without documents become "illegal" and thus immediately criminalized.[35] As the "illegal," the undocumented becomes the impossible subject, someone who lacks rights and who is not supposed to exist.[36]

The militarization of the border escalated with the passage of the Immigration Reform and Control Act of 1986. IRCA's key components included amnesty for those who could prove they had lived in the U.S. on or before January 1, 1982, employer sanctions, and border control. The border was already policed prior to IRCA but not to the same extent. In fact, under IRCA the budget of the then Immigration and Naturalization Services (INS)—now Immigration and Customs Enforcement (ICE)—grew. According to Lytle-Hernández, by 1907, immigrants entering the U.S. were already required to pass through a port of entry. By 1924, the border patrol was created to "enforce U.S. immigration restrictions comprehensively by preventing unauthorized border crossing and policing borderland regions to detect and arrest persons defined as unauthorized immigrants."[37] With the 1924 immigration act came the end of line inspection as U.S. embassies throughout the world were placed in charge of visas, medical inspections, and collecting a head tax; by the time a migrant arrived in a U.S. port of entry, they would do so with legal documents.[38] Arriving without documents meant the migrant was undocumented.

By 1986, border control had become a preventive measure to stop or at least deter undocumented migrants. This altered what had hitherto been believed to be a mostly cyclical movement of migrants.[39] Such focus on the border led to three immediate consequences: lengthier journeys of migrants engaged in cyclical migration to the U.S.; a permanent settlement for migrants engaged in cyclical migration; and the looming of death for those seeking to cross the border as crossing points were pushed east. Prior to IRCA, circular patterns of migration were common among transnational families who expected their relatives to depart for the U.S. during certain months of the year and return during others. With IRCA, the militarization of the border as a form of control escalated in 1986 and accelerated again in the 1990s under the Clinton administration. Measures such as Operation Gatekeeper and Operation Hold the Line (both in 1994) served as deterrents for border crossers along with the military-like equipment used by border patrol agents. Equipment such as "[h]elicopters, night-vision scopes, ground sensors, and computers borrowed from the Pentagon were now used at unprecedented levels," so that "the U.S.-México border became a virtual war zone."[40] Such changes altered the cartography of migration causing routes to move east, leading to thousands of deaths. Estimates include 3,600 disappearances between 1995 and 2004.[41] Today, crossing the border has become a death-defying movement represented by thousands of bodies found in the desert, many of which remain unclaimed.[42] The circular migration patterns also became lengthier and families left behind wait longer to reunite with relatives.

The border has become a site of debate. For those who advocate for border control, Mexicans crossing without proper documents feed into a narrative about the border as a lawless place.[43] According to this narrative, the estimated twelve million undocumented immigrants who have crossed have defied the U.S. nation-state. Peter Andreas (2000) argues that lawmakers have responded to this loss of control by implementing policies that purposely fail to deter immigration.[44] In these policy games, as Andreas calls them, peoples' livelihoods disappear as some migrants literally lose their lives. Andreas argues that "the stress on loss of control understates the degree to which the state has actually structured, conditioned, and even enabled (often unintentionally) clandestine border crossing, and overstate[s] the degree to which the state has been able to control its borders in the past."[45] In other words, in no way has the state lost control of its border. It has reinforced its power over its bounded territory each time an immigration debate arises to assuage nativists' fears.

Robert Alvarez Jr. (2005) points to the power of the state both north and south in manipulating the geographic divide.[46] The U.S. Department of Agriculture (USDA), for example, has extended deep into Mexico, traveling south to inspect Mexican produce before allowing it to enter the U.S. in a move that challenges the sovereignty and the defined boundaries of that nation. On the U.S. side, the border extends and expands as ICE conducts raids deep into the territory. The border, then, follows the migrant. It is in constant motion both before and after migrants physically cross into the United States.

For the girls in this study, the frequency of their fathers' visits usually depends on his legal status, as it provides him with the ability to legally commute or not.[47] According to some of the girls interviewed, their father legalized his status with *la amnistia* (amnesty), making their transnational lives intricately connected to U.S. immigration policies. For those girls who stated that their father lacked *papeles,* the border limits physical visits and commutes.

Mexico's Economic Policies of the 1980s and 1990s

Contemporary Mexican migration can be traced to the late 1970s, 1980s, and 1990s. At the national level, agricultural policies in the countryside and economic restructuring were key factors in pushing migrants north.[48] At an international level, the rise and drop in oil prices, coupled with neoliberal economic policies, contributed to a massive economic crisis.[49]

The 1970s brought an end to the "miracle era" when Mexico enjoyed a relatively stable economy.[50] This period from approximately the 1940s to the 1960s featured import substitution industrialization (ISI) programs that kept trade low and tariffs high, making national products and industry flourish. Mexican industry produced enough supplies to sustain its citizens. The miracle era also included slow disinvestment of government policies in the countryside, causing rural to urban migration.[51] During this era, migration to the U.S was constant but circular, as migrants went north looking for work and returned home after a few months. The border was not a deterrent. This migratory rhythm was also encouraged by the bracero program's contracts, which sought to maintain circular migration by imposing obstacles to permanent settlement and citizenship in the U.S. But this type of migration further developed the links, routes, and destinations carved by earlier generations of migrants.[52] These earlier waves of migration assisted in the production of dozens of satellite communities in the U.S. that also facilitated the continuation of transnational migration.[53]

In the late 1970s and 1980s, U.S.-bound migration was also prompted by a series of international events.[54] From 1973–1980, the Organization of Petroleum Exporting Countries (OPEC) raised oil prices as a response to the Arab–Israeli conflict, causing a worldwide economic crisis.[55] Mexico, which was not part of OPEC but had oil of its own, was affected,[56] particularly after president–elect José López Portillo took office in 1976 and new oil reserves were found.[57] With oil prices high, Lopéz Portillo assumed that the newfound oil would finally allow Mexico to enter modernity and famously told the nation: "There are two kinds of countries in the world today—those that don't have oil and those that do. We have it."[58] Judith Adler Hellman (1983) explores how the newfound oil did not aid Mexico's economy.[59] Instead, "oil revenue was insufficient to underwrite expansion because Pemex, at this point, was investing more than it earned."[60] According to Hellman, Mexico lacked the infrastructure to produce and sustain its newfound oil.[61] The Mexican government increased investments in the oil industry and borrowed money at high interest rates (assuming payments would be possible), with the ultimate goal of morphing into a (what scholars used to refer to as) "First World" nation. At first there was prosperity, but oil prices began to decline and by 1982 Mexico was unable to make debt payments.[62]

Hellman argues that what also affected Mexico's economy was the response of the wealthy to the economic crisis: "The basic strategy of the bourgeoisie was to convert pesos to dollars and get them out of Mexico and into either a Swiss bank account or a piece of real estate likely to retain or increase its value."[63] With capital flight under way, the ominous words—la crisis—rang everywhere.[64] Claudio Lomnitz-Adler (2003) describes this period as "full of events: wildly fluctuating currency values; the daily spectacle of commodity prices in times of hyperinflation; nationalization of the banks as an initial solution to the political crisis followed by an aggressive plan of privatization of state enterprises; company foreclosures, layoffs, calamitous declines in the value of real wages; union mobilizations meeting unexpected responses, including factory closures and government indifference; Mexico's entry into the General Agreements of Tariff and Trade (GATT); elimination of state subsidies; and suspended investment in public goods."[65] According to Lomnitz-Adler, the Mexican government adopted a rhetoric filled with narratives of sacrifice for a future national prosperity.[66] *La crisis,* as it was popularly known, became a suspension in time where people's hopes and dreams were suspended for the good of the nation.[67] The Mexican people were saturated with images of an abstract better future that would come after *la crisis* passed. A permanent state of not now and not yet became the norm.[68]

Fraught with economic woes, the 1980s became known as the "lost decade." Stephen Haber et al. (2008) refer to this decade as Mexico's second revolution, because of its critical shift in economic policies and its radical departure from a nationalist economy.[69] Scholars divide this decade into three periods: 1982–1985, 1986–1988, and 1988–1990, each marked by different adjustments to Mexico's economic policies.[70] The first period saw a drop in wages[71] and the second structural adjustments, including Mexico's entrance to the GATT.[72] During this period, U.S. products began to make their way into Mexican markets, displacing local economies and products.[73] The third period is defined by debt negotiations[74] that eventually facilitated the North American Free Trade Agreement's (NAFTA) approval in 1994.[75]

La crisis caused Mexico's economy to adopt a neoliberal economic strategy, which normalized privatization and foreign investment at the expense of local economies.[76] President Miguel de la Madrid's (1982–1988) transitory economic policy was followed by that of Carlos Salinas de Gortari's (1988–1994), which sealed the deal with NAFTA. The national rhetoric adopted by the Mexican government filled the country with narratives of sacrifice for a future national prosperity.[77] People's lives were suspended for the good of Mexico and what was assumed to be a temporary phase. Everyone was to be complicit in tightening their belts without complaints.[78] For Mexicans with established routes and destinations to and in the U.S., and for those with the means to move, migration became inevitable.[79] Douglas Massey and Audrey Singer (1995) found that the crisis of 1982 led to an increase in "illegal" entries into the U.S.[80] It should be no surprise that 1982 was the last possible year to have entered the U.S. "illegally" and still secure legalization under IRCA.

The end of the 1980s brought a new reality with the signing of the NAFTA treaty that continued the transformations in Mexico's economic policies.[81] NAFTA, at least in Mexico's imaginary, signified once again the possibility of entrance into modernity, the chance to finally become a (what scholars used to refer to as) "First World" nation. The treaty, which facilitated trade between Canada, the U.S., and Mexico, eased trade barriers and, in keeping with neoliberal theory, was assumed to bring jobs and investments to those in need. The latter, once again, did not happen. NAFTA was approved despite criticism for its dismissal of labor and environmental rights. President Carlos Salinas de Gortari expected to finalize the agreement during George H.W. Bush's presidency, but the signing was delayed until the Clinton administration. In November of 1993, NAFTA was signed to come into effect on January 1, 1994.[82]

NAFTA's inaugural year also marked the beginning of the Ejercito Zapatista de Liberación Nacional (EZLN) uprising in Chiapas. They intervened in the celebration of Mexico's so-called entrance into modernity by expressing their opposition and reminding the world of a *México profundo*.[83] 1994 also saw yet another economic crisis, which led to more economic adjustments. The bailout went beyond easing trade barriers and included "further privatization of national enterprises, measures to hold down inflation, and the use of oil revenues to guarantee repayment making them unavailable for economic development."[84] The working class once again paid the highest price.

Some scholars argue that, while NAFTA should not be blamed exclusively, it did deepen and widen existing poverty in Mexico.[85] Penélope Pacheco-López (2005) states that foreign investment after NAFTA has had a negative effect on the Mexican economy,[86] while Jorge Castañeda (2009) notes that it intensified a trend towards impoverishment of the countryside based, for example, on lesser revenues to farmers.[87] Migration to the U.S. increased. Many families from the city and the country migrated to destinations older generations had already chosen for them. The passage of California's Proposition 187 in 1994—an anti-immigrant measure that denied services to undocumented immigrants—was not coincidental, and reflected one response to these changed circumstances.

Structural adjustment policies further impoverished local economies. Because ties to the U.S. were already established, fathers and mothers—including the parents of many of the girls in this study—followed the well-known routes to supplement the livelihoods of their families. Their lives, in part, are consequences of the structural adjustments that have led fathers and/or mothers to make the decision to migrate. Their motives ranged across the economic spectrum, from the desire to pay for a private school education for their children to adding a second floor to a home or opening up their own business. As will be discussed in latter chapters, these girls were able to experience some of the material benefits only because their fathers were able to provide for them from the U.S.

In some ways, transnational families also absorbed and adopted the "suspension in time" Lomnitz-Adler describes during *la crisis*. Families who engaged in varied forms of transnational living were willing to make short-term sacrifices for what they believed would be long-term benefits. During the girls' childhoods, once their fathers left for the U.S., family time became suspended. The same rhetoric of sacrifice used at a national level during *la crisis* can be applied to the girls' extensive waits for their fathers' visits or for the family unit to become united. Zavella describes a suspension of familial formations as a postponement due in part to migration.[88]

Consequences of the Formation of Transnational Families

In this study, fathers' departures are consequences of the context of U.S. immigration policies and of Mexico's economic crises of the 1980s and 1990s. The need for laboring hands within middle-class households in the U.S. was also a "pull" factor. Making someone's life easier may reciprocally mean making someone else's life harder, however. While their mothers and fathers attend to a middle class household in the U.S., girls raised in fractured familial arrangements back home grow up with only sporadic visits from their parents.

With limited educational opportunities or job prospects, fathers leave, usually in their teens, and return to Mexico to marry and form transnational families. They have children and, unable to make ends meet, continue to commute to the U.S. for work. These commutes are an exaggerated version of how we understand commuting as a daily journey from home to work and back. Neil Smith (2002) has noted commute patterns in Sao Paolo, Brazil, which start as early as three-thirty in the morning, or four hours each way for Zimbabweans in Africa.[89] Yet men also commute for months, oftentimes years, for work.

Fathers leave with the idea that the commutes are temporary. Perhaps the saturation of sacrifice as a consequence of *la crisis* penetrated so deeply that his departure as such was not questioned.[90] It became understood as something a family needed to do for its own good. Neoliberal rhetoric and policy sought to inculcate within the individual an imperative of self-management and self-sacrifice, in order to clean up the mess created by plutocratic plunder and its organized abandonment of the working class and the poor. Within these commuting patterns, fathers learned to strengthen and solidify their networks in case they made decisions to bring their families to the U.S.

Many Mexican teenage girls raised in transnational families were actually born into a family that had already agreed to live apart since their fathers were commuting long before they were born. They entered into a family that had agreed to give up intimate affective relations in hopes of meeting basic needs for food, school, shelter, and clothing. This suspension of time resonates with Lomnitz-Adler's analysis of the national narrative of a post-1982 Mexico in crisis, a narrative that centered on sacrifices citizens made based on "viable and desirable images of a future."[91]

Transnational family life then becomes a practice of suspension, of temporariness, of waiting. Fathers commute to the U.S. for work where they may spend months or years working, waiting to return home. Mothers remain behind and become heads of the household in charge of the daily household operations. Daughters grow up thinking of life in the U.S. and, in some cases, imagining their own journeys north.

Caught in Migration: Heteronormativity, Imaginary, and Modernity

The context I provide above aims to show the structural and historical forces that shape the lives of Mexican teenage girls raised in transnational families. The girls' experiences are intricately connected to the conditions—both in Mexico and the U.S.—that pushed their fathers north. First, they were never raised in a heteronormative family. Second, they grew up imagining El Norte. Lastly, that imagining produced desires for modernity. I explore this upbringing as an example of a "structure of feeling" where, as Appadurai states, the global and the local enters their lives.[92] Girls raised in transnational families share that experience and similar desires for a different quality of life. Not all of them develop the same desires, but they share commonalities that are unique to the context and surroundings in which they were raised.

Heteronormative Families and Transnational Families

I use heteronormative families to contrast transnational families. As stated in the introduction, heteronormative alludes to the traditional. In this case, a heteronormative family is one that is understood in the traditional sense of a mother, a father, and children living under one roof. This is not the case for transnational families that are divided and stretched across geographic borders. Transnational families acquire a different meaning. Although they aim to function as families in the heteronormative sense, they are different. In this sense, and as noted in the introduction, I am queering transnational families as not being the norm. Here, I am not advocating for heteronormative families whose realities are often far different from the celebratory ways in which they are described. Their wholeness and coherence are often completely mythical. What I want to note, however, are the temporal consequences of this familial arrangement on children, particularly daughters. Transnational families have a different temporality, a different rhythm, marked by periods of waiting for the family to unite or reunite. In the process of waiting, daughters wait for a date, for a return, for a departure. They imagine a different present and future.

Transnational living is about short-term sacrifices for long-term benefits. Girls are raised in transnational families that are fractured by migratory practices. Assurance that their future will be better is always present. This too has to do with the temporality of transnational families. It resonates with the sacrifices that the Mexican nation-state implemented during *la crisis*. This is a lesson that I argue the girls and their fathers internalized.

Imaginary

Growing up in this transnational familial arrangement allows girls to imagine a different present and future, usually somewhere else. Cole and Durham state that it is common among youth everywhere to desire or imagine alternative possibilities.[93] For some, the imaginary entails migration. In their imagination, the United States is the place that can provide a different promise and a brighter future. The imaginary, as Schmidt Camacho states, "represents a symbolic field in which people come to understand and describe their social being."[94] For Noel Salazar (2011), "imagining is an embodied practice of transcending both physical and sociocultural distance."[95] When the girls imagine their future in the U.S., they think it will be better. Their imagined future in the U.S. is one where they imagine they will have more control over their present and future. The girls in this study then also imagine that it is there where they can become engineers, doctors, or nurses, or where they can save money to construct their future. They imagine a life in the U.S. that will be filled with opportunities for upward mobility, with access to modern clothes, gadgets, travel, and other things they attach to their understanding of modernity.

Because the girls in this study are growing up in transnational families, direct ties and connections to Napa or other cities in the U.S. are present while they are in Mexico. The way they imagine life in the U.S. is not simply based on the hegemony of the U.S. popular culture that they see on the television set, or the flow of images from elsewhere common in a global world. Rather, they see it directly when their fathers return from the U.S. with T-shirts, sneakers, necklaces, stationary, and stories about El Norte that fuel their imaginations. Their father left to provide for them. The U.S., they imagine, is also the place to go to provide for themselves.

Modernity

I link girls' imaginaries to expressed desires for modernity. As Appadurai states, modernity aims for "universal applicability."[96] The West and its representative nation-states, as Enrique Dussel (2016) tells us, express those universal ideals,[97] with the underlying assumption that the West, its citizens, and the rest aim "to become modern."[98] Of course, that assumed universal ideal has been critiqued by decolonial scholars, including Dussel and Anibal Quijano (2007).[99] Historically, modernity is situated within the industrial revolution, although Dussel traces its roots to 1492 and the aftermath of the conquest and colonization. Conquest, colonization, and slavery have been foundational acts in the making of the modern world, producing a racialized capitalism replete with exploitation and hierarchy. Modernity's mystifications hide its oppressions by relegating the exploited peoples of the global south to a previous time in history, diagnosing them as in need of modernity rather than in need of justice and freedom.

As a universal expression, modernity disavows the historic underdevelopment that intrinsically connects the West to the rest. From this perspective, modernity obfuscates how modern societies emerged.[100] Its systems of knowledge—political, economic, cultural, and social—are assumed to be the norm to which all should aspire. This is the desire that the imaginary Mexico expresses and that Bonfil Batalla critiques.

These universal claims, including desires for a modern experience, pervade the ways young Mexican teenage girls talk about their existence. They are responding to a desire embodied by the imaginary Mexico. For them, the embodied sensations for modernity lay in the U.S. What is unique to the girls' experiences in this study is that they receive firsthand accounts of modern life in the U.S. via their fathers' commutes, remittances, and tales. Modernity, then, is expressed via the girls' desires for that modern experience. They develop modern aspirations of a modern adolescence.

Conclusion

Whether transnational families reunite in Mexico or in the U.S., they do so after having experienced a type of familial fracturing. If the family is reunited in the U.S., their reunification will depend on their legal status. The increase in deportation practices in recent years has introduced real fear in families that have already experienced separation. The fear of further fracturing looms large. In some cases, families are reunited in Mexico as a consequence of the father's permanent return. This fulfills the ideal hope from the beginning that led to transnational familial arrangements. Yet the possibility of commuting again if money runs out, a business fails, or a new debt is incurred is always present as well. Migration, in this sense, also always looms large.

The formation and fragmentation of transnational families is a product of twentieth-century U.S. immigration policies and of economic restructuring. Current debates on U.S. immigration policy illuminate the fate of children of undocumented workers who experience their parents' deportations, a phenomenon that increased during the Obama administration. This raises questions about the rights of U.S. citizens of Mexican descent to live with their parents. At the end of 2014, President Barack Obama signed the Deferred Action for Parents of Americans and Lawful Permanent Residents (DAPA) executive order precisely to address this point. DAPA was challenged on February of 2015 by twenty-six states including Texas. The case went all the way to the Supreme Court where a four to four split prevented its implementation.[101] Yet, for girls like Elena, whose family reunited in the U.S. after having lived in a transnational family for thirteen years, her family was fractured long before her own migration. How can this injury be repaired? The same system that produces transnational families in Mexico breaks up undocumented and mixed status families in the U.S. Here, the question lies on who has the right, as Abrego asks, to live as and in a family unit?

This type of familial arrangement continues. As a product of twentieth-century U.S. immigration policy and a response to Mexico's economic policies, men, women, and children continue to migrate. The roots of a transnational living are so entrenched in certain segments of Mexican society that migration becomes expected. Massey et al. (1993) found that "causation is cumulative in that each act of migration alters the social context within which subsequent migration decisions are made, typically in ways that make additional movements more likely."[102] The consequences of transnational living will be explored in the rest of the book.

The girls in this study come from the typical transnational family where the father leaves and returns sporadically for short-term visits. Chapters 2 through 4 present a more thorough analysis of the father-daughter relations within this familial formation. It explores the reasons as to why some fathers refuse to bring their daughters to the U.S. and thwart their desires for movement. Girls then remain as migrants in waiting for an indefinite period of time.

2

Growing Up Transnational

*Mexican Teenage Girls and Their Transnational
Familial Arrangements*

I sit on a bench at Nadia's mother's beauty salon waiting for a haircut. Vero, a small-framed woman in her fifties, charges approximately thirty pesos (three U.S. dollars) for a dry cut.[1] She was about to finish with a client when I arrived. While I waited, two women popped their heads in and asked how long before she was available. They were in a hurry and did not have time to wait. Though clients can make appointments in advance—Vero has a visible appointment book—she tends to run a first come, first served business. Vero assured them it would only take half an hour to do my hair so they could return then.

The beauty salon called "She and Him" is a space that Vero rents from a relative. It is in a very central location in downtown Zinapécuaro, which makes it convenient for customers to drop in for a quick haircut in between errands. Her salon provides full services including waxing, *rayitos* (highlights), hair perms and coloring, manicures, and pedicures. The salon is a large room with two stations, one hair-washing station, and a long bench for customers to sit as they wait. There are mirrors along the walls for customers to view their haircut in progress from all angles. A large television set sits in the middle of the room for customers to view the latest *novelas* from Televisa or Hollywood films from the "Golden" and "Golden Edge" channels. When the television is off, Vero plays 1980s *baladas* and hums along to songs by Mexican icons like Los Bukis, Marisela, José José, and Emmanuel.[2] When Vero feels more upbeat, she jams to Juan Gabriel as she washes or trims her client's hair.

Vero enjoys chatting with her customers. Because she had given me permission to interview her daughters—seventeen-year-old Nadia and nineteen-year-old Alba—as she trimmed my hair, we spoke about her living arrangements. She tells me she is finally ready to move forward and will file for divorce soon. Vero has lived in a transnational family with her husband away since she returned from Arizona in 2002. Her husband, who remained behind, does not send any remittances and has only visited twice. "A three day retreat I attended in Guadalajara," she said, "provided me with some tools to heal, to forgive, and to move on. I wish I had the money to send Nadia and Alba. They hold so much resentment." Vero is worried her daughters are carrying the pain and betrayal over what feels like abandonment and a violation to an agreement made between them and their father when they returned to Zinapécuaro in 2002. That arrangement includes him sending money to improve the material conditions of Vero, Nadia, and Alba. They are still waiting for that improvement.

Girls like Nadia and Alba were raised in transnational families. Their father left when they were young and has only returned twice. In many ways, both girls are accustomed to their familial arrangement, but there is a continuous feeling of waiting for their situation to change. Their mother Vero has become the sole provider and breadwinner. It is Vero who is raising her daughters on the income she receives from "She and Him." Their story, however, is only one among varied transnational familial formations I found in the town of Zinapécuaro.

The majority of girls that I interviewed in Zinapécuaro were raised in transnational families. Not all harbor feelings of resentment and betrayal. Some have developed healthy relationships with their fathers and express gratitude for what they interpret as his sacrifices for them. In this chapter, I explore the fragmentation produced by migration, and the affective "structure of feeling" accompanying it. The stories related by my interviewees testified to the key role their mothers played in arranging and re-arranging family dynamics. They voiced unhappiness about the uncertainties and interruptions to their young lives caused by the transnational form of their families.

This chapter begins to highlight the experiences and consequences of girls raised in transnational familial arrangements by first situating the town of Zinapécuaro and its diaspora. I then provide a brief overview of the girls' lives followed by concrete details of their varied familial arrangements. The goal of this chapter is to examine girls' familial formations, their shared experience or "structure of feeling," and the development of a fragile yet very real agency. I argue that, in some ways, Mexican teenage girls inhabit the borderlands—a place where cultures meet[3] and different ideas are circulated, producing multiple desires that are explored in chapters 3 and 4.

The Town: Zinapécuaro

The town of Zinapécuaro has a population of approximately 46,000 and an atmosphere similar to many migrant-sending towns outside of Mexico City.[4] It has a *plaza* or *zócalo*, known as *el centro*, where the market, most stores, and government offices are located. Downtown—also known as *el jardín* or the garden for its central fountain and greenery that surround it—is where fruit and ice cream vendors, shoe shiners, and newspaper stands are found. There are private and public schools from kindergarten to high school with the nearest universities located in the state capital of Morelia, a forty-five-minute bus ride away. A Catholic church sits atop a hill with one of the best views in town. Each night at the end of the seven o'clock mass, bells are rung and heard throughout the town, suspending any private or public activity for what is known as *la bendición* (blessing). Wherever a devout Catholic is located, when the bells begin to ring, s/he stops and turns to face the church. The town is still until the bells stop ringing. Activities resume when the ringing comes to an end.

The town is fairly quiet throughout the year—with two exceptions. The first takes place the week before Holy Week, when the tourists and the diaspora arrive. The second occurs during the month of December, when the diaspora returns from U.S. states including Wisconsin, California, Illinois, Nevada, North Carolina, Virginia, Indiana, Michigan, Georgia, Louisiana, and Alaska. The return of the diaspora highlights the town's multiple satellite communities north of the border.[5] These communities shape and influence the town of Zinapécuaro, thus providing multiple U.S. experiences available for Zinapecuarenses. For example, migrants who go to Louisiana adopt styles, tastes, and accents different from those who live in Chicago. The former is more rural while the latter is more urban. These multiple diasporas come together twice per year, making locals extremely familiar with U.S. geography. Families and neighborhoods are known for their U.S. destinations.

The week before Holy Week heralds the arrival of El Señor de Araro (Figure 2.1)—a wooden-like figure of Christ made from cornhusks—which represents a long-standing tradition between Zinapécuaro and the neighboring town of Araro.[6] El Señor de Araro is a saint-like patron with many followers due to his believed miracle-making abilities. Each year, Araro allows Zinapécuaro to borrow its Señor for display at the town's main church for fifty days. Followers walk the three-hour distance that separates the towns to pick him up. He is placed inside a box in the shape of a cross lined with velvet cloth, and is carried by men who sign up months in advance to have what for them is an honor and privilege to carry the box into town.[7] Only men are allowed to carry El Señor. Women are expected to follow behind praying. According to this tradition, men and women are expected to play different roles in this pilgrimage. When El Señor enters the streets of Zinapécuaro, he encounters colorfully decorated streets, confetti, music, and fireworks that echo throughout the town, announcing his arrival (Figure 2.2). It is a celebration that attracts national tourists and members of the diaspora who flock to town, fill the hotels, enjoy the aquatic park of La Atzimba,[8] and savor the local cuisine, which typically includes *corundas* served with salsa, pork, and sour cream.[9] The diaspora returns to thank

Figure 2.1. El Señor de Araro inside the church in Zinapécuaro. Photo taken by Lilia Soto.

Figure 2.2. Men in the town of Zinapécuaro carry El Señor de Araro.
Photo taken by Lilia Soto.

El Señor for any blessing or miracles they have received. Celebrations begin the Wednesday before Holy Week and continue throughout the weekend. Students are excused from school, soccer practice and matches are cancelled, and going swimming in La Atzimba on a Friday morning is common as the whole town partakes in the very Catholic celebration.

December also means the return of the diaspora yearning to spend the holidays with their loved ones. When they return, they bring with them commodities and customs from the U.S. states where they reside. A single family may have immediate family members in Virginia, Indiana, Utah, and California—all of which shape the imaginations and cognitive mappings of those who remain behind.[10] Their arrival means weddings, baptisms, and celebrations that become common any day of the week at this time of year, as opposed to the usual Saturday or Sunday. Halls for large receptions need to be reserved months in advance. Neighborhoods throw parties known as *fogatas* with bonfires that close down streets. DJ's are hired and dancing is required. The diaspora tends to throw the most opulent *fogatas* and parties, as these become a way to display visibly and sometimes ostentatiously the success they have garnered from labor in the U.S. They bring what locals interpret as the most up to date music, dancing, and styles, emblematic of the promises of modernity that fuel girls' imaginaries. Families return with children and teenagers. Relationships develop over the two-to-three-week span of the visit and are often nourished across international borders. When Holy Week ends or Christmas and New Year's Eve is over, the diaspora returns to the U.S. and the town resumes its normal activities. Teenagers in Zinapécuaro are left with new musical tastes, dance fads, and styles of dress that they have picked up from the diaspora.

These visits also occur throughout the entire year, but not to the same degree. It is not uncommon at those times to walk down the street, visit Internet cafés and local shops, and hear teens or adults speaking in English. Vero's daughters learned English while they lived in Arizona. There are other girls who also share this experience. Seventeen-year-old Mariana also learned English during the three years that she lived in San Jose, California. Girls like Mariana, Alba and Nadia like to put their English-speaking abilities on display when they are out and about as a way to showcase their cosmopolitanism. The constant and continuous visits of the diaspora throughout the year make the town of Zinapécuaro seem quite unstable and transient. For teenage girls, the diaspora is made up of former compatriots who, though they have roots in Zinapécuaro, are no longer from there. The idea that Zinapecuarenses living elsewhere are no longer viewed as locals points to the changes caused by migration. Girls grow assuming places are like this—transitory and not quite rooted, with migration and movement always present. Deep inside Mexican territory, they are living in borderlands.

The Girls: An Overview

In examining the lives of Mexican teenage girls raised in transnational families and transnational social fields, my goal is not to create a type of girl growing up in this familial arrangement that can be generalized and whose experience may be applied in a broader context. Instead, I want to highlight "how specific local processes condition each other," applying Weinbaum et al.'s method of connective comparison that avoids sameness and equivalence when describing girls' experiences.[11] Weinbaum et al. negotiate multiple languages and contexts when studying girls. Here, I examine how their lives are shaped and influenced by the local, national, and transnational, each with its own contexts where I trace the unique and common practices of Mexican teenage girls within the place in which they live.

In some ways, Mexican teenage girls resemble a typical teenager from the U.S. or any so-called modern nation. There is also something unique and specific to being from Zinapécuaro. Style-wise, they prefer to wear skinny jeans, flats, and colorful jewelry—a style of dress similar to that of U.S. teenage girls. Musically, they listen to U.S. pop stars such as Katy Perry, Kesha, and Rihanna. More locally, they also listen to *banda* music and *reggaeton*. The Puerto Rican duo Wisin y Yandel are frequently cited as the favorite *reggaetoneros*. Girls carry cell phones, text one another, and enter chat rooms. Facebook and Myspace accounts are part of their daily lives. Some have laptops they carry to school for note-taking purposes. They watch *telenovelas* and music channels, including *Banda Mix* and *Tele Hit*. Films, such as *Crepúsculo* (Twilight)—based on Stephenie Meyer's vampire novels—and series such as *La Ley y El Orden* (Law and Order), *La Anatomía de Gray* (Gray's Anatomy), and *Mentes Criminales* (Criminal Minds) are some of their favorite television shows. Two television channels—Golden and Golden Edge—show subtitled Hollywood films all day, which girls enjoy watching after school and on the weekends. This points to the hegemony of U.S. popular culture where the global is adopted into the local. Despite the abundance of material gadgets in their lives, most of the girls are working-class, attend public schools, and come from families with very limited schooling.

The girls' seduction by U.S. pop icons, television shows, and Hollywood films represents the penetration of a dominant U.S. popular culture, where a type of "sameness" is produced. Yet, there is also a local feel to their taste, for example, in hairstyles or schooling practices that set them apart from other diasporic teenage girls who visit during Holy Week or December. As will be further explored in chapter 3, I situate this sameness within the town of Zinapécuaro where I highlight girls' daily practices to point to "specific local processes" that shape their lives.[12]

Familial Arrangements

In this study, girls' fathers usually first left to the U.S. for work during the 1980s and the 1990s. Fathers are part of the exodus of migrants who went north during a period of monetary devaluation and imposed austerity known as *la crisis* and its aftermath. As teenagers, they followed the footsteps of their own fathers or other members of their community who were looking north for the jobs they could no longer find in Zinapécuaro. When a girl is asked why her father left for the U.S., she typically explains that he left to be able to provide their families with a better chance at life—more education than their parents, a home, an extra room, a second floor to the house, or a business so the family can become independent. As I argue in chapter 1, the lack of means to provide for a family is a result of Mexico's changing economic policies. In other words, fathers cannot provide for their families because the state has not invested in them. Fathers then turn to the U.S., a place many of them have commuted to for work long before marriage, the formation of transnational families, and the birth of their daughters. They turn to the place that historically has recruited their fathers, grandfathers, and other relatives for employment.

Transnational familial arrangements vary widely, with some being more permanent, others continuous, and some short-term. Five of the forty girls interviewed live in transnational families where there has been limited contact with the migrant father. Within this arrangement, the girls' father does not send remittances, does not return to Zinapécuaro regularly for visits, and does not call regularly. He is almost a ghost-like figure in the girls' lives. They cannot quite feel him, but know of his presence. Like a ghost, he makes irregular apparitions. For the girls, this insecure and unstable living arrangement feels permanent. Fifteen of the girls live in transnational families with a father who returns and departs to and from the U.S. regularly. This arrangement feels more constant and continuous as fathers visit, call, and send remittances home routinely. Within this familial arrangement, fathers occupy more prominent roles in the girls' lives. Eleven of the girls were once raised in a father-away transnational family, but their father no longer commutes, making their earlier transnational familial arrangements short-term. Finally, nine of the forty girls live in seemingly heteronormative families with parents who have never commuted to the U.S. for work. The girls in this last group have relatives—aunts, uncles, cousins, and grandparents—who live in the U.S. and visit regularly. This means that a total of thirty-one of the girls were either once raised, or are growing up in, a father-away transnational family. All of the girls live within transnational social fields.

Growing up in these transnational living arrangements exposes girls to different forms of mobility. For those growing up in father-away transnational families, their father's commutes force them in some manner to move with him, to experience his departures and arrivals. For all of the girls, growing up within a transnational social field also exposes them to a different form of mobility as they witness the return and departure of the diaspora, cars with U.S. license plates, and names on eateries and restaurants they may not recognize. This places girls in a border-like living situation of continuous movement. Coupling this movement with the television shows and Hollywood films allows girls to imagine a particular *norte*. In the section below, I provide a profile of girls raised in each of the familial arrangements, highlighting their parents' educational background and reasons given for migration.

Girls Raised in Transnational Families: Ghost-Like Fathers

Girls raised in this arrangement generally come from families with limited schooling practices. In fact, they feel this contributed to their father's decision to move. According to the girls, fathers lacked access to good jobs and had limited options to improve their economic status. Because fathers hoped to provide their children with a better chance at life, they left.

Girls raised in this arrangement describe having limited contact with their father. They hardly see him. They understand the reason behind his departure but have yet to see the rewards for the sacrifice they feel they made. Part of his absence is due to a strained relationship with the girls' mothers. In "Honor and Virtue," Joanna Dreby (2006) found that, when relationships between a husband and wife weaken, so do the relationships fathers have with the children they leave behind.[13] Yet Abrego found this is not the case for transnational mothers.[14] When mothers depart—leaving the children under their husbands' care—and the relationships weakens, transnational mothers continue to provide for their children. On the surface, girls develop an "I don't need him" attitude. When asked how they feel about his absence, they reply: "*ya estoy acostumbrada*" ("I'm used to it"). They feel they are better off not having him be part of their lives. Contradictions, however, arise when they speak of growing up without him.

Nadia's interview presents internal turmoil resulting from the contradictory and conflicting emotions she feels toward her father and his ghost-like presence. I visited seventeen year-old Nadia at her home in April of 2010. The home belongs to her maternal grandmother. She lives there with an aunt, her older sister Alba, and her mother Vero. There are enough rooms for everyone in the modest two-story brick home. Nadia, however, shares her room with her grandmother. It was an unusually hot day in Zinapécuaro, particularly for the late afternoon. The town's Holy Week celebrations were already coming to an end. Nadia took me into the room she shares with her grandmother and said we could talk there freely. There were two beds in the room, a big dresser on the opposite end of the room, and a small window looking out onto the patio. We sat on the bed closest to the window to catch the afternoon breeze. Nadia was wearing cargo pants, flip-flops, and a pink sweatshirt. Still recovering from a cold, she was bundled up. Her black hair was pulled back in a ponytail and she coughed repeatedly. When asked about her father, she said: "my father went to El Norte after I was born. He went to Arizona to stay with my uncles [mother's brothers]. Two years later, my mom, my sister Alba, and I joined him. We lived there for five years. I did kinder, first, second, and third grade. I think about my life there often. I had friends and liked the school, the cafeteria, the food, the malls, and swimming pools. I also liked Halloween and Christmas because we got presents. At times I'd like to go back. I'm just not sure it will happen." Nadia compares her life in Zinapécuaro to Arizona, practicing what

Zavella describes as "peripheral vision."[15] She highlights what she liked about living in the U.S. and her hopes to return one day. Because she lacks documents and is unlikely to get a visa, though, she does not think she will be able to. Nadia returned to Zinapécuaro after completing the third grade. By then she mostly spoke English and found it difficult to re-adjust to life in Zinapécuaro. While in Arizona, she used to get massive headaches. Doctor's visits confused Vero, who decided it was best if she were treated in Mexico where they "didn't give you the run around," as Nadia said. They returned in 2002 and her father stayed behind. The agreement was for him to send money regularly. With Vero's income and the remittances, a middle class lifestyle was guaranteed. However, it did not work out that way. Since that time, he returned for Alba's *quinceañera* in 2006 and a second time to attend the funeral services for Nadia's maternal grandfather. There are rumors of him having another family, of gambling issues, and of being unable to keep a steady job—all common stories circulating among father-away transnational families. As Joanna Dreby (2009) notes, gossip and rumors are recurrent aspects of transnational migration.[16] Nadia believes they are just rumors. What she knows for certain is that he does not send money and rarely calls.

When he returned in 2006, Nadia cried. In her soft tone and with her eyes glittering with tears, she recalled: "I miss him, usually on holidays like Father's Day. When he came for Alba's *quince*, I was thirteen. I cried when I saw him. He took me to the plaza, the *jardín*, and bought me hamburgers. I also cried when he left. He came again for a little bit. Now I'm used to it. When he calls, I'm usually not home. I don't want to talk to him. I don't think he'll ever return." Nadia's brief narrative reveals mixed feelings about her father's absence that are part of a complex personhood entailing multiple contradictions.[17] She feels nothing and everything when she speaks of his absence. Emotions and tears betray her "I don't need him" proclamation, displaying complex and simultaneous feelings of love and anger that highlight the multiple dimensions of her character and experiences, which are often difficult to balance.

Nadia's contradictory responses are similar to those of eighteen year-old Yola and her younger sixteen year-old sister Sara. Yola and Sara see their father at most once per year when they visit him in California. He has only been to Zinapécuaro once, when he married their mother Aurora. They live with their mother—a hairstylist—and an older sister.

Both Yola and Sara were born in California, the place where their parents moved after the birth of the first daughter.[18] They lived there until their parents divorced. Yola was six and Sara was four. Since their return to Zinapécuaro, they have had limited contact with their father. Yola describes how she used to miss him when she was younger, particularly during school events. Wearing a pink tank top with sequined flowers—purchased at Forever 21 on her last visit to the U.S.—with blue jeans and white sandals, she described what it was like growing up without her father in a matter-of-fact manner:

> Y: [When I was younger,] I didn't look for him, but had hope he would show up one day and stay here and live with us, but not anymore. I don't feel that way anymore.
>
> LS: When you were little, were there moments when you wished he were around?
>
> Y: Yes, like, we really like sports, my sisters and I. I think we got that from him because he does too. He does a lot of sports and we do too. We play all kinds of sports and, in all sports, there are events where parents and children can go, and my mom, she didn't let us do any sports because usually, I mean, we always came home with bruises and she didn't like that. So she hardly let us go. The few times she did, we'd go by ourselves. All of the other girls' parents were there, supporting and cheering them on, and my mom wasn't there. That's what I remember the most.

Yola noticed the absence of both, but for varied reasons. It is what she most remembers. This served as a reminder of their familial arrangement, which was different from her classmates' heteronormative appearing families. Though she was mostly used to it, such moments stood out for her. They singled her out as different from the rest. School events like graduation parties and scholarly celebrations were sad reminders of her father's absence. It is a shared experience among girls with ghost-like fathers.

According to Sara, her father does try to call, but at times when they are usually not home. As Yola said, "the conversations with him are awkward." He does not send money but they feel they do not need it, as they are used to their mother taking care of them. In some way, they have control—agency—on whether or not to be around when their father calls. They decide on the frequency and the kinds of exchanges they will have with him.

For girls like Nadia, Yola, and Sara, living in a transnational family is as normal as going to school, yet they do not necessarily enjoy it. This group of girls is arguably the most affected by migration and transnational familial formations as they have yet to experience the promised material benefits of living with a father away. Yola mentioned that, when she was little, she wished the living arrangement would change and that her father would return to Zinapécuaro. At eighteen years old, however, Yola no longer hopes for that. The strong relationship she has built with her mother and sisters is one she hopes will last. Sara, the youngest, wishes to migrate to the U.S. For Sara, Zinapécuaro does not have much to offer and she wants a different lifestyle. Seduced by an embodied sensation of modernity, Sara would much rather do high school, and perhaps college, in California.

Transnational migration scholars have pointed to the critical role women play within the home while husbands are away. This dynamic applies in Nadia, Yola, and Sara's homes as their mothers become the breadwinners. With limited schooling, mothers have few options to make ends meet. Vero, however, has steady employment. She has been in the hairstyling business since long before she married. The clientele she has built over the years is faithful to her. As the breadwinner, Vero takes care of her daughters and her ailing mother. Alba has been able to study in Morelia and in Mexico City. Her expenses are covered by Vero's earnings. If or when business is slow and Vero cannot pay the weekly or monthly expenses, she calls her brothers in Arizona for economic assistance. In this case, Vero is extremely lucky, not only because of her steady employment but also because of the relatives she has in the U.S. She worries little about day-to-day expenses, yet does not have extra cash to spend. In this sense, the ream of a middle class lifestyle has evaporated.

Yola and Sara's mother similarly attends to all of their needs. Aurora is also a hairstylist. Unlike Vero, she owns her own salon and her own home. It is a modest salon called Atzimba that offers haircuts, waxing, highlights, and perms. The salon is on the first floor of a three-story building that Aurora inherited from her father, once a bracero. She and her three daughters live above the salon in a two-story apartment with two bedrooms, one bathroom, a kitchen, a living room, and a dining room on the main floor. Each room on the first level is fully furnished. Upstairs are two more rooms, a laundry room, and a second bathroom. Though the home has enough bedrooms for each one, all four sleep in the two rooms on the main floor. All three girls fully depend on their mother's salary. Aurora does not have to pay rent of any sort, so all of the money she earns is for her and her daughters. Aurora's earnings provide Yola with a college education.[19] The girls—Yola and Sara—take pride in not needing their father, and feel they are better off without him. Like Vero, Aurora also has family in the U.S. If Aurora, too, were to fall short on her monthly expenses, her sisters who live in California and Illinois would immediately send her money to assuage any financial shortcomings.

Mothers like Vero and Aurora become the breadwinners in charge of raising their daughters. They make decisions, grant permissions, and encourage their daughters to do better. For Yola and Sara, this is a source of pride, but for sisters Nadia and Alba it only causes further resentment. All of the girls in this familial arrangement are quite critical of their fathers. They cannot change their arrangements, but they do get to display their agency, and disapproval, by refusing to talk to their father when he calls. It is how they assert a certain level of control over their situation.

Girls Raised in Transnational Families: Fathers Present

Fifteen of the forty girls live in transnational families with a father who is present. Within this arrangement, fathers visit regularly, send remittances, and, while away, remain in touch with them. Girls in this group have varied opinions about their arrangements and fathers. They understand fully why their father left. Most of them have witnessed the material benefits via the American clothing or jewelry he brings them upon his returns. I should add that, when fathers bring clothes, it is not uncommon for them to bring the wrong size because they may not be aware of the growth of the children they are buying for. Because of this, jewelry and toys seem like a safer option.

Within this arrangement, girls are still enrolled in school and usually live in a home owned by their parents. Because girls' fathers have been commuting for a very long time, they have had the means to save, build a home, and take care of their family. In other words, fathers have further developed their own social capital and are able to provide their families with a "better" lifestyle. Some girls feel the sacrifice they have made by growing up in this arrangement is well worth it, and hope to repay their father with good grades and a college degree.

Within this group, there are girls with great relationships with their fathers. Fifteen year-old Emilia and her sisters, seventeen-year-old Marbe and thirteen-year-old Toñita, describe having an excellent relationship with their father Sixto. While he is in the U.S.—whether in Chicago, Oregon, or Alaska—Sixto calls regularly, sends money, and assures them of his imminent return. While he is away, they feel a void, but want to behave well. They look forward to the material gifts he will bring. Toñita, the youngest of the three, walked into the interview wearing U.S. clothing her father bought for her on his last trip: white jeans, slip-on checkered Vans, and a black Gap T-shirt. A week away from turning fourteen, Toñita is very mature, curious, and laughed a lot during the interview. In relation to her father's absence, she said:

> Well, two years ago when he left, um, I didn't feel bad because I thought, he'll bring me tons of things, right? But later I realized I was wrong because like, only when your family is apart do you value them because I needed him lots of times, and like, he wasn't there. We only talked over the phone and when we needed him, well, he couldn't [be there]. But like, I didn't feel too bad because two years ago, even last year, even before that, there were too many problems at home, so my dad would leave and then they [her parents] wouldn't fight anymore. I didn't see them fighting and all that. So, like, when he left, I didn't miss him as much, but now, things have changed at home . . . and like now that he is leaving, I feel bad.

Toñita expressed mixed feelings of love, joy, and sadness, all of which she surrenders to because she understands her father must leave. She desires the material goods, things that will compensate their sacrifice. The material goods allow her to feel modern. Part of the reason she feels fine when her father leaves has to do with those U.S. products he will bring back to the family. The dynamics at home also push her to agree to live with her father away, as it means fewer fights between her parents.

Girls like Toñita lead complex lives, not only because they live in transnational families but because life is filled with contradictions. Perhaps her father's departure is a temporary fix to marital problems, yet his decision also needs to be situated within broader structural forces that forced him to make this decision. He left to improve his family's economic situation. They could not have survived otherwise. Because his commutes have been taking place since the 1980s, Sixto has developed routes and destinations for work that he knows will bring higher wages. For Toñita, a temporary fix also brings the possibility of another Gap T-shirt, a pair of sneakers, or colorful jewelry—things that will set her apart from girls in her neighborhood. She catches herself, however, in not being too seduced by material goods.

Other girls like Carmen and Paloma prefer their fathers' absences. In her research on transnational families, Stephen found that some adult women with a husband away prefer the absences and feel freer because of them.[20] In Carmen's case, her father is a prominent figure in her life, but he fails to provide any support other than his financial contributions. She is a sixteen-year-old, petite girl who walked into the interview wearing dark blue skinny jeans, a tight black T-shirt with golden letters that matched her sandals and bracelet. It was quite warm that day, so her hair was pulled back in a ponytail with two bobby pins holding back her bangs. She was born into a transnational family as her father began commuting to Virginia long before she was born. His shortest commutes last three months, while the longest one was two years. The reasons for his departures changed. At first, he left as a teenager to look for work. As an adult with a family, he continued to commute to be able to provide for them. Like Sixto, he has been able to amass knowledge of where to go for work. I asked Carmen how she felt about her father's commutes. In her soft-spoken voice, she said: "when I was little, well, I do remember that I felt bad, like, really bad because well, when he was gone, he wasn't here and like, I'd grab his clothes to smell him because like, I really did miss him when I was little. But now, I, I almost don't. Now I could care less if he comes and goes, if calls or if he doesn't." There is an obvious shift in attitude and detachment as she grew older. Her father developed a drinking habit that Carmen disapproves of, which makes her wish him gone (I discuss this further in chapter 4). There is an emotional adjustment Carmen needed to make to get used to his absence. Part of that adjustment was a response to her father's behavior, and the rest is perhaps a choice Carmen needed to make to avoid the pain and need to look for him, to smell him. Like Nadia and Yola, she concludes by stating that now she is accustomed to her living arrangement. A change to that arrangement would mean her father would most likely return to Zinapécuaro. As will be further explored in chapter 3, this is not something Carmen wishes.

Paloma, who has lived in a transnational family from birth, experiences similar feelings. She was interviewed at El CBTIS during one of her free periods.[21] At fifteen, she is in her first year of courses in business administration. She walked into the interview wearing the school uniform: a plaid blue and red skirt down to the knees, white knee-high socks, black flats, a burgundy V-neck sweater with a white shirt underneath. Her straight black hair was pulled back. I found Paloma to be very intense, smart, and emotional, carrying her heart on her sleeve. During the interview, there were moments I thought she would cry. She lives with her mother, sister, and three nephews. Her father Pablo has been commuting for such a long time—long before Paloma was born—that now she simply says that it is what he does. I asked her how she feels about her father's absences: "I used to get real sad when he'd leave because between my mom and my dad, I am closer to my dad, well, I was closer to my dad. Wherever he'd go, I wanted to follow. I wanted to go everywhere with him. Maybe I always wanted to be with him and go everywhere with him because he was usually gone. Now, um, not anymore, like, I'm grown now, like, we're not as close anymore." Paloma made sure to underscore that she no longer feels close to her father. Pablo's yearly commutes last from nine to ten months, while his stay in Zinapécuaro is between two to three months. Paloma's response points to an emotional distance that seems inevitable within this arrangement. Now she is used to his absences.

None of the girls in Zinapécuaro cried or became angry as they described their fathers' absences. They spoke in a very matter-of-fact tone. On the surface, they seem to understand why their fathers left. Some even expressed appreciation for the subsequent material benefits. Yet, as teenagers, they also hold a romanticized notion of what a family should consist of, even if they never grew up in one.

Like those raised with completely absent fathers, these girls have parents with limited formal education. Paloma's mother Amparo, for example, only completed elementary school, while her father Pablo never attended. Poncia—the mother of Marbe, Emilia, and Toñita—studied to be a secretary. With six children, Poncia felt she needed to stay home and raise them. But, unlike girls raised in ghost-like father-away transnational families, these mothers did not necessarily have to worry about finding the means to financially provide for their family. They did, however, have other augmented responsibilities. For example, while Sixto is away, Poncia's role is to take care of the household. She makes sure the family business continues to run smoothly, and sees to it that Marbe, Emilia, Toñita, and the three younger children maintain high grades. It is Poncia's responsibility to discipline the children. She is the one who grants or withholds permission for the girls to go out on dates and have boyfriends. Since Sixto does not approve of their daughters dating or having boyfriends, Poncia becomes their accomplice. When Sixto returns, he will reclaim his seat at the head of the table, and Marbe, Emilia, and Toñita resent him for this because, when he is gone, Poncia is successful as the head of the household.

According to Marbe, Emilia, and Toñita, their mother Poncia has never wanted to join Sixto in the U.S. She sees her role as a mother as being present with her children. In recent years, the family has requested loans from the bank to keep the business afloat. The high interest rates are accumulating and need to be paid off. They are barely making ends meet. Toñita has suggested to both parents that, if Poncia joins Sixto in the U.S., they would get out of debt quicker. Toñita thinks both parents could stay in the U.S. for a couple of years and return debt-free:

> I told my dad, "you know what?" I said, "if you want to fix my mom's papers, go ahead. I'll take a year off school." I told him, "I think a year or two would be enough for my mom to go over there so that she could work, to try really hard and I'll stay over here, like, I'll take on the motherly role." I said that because my oldest sister [Marbe] is almost done with college. For her to take a year off school, I don't think so . . . like, I wouldn't do it, if I was almost done, I would not take a year off. My other sister [Emilia], the one who is almost done with high school, she's the type of person that, she just leaves things there, a negative person at times. If she were left in charge of the household, she wouldn't do it. She's not strong enough, um, she gets too emotional and feels bad. She wonders too much and so she

does not have the right character to run a household, the right attitude. Me, to be honest with you, I am quite strong headed. Lots of times when my parents aren't home I start to take charge. If my sisters, the oldest even, if she wants to go out, I tell her, "you aren't going anywhere because of this or that. You will stay here and you won't go, you just won't, I am not letting you." I feel that when I'm not there, they'll do what they want or a different decision will be made. So, I've noticed that like, that I have the strength to be the leader, to be in charge of a group, or something like that. So then I told my mom and dad. They thought it'd be a good idea for both to leave and I'd stay here. They thought about it but then my mom said no. She said, "no, *hija*," she said, "we'll see how we can get by." To tell you the truth, I think that we had less expenses when we were little. We needed less money then. Now we need more. Like, when you are little, how much can you need? Right? And so now I need money for this or that, and for school, forget about it! My mom says that she spent all this time caring for us, looking after us. She does not regret having quit her job as a secretary. "I did it for you," she says, "and now it would hurt too much to leave you." So I don't think she'll go.

This narrative came from a 2012 follow-up interview with Toñita who at that time was fifteen years old. By then, her sister Marbe, as she notes, was almost done with her nursing degree. Because expenses at home were accruing, the family's income needed to be stretched out. Toñita feels her life is a bit more precarious than it was in 2010. She is willing to take a couple of years off of school to help contribute to the household, a role her brothers are never expected to fill. She feels more ready to do so than her siblings, but all she can do is express her thoughts. Her father is ultimately the one who would make a final decision on who goes and who stays. Perhaps Toñita, who is eager to migrate to the U.S., hopes that, if her mother leaves, the rest of the family would soon follow.

Carmen's mother Connie has a different life than Poncia. While her husband is away, she is a full-time wife. With a sixth-grade education and five children under her care, she does not have much time to work outside of the home, nor would her husband allow her to do so even if she could. Connie feels that her daily life is under constant surveillance. The home her husband constructed for her and her children is in the same neighborhood as her in-laws. His relatives always seem to be lurking around to make sure Connie does not misuse the money he sends her. Carmen confides that, if her relatives on her father's side feel that her mother spends too much money on clothing, they call and complain to her husband in the U.S. If they see her leaving the house more dressed up than they consider proper, they suspect infidelity. When Carmen talks to boys, they tell her father that she is promiscuous. Carmen resents the ways they behave towards Connie and the children. "They make up lies and tell my dad," says Carmen, "and he always takes their side." When her husband calls or visits, Connie constantly feels she needs to advocate for herself. She has to endure the treatment she receives, because she does not want any problems with her husband's family. Although she appreciates the money he sends regularly while he is away, Connie dislikes not feeling free. When her husband returns, all he does is drink, which makes her feel extremely nervous. Connie has a sister she leans on who always warns her not to share her grief with her brothers, as she fears that would lead to fights between them and her husband. Connie's options are limited. She can either continue to endure the relationship—which she has for almost twenty years—or migrate to the U.S., because there are not many jobs available in Zinapécuaro, particularly for someone with a sixth-grade education. Connie, however, has been unable to make such a decision.

Girls grow up having to negotiate gender dynamics at home. Sisters Marbe, Emilia, and Toñita have to hide boyfriends during their father's return visits, while their mother takes a temporary back seat when it comes to family discipline. For Carmen, even though her father is usually gone, he always seems to be present as the head of the household. At times, family life seems to be getting better, but it worsens at others. As the girls get older, they become more critical of their living arrangements.

Girls Once Raised in Transnational Families

Eleven of the forty girls were raised in what once were transnational families, whose fathers have not commuted to the U.S. for work in the last five years and have no plans to return. In some cases, fathers made said choice because they earned enough money during early commutes to enable them to stay in Mexico. Gisela's father, for example, left for the U.S. on different occasions for three years at a time. At sixteen, her father's commutes seem so long ago that she does not recall the cities or towns in the U.S. where he worked. During his absences, he sent money home that enabled them to finish constructing their home. He now works as a plumber and electrician while her mother sells cactus salads—which are especially popular during the warm season—at the market downtown. Wearing jean shorts with sandals and a bright summer top, Gisela walked into the interview with her long curly hair down. She said: "[he hasn't gone] because, moneywise, we're all right, and like, well, he didn't want to go anymore. [When he used to go], I was little, I suppose I felt strange. Moneywise we were never that bad, but the thing is, he left to finish building the house." Although the family was not in dire economic need, commuting to the U.S. enabled her father to obtain the extra money they needed to add a second floor and extra bedrooms for Gisela, her older sister, and her younger brother. Gisela assumes she must have felt strange while her father was away, but she does not really recall any troubling family dynamics or unhappiness when her father was absent. Before her father's departures, they had enough to get by, but not for extra expenses. While away, Gisela's father earned and saved to finish their home; when he came back, he opened his own business. Gisela worries what would happen if the business fails. Would her father have to return to the U.S.? Gisela has relatives who live in Sacramento, California, which looms as a possible destination for her father. Gisela hopes to follow in the footsteps of her older sister, who is already in college. With a college degree in hand, she believes she would never have the need to move to the U.S. for work, although she says she would not be opposed to travel on a temporary work visa.

Like Gisela, Margarita was also little when her father left. The goth-looking sixteen-year-old likes to wear black clothing and listen to punk music and *rock nacional.* In her neighborhood, this gives her an outsider identity, since the popular musical trends coalesce around *banda* and *reggaeton.* At times, Margarita feels like a target, teased as an *emo* or punk, labels that she refuses. When she was younger, her father lived in southern California for two years. He left to stay with relatives. Upon his return, he began to do carpentry and opened his own business. Business began to flourish and there was no longer a need for him to work in the U.S. Margarita hardly recalls having any reaction to his absences, a common response from girls in this group as they were simply too young when their fathers left to remember it clearly now. She knows she stayed with her paternal grandmother during those years, but does not recall having any particular emotional reactions. Margarita did express having a very close relationship with her grandmother, perhaps a consequence of living with her while her father was away.

Most girls in this group said their fathers simply no longer wanted to commute to the U.S. Perhaps their initial departure was a response to the economic crisis of the 1980s and 1990s, a promised quick solution to many problems. Having relatives in the U.S. facilitated departures. At the same time, mothers and daughters began to work more outside of the home. Gisela's mother became a vendor downtown. Seventeen-year-old Marifer, whose father once migrated to the U.S. for work, found employment making bricks and selling sheep while her mother breeds chickens and sells them at the market. Fourteen-year-old Esme's father works at a shop making wooden boats while her mother sells beauty products in the evening. These varied kinds of employment provide enough to get by, but the jobs are not stable. It remains unclear how these families would get by if new economic hardships arose without having some family member journey to the U.S. and send remittances back home.

Like the others, these girls' parents have had limited schooling. The fathers tend to have completed elementary school, while the mothers at best had only one or two years of middle school. They have limited job options. Thirteen-year-old Valentina is an exception. She is in her first year of middle school. Small-framed with shoulder-length straight hair and wearing her physical education uniform—blue sweats and a matching sweatshirt—she explains that both of her parents have degrees in engineering from El Tecnológico de Morelia. They both lost their jobs in the late 1990s and divorced soon after. Valentina's father tried his luck in the U.S. where he migrated for work, but returned after his visa expired. Her mother now runs a parking lot downtown. The profits she makes there are enough for the family's subsistence.

Long commutes to the U.S. in these girls' families stopped when fathers seemed able to start a business and maintain its success or found other means sufficient for daily survival. This relative prosperity allowed the girls to remain in school and their families to return to a seemingly heteronormative appearing family unit. Being able to sell bricks, chickens, or goats may not be sufficient for securing a long-term steady income, however. The lack of employment and the paucity of business opportunities in Mexico make traveling to the U.S. for work a constant, looming possibility.

Girls Raised in Heteronormative Families

Nine girls live in seemingly heteronormative appearing families with parents who own their own homes and have never worked in the U.S. Although they have cousins, aunts, and uncles who live and work there, and whom they visit regularly, their own parents have never left Mexico. They share similar profiles with the girls in other familial arrangements. The girls' mothers and fathers also have limited educations. Sixteen-year-old Estrella's mother, for example, completed her first year of high school, while her father only finished middle school. A petite girl, she came into the interview wearing blue jeans and a short sleeve magenta hoodie over a white tank top and matching flats. The hoodie had silver stars that matched her silver earrings and headpiece over her black curly hair. I asked Estrella why her parents never left. She explained that they "found a way to make it. They are business owners and both work together." Their business is a shop where they sell perfumes, jewelry, and make-up that her relatives supply from the U.S. They work together and have managed to put their older children through college in Morelia. Estrella has a brother who is in his last year of high school and plans to attend university in the fall. Once Estella graduates from high school, she will follow the same path.

Sixteen-year-old Yuri comes from a similar background. She is one of four children. Her parents work in local businesses and have never thought of moving to the U.S. for work. They have heard plenty of tales of the difficulties migrants encounter in El Norte and, as Yuri says, they concluded they could live better in Mexico without suffering. Like some of the other girls, Yuri's style resembled that of a typical teenage girl in the U.S. She walked into the interview wearing black skinny jeans, black flats, a purple long sleeve top, and matching earrings. Her eyebrows were nicely shaped. She wore her long, straight brown hair tied in a side ponytail and her hands were manicured. She expressed judgment and condescension for those Zinapecuarenses who have migrated to the U.S.

because they are unable to make ends meet in Mexico. Like Estrella, she proudly assured me that her parents have never had to leave for work. Her beliefs reflect a long history of political and cultural discourses in Mexico that blame Mexicans for not making it at home and leaving to the U.S. for work.

Fourteen-year-old fraternal twins Luli and Laura share a similar story. Their father only completed middle school and their mother high school. Both sell dairy products and bread seven days a week in Morelia, the state capital. They have quite a following among their customers, which means business is good. Luli and Laura have family who reside in the U.S. I asked Luli why her parents never left to the U.S. like her relatives. Luli—wearing plaid shorts, a white shirt, and a pink sweater—fixed her white headband that held her long brown hair back as she sat on the sofa in the living room. Luli, who looks young for her age, yet spoke in a mature and thoughtful manner, said: "well, my uncles [left because they] had passports, but neither my mom nor dad were able to and my dad didn't want to go. I don't know why he didn't want to go, but he didn't want to and stayed here. It never crossed their mind [to go]. My dad is a businessman, things are fine. He's got a bunch of clients. Things feel stable. Slowly we've been building the house adding rooms [as money comes in]. We're doing well." The relatives who live in the U.S. left with a passport, which indicates a middle class status. Unlike Gisela's father, Luli's father made enough money to slowly build the two-story home without having to migrate to the U.S. They began with the first floor, adding windows and doors as income came in. If business slowed down, they placed doors where it seemed most necessary. The second floor was added with the same plan in mind— bathroom walls, windows, doors, and bedrooms for the children. With five children in the house—all expected to go to college—"money," said Luli, "was spent and saved wisely." There has never been any talk of moving to the U.S. I realized my questions surprised Luli. Her family is quite removed from migratory practices. The U.S. has never been on her family's radar as an option. Within this group of girls, eighteen-year-old Jessica is the exception, as her parents once lived in the U.S. They migrated to Illinois where Jessica was born, but decided to return to Zinapécuaro to raise her and her younger brother born five years later. Neither parent enjoyed the cold and the rigors of city life in the

Windy City, vowing never to return. Her immediate family has never lived apart. She does have aunts, uncles, and grandparents who live in the U.S. Her mother is a housewife and her father sells socks and bread. They get by living in her grandmother's house. Their U.S. relatives send remittances to assist them. Jessica, whose story is discussed in chapter 4, hopes to return to Chicago.

With the exception of Jessica, the girls in this section come from a more middle-class upbringing and enjoy an inherited status that has allowed their fathers to drop out of school without negative consequences. Estrella and Yuri, in particular, pride themselves in growing up in families who have never needed to migrate. Their life in Zinapécuaro, they feel, is good and their future is bright. Luli understood that her parents have a successful business that allows her to focus in school. As will be discussed in chapter 3, despite their lack of immediate connections to the U.S., they are still growing up in a Zinapécuaro where the diaspora returns frequently enough for them to be aware of life on the other side of the border. Although migration is not present at home, it surrounds their lives whenever they step outside.

A Connective Comparison

Following Weinbaum et al's method of connective comparison, I argue that the four groups of girls share much in common. They all are raised within transnational social fields in the town of Zinapécuaro and most reside, or at least did at some point, in transnational family arrangements. Their exposure to movement and mobility provide them with insights about why people leave and why they are growing up in the kinds of families they have. On the surface, most girls share a similar profile— they are raised in households with parents who have limited schooling in the town of Zinapécuaro, where they see each other at school or in their neighborhoods. They enjoy similar tastes in clothing and music. These similarities make it difficult to identify why some of the girls' fathers leave and others do not. Estrella's father's educational background, for example, is similar to Toñita's. He was not more objectively prepared to open his own business, yet he has never left for the U.S.

Within each group of girls, there is a shared experience influenced by their living arrangements. The manner in which they respond to an absent father, for example, or the changes in dynamics when fathers arrive are all part of that shared experience. Each group responds differently to this, though. For example, girls who are raised with ghost-like fathers develop a stoic position in relation to their absence. They are accustomed to it and have not enjoyed any of the material benefits promised by migration. The girls raised in father-away transnational families with the father present in spirit share the experience of growing up with interruptions and at times desires for change. The economic improvements some of them are able to have are also because of an experience they all shared. They can have extra schooling or perhaps their own room because their father is away. Growing up in a father-away transnational family also provides girls with certain expectations about what or who they should aspire to be as they are the reason for their fathers' departure. This reason constantly looms. For those who once lived in transnational families, the benefits gained during their fathers' absence were felt with appreciation when they returned without any further plans for migration.

In all cases, girls already have more schooling than their parents, who hope their children will attend college, earn a degree, and have a better chance at life. As will be examined in the next chapter, however, the girls' goals may not align with those of their parents. Some may want to move to the U.S., while others have dreams about staying in Mexico. No specific familial arrangement leads to a particular outcome as there are girls in all groups who express desires to stay or to migrate.

The lives of all of the girls in Zinapécuaro are affected by the possibility of migration. It is an option, even if their family chooses to remain in Mexico. Massey's cumulative causation framework establishes that, once migration patterns begin, it becomes easier for subsequent generations to follow. As the next chapter shows, however, for those girls who do desire migration, it is not a simple matter due to the power of patriarchy in their lives. Desires for migration are stoked by the advertising and entertainment industries, by the conspicuous consumption of the diaspora on visits back home to Zinapécuaro, and by the central roles played by remittances and gifts in legitimating and justifying absences of fathers from families. Inhabiting the borderlands as Mexican teenage girls means exposure to other ways of being and to other ways of living.

3

Muchachas Michoacanas

Portraits of Teenage Girls in a Migratory Town

It is April of 2010 in Zinapécuaro, Michoacán, Mexico. Celebrations for the centennial and bicentennial of the Mexican Revolution and Mexico's Independence, which began on January of 2010, are difficult to ignore. Televised advertisements and public service announcements highlight the country's tourist attractions and celebrate a much-sanitized indigenous presence as a scenic backdrop that places the Other in a distant past.[1]

Televisa's ads, popularly known as *Las Estrellas del Bicentenario,* range from thirty seconds to three minutes. They are aired daily in between *telenovelas* (soap operas) and the nightly news, including *Las Noticias por Adela.*[2] The ads feature three young Mexican models—Edsa Ramírez, Fernanda Vizzuet, and Alejandra Infante—who responded to a call for an audition in which over fifty thousand young women participated. These three girls—all brunettes—are meant to represent the typical *mestiza* beauty. The theme and motif of the ads are always the same, highlighting the raw beauty and tourist attractions of each state in the Mexican republic. The ads do not reveal that tourism and monocultural production of crops like coffee leaves have mired these states in austere economic conditions.[3] The models are featured alongside animals from the region. A song in an indigenous language—presumably sung by an indigenous woman from the state where the ad is filmed—plays as background music. Despite the ethnic and linguistic diversity within each state, the producers assume one indigenous experience. In the Chiapas ad, for example, the tourist attractions of Las Cascadas de Agua Azúl and Palenque are beautifully highlighted. The three young models wear gowns of various colors. Animals accompany these young models posing in rural locations. In the background, indigenous men stare—perhaps protectively—at the young *mestizas* who are at the center of the frame. The ad concludes with the phrase: "*Esto es México, El Estado de*

Chiapas, una estrella más del bicentenario," (This is Mexico, the state of Chiapas, another star of the bicentennial). In an unproblematic way, the ad captures a superficial and much-sanitized hybridity in Mexico.

Televisa's ads were not unique to 2010. In fact, in the late 1980s and early 1990s, Televisa's El Canal De Las Estrellas also produced similar ads titled *El Canal de las Estrellas Promocionales.* The goal was to promote tourism and invite nationals to visit Oaxaca, Chiapas, and other states. Like the 2010 ads, these were aired in between *telenovelas* and the nightly news. There was no call for models, however; they featured only Eugenia Cauduro, a popular young model turned actress, and were not meant to mark a particular celebration. They were most likely aired to distract viewers from Mexico's economic crises caused by the nation's move toward neoliberal policies of free trade and open markets.

The ads produced by TV Azteca to commemorate the anniversaries were a bit more modest. Known as *Imágen de Nuestro México,* the ads featured *telenovela* actors and actresses from TV Azteca as well as singers and talk show hosts.[4] Like the Televisa ads, these celebrated the beauty of several states of the Mexican republic. Lasting anywhere from thirty to sixty seconds, each ad focused on an actor, singer, or talk show host walking through a city in Oaxaca or the *malecón* in Veracruz, concluding with the phrase: *"Te invito a festejar el cumpleaños número docientos de mi México. Mi México, docientos años de Libertad. TV Azteca"* (I invite you to celebrate my Mexico's two-hundred-year anniversary. My Mexico, two hundred years of freedom. TV Azteca). Like the Televisa ads, these were only aired in Mexico during the 2010 bicentennial and centennial celebrations.

Perhaps the goal of these ads is to appeal to Mexicans' sense of heritage through the natural landscapes of their country. Perhaps it is to bolster a Mexican national identity—part of the legacy of intellectuals like Octavio Paz, Carlos Monsiváis, and Carlos Fuentes[5] —that sanitizes hybridity and *mestizaje,* disavowing the African root (or the third root) and portraying indigenous peoples as objects and part of the scenery.[6] Perhaps it is to divert viewers' attention from the war on organized crime, which since 2006 has unleashed rampant violence and death among citizens. Though these ads are easily accessible on YouTube, they were not aired outside of Mexico, and so evidently are intended to elicit an affective reaction from the local viewer.

The ads, particularly those produced by Televisa, display specific gender dynamics. They place young women at the center of the frame—they are the main focus, always under surveillance, a symbol to be protected and contained like the animals, indigenous people, and natural scenery they are surrounded by. These gender dynamics reflect the lives of the girls, like fifteen-year-old Emilia, that I interviewed.[7]

For Emilia, it may seem like the 2010 ads have little meaning. She is a tenth grader at a well-reputed public high school located approximately twenty minutes from the town square in Zinapécuaro. Students who do well there are rewarded with scholarship money that is deposited in a bank account under their name. Emilia has been a recipient of this largesse a few times. In order to catch the school bus, she leaves her house at seven in the morning and does not return until at least two-thirty in the afternoon, and sometimes past four, depending on her class schedule. As she makes the fifteen-minute walk from her home to the bus stop, Emilia sees trucks and cars with license plates from the United States.[8] She notices Oregon and Illinois, two states where her father has lived. She makes a turn onto Calle Hidalgo and sees the breakfast eatery Toñita Lunch's, where they sell *quesadillas, tortas, burritos*, and hamburgers (Figure 3.1). Perhaps she does not notice the misspelling that should read Toñita's Lunch.

When she returns home, she heads straight to "*el café a conectarme*" ("the café to go online"). *El café*—an Internet café—is a room in a house across the street from hers with a row of computers on each side of the wall. A teenager is in charge of collecting the money, usually ten *pesos* per hour or approximately one U.S. dollar.[9] The café offers printing services, soda, and potato chips for sale. Some Internet cafés sell flash drives to facilitate saving documents or blank CDs for customers who prefer to download music. Emilia likes to go on chat rooms and "*conectarse*" ("go online") for about an hour. As she says, she likes to "*chatear en el cyber*" ("chat online") with classmates, her boyfriend, or cousins who live in the U.S., and check her Myspace and Facebook page. After an hour, she returns home, does her homework, and helps her mother around the house.

If she is not in school or at the café, Emilia enjoys listening to music, usually *banda, norteño, corridos*, or American pop, with Katy Perry being one of her favorites. Like many teenagers, she likes to walk to the

Figure 3.1. This is the eatery that Emilia sees every day on her walk to school. Photo taken by Lilia Soto.

town's square on Sundays, preferably in the evenings, to enjoy a Frappuccino at a local café, a hamburger, pizza by the slice, or the famous *tacos* from the *plaza*. When there are *jaripeos* (rodeos), she also goes with her sisters and older male cousins. Because she is only fifteen and her parents are quite strict, she rarely goes to the discos or nightclubs as these usually only open late in the evening.

Emilia's life is representative of most of the girls interviewed in Zinapécuaro in 2010. Her life, in many ways, appears quite common for a fifteen-year-old high school girl. What is also very common is her familial arrangement. Emilia is in a father-away transnational family with a present father. Her father Sixto commutes to the U.S. for work once per year. When Sixto leaves, Emilia feels lonely, sad, and eagerly awaits his letters and weekly phone calls. She begins to mark her days by the weeks and months that he is gone, always awaiting his return.

Growing up in this arrangement has made Emilia fall in love with the idea of the U.S. She, along with her sisters Marbe and Toñita, have always wanted to migrate, even if just temporarily, or to visit. Receiving postcards her father sends from Alaska and Portland only fuels Emilia's imagination and desire. When her father is around and they watch a Hollywood film that shows streets of cities in Los Angeles or Chicago, her father says: "hey! I've been there, I've driven through those streets!" To this, Emilia invariably replies: "I want to go there too!" Her father returns bearing gifts for Emilia and her siblings. When she gets new clothes, shoes, or jewelry, Emilia feels she is at the cutting edge of fashion. She imagines life *en el otro lado* as very pretty, as life in a place that will provide her with a good education and a bright future that she can control. In this sense, her story is also representative of girls her age.

The ads from 2010 depict a Mexico that girls like Emilia are a part of, but feel disconnected from—a Mexico negotiating its identities during tumultuous historic times. It is a Mexico that is also shaped by the local and the transnational as manifested in migrants' returns and departures, such as Sixto's. It is a Mexico that also includes the penetration of U.S. life via popular culture, which allow girls like Emilia to dream of the possibility of obtaining what they perceive as modern.[10] Girls like Emilia inhabit a place of constant movement, of both limited physical and unlimited imaginative mobilities that they must negotiate. They witness the regulated and laborious physical movements of their fathers and other Zinapecuarenses around them, while experiencing the rapid, relentless, and seemingly unbounded movement across borders of advertising, entertainment, culture, and commodities. I borrow Salazar's definition of "mobility imaginaries" to explain how girls like Emilia long for greener pastures in the U.S.[11] This place of limited and multiple mobilities, of crossings and imaginaries, provides them with possibilities to study, get married, or migrate, all of which are influenced by their age, class, gender, and sexuality.[12] The lure of these options allows them to feel they can control their present and future. While some girls in this study dream about the U.S., others seek a life of fulfillment in Zinapécuaro. These options are also conditioned by the Mexico in which they live, as it sends girls mixed messages that they have to negotiate.

This chapter explores the girls' stories, options, feelings, emotions, and daily practices that allow them to harness agency, however fragile, while growing up in a migratory town.[13] It is within their daily lives, including their imaginaries, that we see the girls' power. Borrowing the words of Renato Rosaldo (1993), I situate their lives in "a place where a number of distinct social processes interact," including the local, the national, and the transnational.[14] This snapshot will first discuss the schools they attended, as these are critical components of their social worlds, followed by afterschool, weekend activities, and future plans. The girls' answers to my questions reflect their complex personhood in relation to their hopes, dreams, and one another.[15]

Schools: *La Secu*, El CBTIS, *La Prepa*, and La Michoacana

Whatever the familial arrangement, Mexican teenage girls are expected to follow a prescribed script: go to school, get good grades, behave well, don't run away with a boyfriend, and complete a college degree. This is a message they receive at home, usually from their parents. On the one hand, parents expect their daughters to practice what Lorena García (2012) describes as sexual respectability.[16] On the other hand, parents also hope their daughters will be equipped for a better, and much brighter, future than their own.

Fulfilling parents' desires, most girls interviewed were still in school, and even those who were not dreamt of becoming a lawyer, a teacher, an architect, or a *persona realizada* (an accomplished person)—as mentioned in the introduction, these are modern aspirations of adolescence. Most girls had already received much more schooling than their parents. When asked what parents expected from them, three seventeen-year-olds responded in consistent ways. Mariana related: "My parents expect a lot from me. I'm doing what they were never able to do and I get to enjoy my youth." Camila responded: "My parents wish that all my dreams come true. I want to finish my degree." Belen replied: "they want me to do better in school, to finish my degree, to not run away with my boyfriend, to be better each day." Similarly, eighteen-year-old Fabi answered: "They say that my future is in my hands, that I should finish school and go get my B.A. in nursing." Sixteen-year-old Carmen explained: "My mom wants me to stay in school and to finish my degree." Thirteen-year-old Toñita stated: "My parents want me to finish college, to do things right, to not forget God." These quotes point to parents' desires for a good education and sexual respectability for their daughters.

Girls also receive messages from their television sets and their schools. Televised messages, including the ads that open this chapter, promote pride—an *orgullo Mexicano*—designed to engage the viewer and make her feel connected to the broader national project of Mexico. Schools also disseminate ideas and values surrounding Mexican citizenship. School-aged children are taught to prepare for their adult roles in society.[17] Girls, however, receive a range of mixed messages from school, and other institutions, about what is expected of them, which only become more difficult to negotiate as they enter high school and college.

The majority of the girls expressed the belief that, in this day and age, it is imperative for women to have a college degree and not depend on a man for economic support. Some said, carefully, that there was nothing wrong with a woman choosing to rely on a man, but most girls expressed the opinion that it is possible for today's woman to have it all: a husband, a house, children, and a career. As García writes about girls in the U.S., "in the current neoliberal context, a new category of girl or young womanhood has emerged that is defined by individualization, choice, and capacities."[18] This neoliberal thinking states that, with hard work and discipline, girls can achieve it all. This, of course, is supposed to take place despite deep structural, sexual, and racial barriers that limit opportunities. The fact that girls desire success is not the problem. What García is concerned with is the manner in which such beliefs are oblivious to any of the structures of power that place limits on the girls' imagined dreams.[19] García describes this as "a 'successful girl discourse' that has interfaced with neoliberalism to reproduce a new category of womanhood grounded in disciplinary notions of meritocracy."[20] What García found in her research about Latina girls in Chicago resonates powerfully with what I discovered in the girls of Zinapécuaro. The contradictory and conflicting messages they receive, allegedly to encourage them, can actually impede them from becoming *personas realizadas*. Girls hear the "successful girl discourse" and desire it. They also are disciplined to pursue the traditional roles that young women are expected to perform. When they enter middle school, the message becomes louder. Some girls are able to handle the contradictory messages and negotiate the demands of school and their personal lives. Other girls drop out, marry young, or become young mothers. Both are regardless expected to overcome enormous structural and institutional obstacles. Neoliberal discourses promote personal and individual solutions to what in reality are structural and collective problems.

The girls in this study attend four types of schools: a middle school, a technical high school, a regular high school, and the college at La Michoacana. In 2010, only one of the forty girls interviewed was in college. By 2012, four were pursuing bachelor's degrees. In this section, I group and divide girls according to the schools they attend.

La Secundaria or La Secu

Ten girls are enrolled in the middle school located downtown that is known as *la secundaria* or *la secu* for short. It offers three grade levels: first, second, and third—for twelve- and thirteen-year-olds, thirteen- and fourteen-year-olds, and fourteen- and fifteen-year-olds, respectively. There are cohorts within each group: for example, cohort 1-A, 1-B, and so forth, which are used to group students. Uniforms are mandatory. Girls' uniforms are color-coded based on grade level: first grade wears pink, second blue, and third burgundy, which means they have to purchase a new uniform each year. All boys wear green pants, green shirts, and a green tie. Physical education uniforms are also mandatory. The school day is divided into two shifts to accommodate the larger student population of the town and its surrounding smaller towns. The morning shift runs from seven-thirty to two o'clock in the afternoon, and the evening from two-thirty to approximately eight in the evening. The students stay in one classroom. Teachers come in and out to teach a wide range of subjects, including English language, Civic and Ethical Formation, and Literature. Along with two uniforms, students need to purchase notebooks, pens, pencils, and books for each course, and materials for any extra-curricular activities.

There is another type of middle school known as *tele secundarias*, or televised middle schools. Valentina is a thirteen-year-old first grade student who attends a *tele zecundaria*. These are schools located in towns that lack enough teachers and resources to hire staff. Instead, students in *tele secundarias* sit in one classroom and are taught by a television monitor—a type of distance learning through online hybrid courses that are becoming popular among colleges and universities in the U.S. hoping to make profits in times of recession. Students learn biology, chemistry, literature, and all other required courses from the teacher they see on the monitor.

Middle school is where girls begin to experience significant change. Heavy drinking, smoking, skipping school, dropping out, running away with boyfriends, getting pregnant, and getting married can derail their progress. When Luli, a fourteen-year-old second grader at *la secu*, was asked about girls her age, she said: "well, when we all started middle school, we all tried real hard, but some started losing interest because they didn't really care anymore. They started skipping classes and you can't do much that way. They start missing school and begin to think differently. They don't feel like studying anymore." Luli was referring to girls like Valentina that she sees at her school. I interviewed Valentina when she was thirteen years old and in the second semester of her first year at a *tele secundaria*. She was already skipping school, often coming home as late as nine in the evening. During the fall semester of her second year—months after our interview—she became pregnant. Her mother pulled her out of school. By 2014, Valentina was a stay-at-home teen mother with no plans to return to school. She only completed eighth grade. Her mother, however, is economically stable and is helping Valentina raise her son.

Seventeen-year-olds Nadia and Sol completed only middle school and did not pursue high school. Nadia dropped out due to health problems. Her constant headaches and the stress she felt taking tests made it difficult for her to focus, so her mother thought it best to not enroll her in high school. For Sol, it was the money required to purchase uniforms and school supplies that prevented her from pursuing high school. Her parents had already spent more than they could afford during her three years of middle school. By 2012, Nadia was in charge of her grandmother's minimart where she worked every day until two in the afternoon. Sol was a young mother and a new bride. Neither had plans to return to school.

El CBTIS

Sixteen girls attend the Centro de Bachillerato Tecnológico Industrial y Servicios (El CBTIS), a technical high school that offers degrees in nursing, business administration, computer science, and electronics. Upon registering, students select one of the tracks. Like middle school, there are three different grade levels. Students are placed in cohorts and remain together for the six semesters enrolled. Most of the girls I interviewed were sixth-semester nursing students. As part of the requirements for graduation, they do *prácticas*—a sort of internship—at the Hospital de la Mujer in the city of Morelia during their last semester. The school rents a bus that takes all of the students on Saturdays and Sundays for a twelve-hour shift where they shadow nurses. For girls like Marbe, this internship is very inspiring, and she speaks highly of the *señoritas* she works with:

> . . . the misses from there, well, that's how we call them in the hospital. We are not allowed to call them by their first names. They are the nurses. Most of them are married and I see they have a good salary. They have a full-time job, a family because most of them are married to a doctor, a male nurse, or to someone who works in the health department, um, they have children, and have time for themselves. They do their own thing, rest twice a week and work eight hours per day. I think it is a must to have a career nowadays to live better, now that doesn't make us [young women] feminists, but we want gender equality, to feel better about ourselves.

Marbe has long curly hair and walked into the interview with her hair pulled back in a bun. She was wearing her school uniform—P.E. sweats and a white cotton T-shirt. Pearl white earrings decorated her ears. Her post-CBTIS goals include a college degree in nursing. She is, however, also very careful in not calling herself a feminist as this is not a message she receives at home. Her parents approve of her educational goals but would frown on feminist views. For Marbe, her degree is a way to repay her father for the sacrifices he has made living abroad and missing important family milestones.

Once El CBTIS students graduate, they have the option of either attending college to pursue a bachelor's degree in nursing or another health-related field, or do a one-year unpaid residency at a hospital, after which they can be hired as technical nurses. Most of the girls want to pursue a degree in nursing, as it would open up more options and generate a higher salary. Other girls anticipate going to medical school or getting a degree in nutrition or the hard sciences, including chemistry and biology. Girls who chose to attend El CBTIS do so to have the option of either college or work upon graduation.

Like middle school, high school is a time when girls may drop out, get married, or run away with a boyfriend. Fifteen-year-old Paloma noted that most girls her age are no longer interested in school: "it has become a common practice when we return to school after a long break to ask, 'who's back? Who got married? Who ran away with the boyfriend?'" For Paloma to call this a "common practice" means that enough girls drop out for it to be considered common place. Since they spend six semesters with their cohort, it is quite obvious when students, and particularly females, do not return to class. This also means that fewer girls complete high school as they slowly begin to drop out.

Seventeen-year-old Jessica completed El CBTIS in 2009 with a technical degree in business administration. She did not pursue college because her family did not have the means. Going to college usually means either commuting daily to Morelia, which requires round-trip bus fare plus any innercity transportation, paying for breakfast and lunch, or renting a place there. If Jessica were to commute daily, she would need approximately one hundred *pesos* per day. This would be a total of five hundred *pesos* a week, approximately fifty U.S. dollars.[21] The other option would be for her to rent a room, which would still include some of the expenses mentioned above. Her parents simply do not have the means to help her. Instead, Jessica decided to look for a job. With her degree, the ideal job placement would have been as a teller in one of the two banks in town. Jessica was unable to land a job there, however, and instead worked at a coffee shop making three hundred *pesos* per week, approximately thirty U.S. dollars in 2010. By 2012, Jessica found work at a boutique earning a bit more. By 2013, she had migrated to the U.S. Jessica's inability to land a job in her field of accounting points to the sparse opportunities available for girls like her.

Regular High School: La Prepa

Ten girls attend a regular high school. Nine of these attend high school in the town of Querendáro, located approximately twenty minutes from downtown Zinapécuaro. Only nineteen-year-old Alba attends the local *prepa*. Those who commute to Queréndaro ride vans provided by the school. By seven thirty each morning, three vans await to take the students on a twenty-minute bus ride to their first class at eight o'clock in the morning. At school, all students take four fifty-minute courses before lunch and four more after lunch. They are required to wear uniforms on

Mondays, Tuesdays, Thursdays, and Fridays. On Wednesdays, they have *día cívico* (civilian day), when they can wear quotidian clothes. According to sixteen-year-old Gisela, this high school has a good reputation, as there are hardly any teacher strikes or disruptions in the daily schedule. For Gisela, the prospect of teachers on strike connotes schools that provide a less rigorous education. Since she wants to attend college, disruptions would mean less preparation for college. Like the girls from El CBTIS, those who attend high school speak of how abnormal it is for girls their age to keep studying. Sixteen-year-old Sara noted that "there are some girls that, I don't know, they're very *locas* [wild]. They always have new boyfriends. Then there are others who like school and some who like trouble. There's all kinds of girls." Emilia agreed, relating:

> Well, how should I say it? Girls my age? I don't really hang out with them. I do, but it's just like, "hey," and, "I'll see you," or, "how are you?" When I used to go to *la secu*, I used to hang out with girls from this neighborhood and we'd chat all the time. Now, we all went our separate ways. I hardly see them or talk to them. Girls from this neighborhood hardly go to school. They all have boyfriends, are married, pregnant, others already have babies . . . but like, I do see [girls my age] going down the wrong path. Some do go to school but when school's out, they go out drinking. They want to know if I'm down. I tell them that I don't drink, I do drink but like I see them getting in cars with boys, they go swimming [to La Atzimba] and for a minute I think, "how fun!" But you never know what'll happen. They may get into accidents, or get home drunk. I [would] rather be at home, bored.

Both Sara and Emilia distance themselves from the *locas*, a term they used often to describe girls who like to hang out with boys. Their comments point to differences they themselves create and reinforce. Emilia's comments refer to *locas* from her neighborhood, but not her school. There also seems to be a perceived slight difference in attitude among girls who attend high school in Queréndaro. Comments such as "it's more rigorous than the El CBTIS" or "it's better" were very common, with the underlying assumption that being a *prepa* girl means they will have more options and fare better, or that they belong to a higher-class status. These again point to class differences that girls perceive and perform.

The College Girls

Among my 2010 interviewees, only eighteen-year-old Yola attended college. She was a first-year student at the Escuela Normal Urbana Federal, or La Normal for short—the school in Morelia that specializes in bachelor's degrees in elementary education. She moved to Morelia where she resides Monday through Friday. Her mother Aurora found a room to rent in a home, which Yola shares with a former high school classmate. Aurora bought Yola a bed, a desk, and a television set. As mentioned in chapter 2, Yola's mother is the breadwinner, as her ex-husband who lives in California does not send remittances to help raise his daughters. Yola lives close enough to school and does not need to spend too much time commuting. When her school day ends on Friday afternoons, she takes the four o'clock bus and is back in Zinapécuaro by five. She stays until Sunday evening or Monday morning. Living in Morelia has exposed Yola to different forms of living and new ways of thinking that in some ways are incompatible with a small town mentality. As she says, "in Morelia everyone's a bit more liberal, especially the youth. I see that my friend's parents let them go out and give them like a four a.m. curfew! That would not fly here [in Zinapécuaro]. Here, you have to get home early. I don't know! Over there, they're used to it, even girls are allowed to be out and about and, here, things are just so different." I interviewed Yola again in 2012. She was still in college, still living in Morelia, and only one year away from completing her degree. Once she receives her degree, she will need to do a type of residency wherever the secretary of education places her. After that, it will depend where she finds a *plaza*, or job placement. She hopes it will be in Zinapécuaro as she wants to stay close to home.

By 2012, Marbe was also in college in her second year as a nursing student. She moved to Morelia during the fall of 2010 after completing her nursing degree from El CBTIS and then enrolled in the Universidad Michoacana de San Nicolás de Hidalgo—Morelia's most important public university—to pursue a bachelor's degree in nursing. For Marbe, commuting was not an option. With the help of family friends, Marbe moved into a retirement home run by nuns. In lieu of rent, she worked every other weekend assisting the nuns. This prevented her from going home every weekend. Part of the contract also included daily chores.

When Marbe's grades began to suffer, she felt it was time to move out. Her parents' *compadres*, who live in Morelia, offered to rent her the extra room in their home so Marbe could focus fully on school. This also allowed her to return home every weekend to recharge. Marbe has found a balanced approach to school and to her social life in Morelia. Her college friends describe her as "*alebrestada*." I did not know what the word meant, so Marbe explained: "it's like someone who is always on the go, like, I'm not afraid of anything. Things don't frighten me. That's what it means to me, a go-getter. But I try to find a balance. I like to go dancing. I like to dance, dance, dance. I dance to dance music, electronic, or when they play *banda,* I get very excited. I'm not a very good dancer, sometimes I just start jumping up and down, but I don't care."[22] Marbe is doing exceptionally well in school and has found a way to succeed and enjoy herself as a college student in Morelia. Her views on women's rights and roles have also begun to change. She no longer apologizes for her feminist views, which becomes apparent when she argues with her father about decisions she makes, including who she dates. Her father is not fond of Marbe's choices and thinks her current boyfriend will take advantage of her. This attitude is similar to what García found confronting young Latinas in Chicago. She argues that, "while teenage boys are readily acceptable sexual beings overrun by their hormones and/or efforts to assert their masculinity, teenage girls are generally constructed as their sexual prey, susceptible to trickery by boys and men."[23] Although García is speaking of sexuality in a different context, Marbe's arguments with her father resonate with García's analysis. In her strong-minded tone, Marbe says:

> [I tell him], "come on dad, I've never believed that, that men take advantage of women, I mean, they do play us, of course they do, but we always have the upper hand, to put it in those words. We always know our limits and if we want them to change, they either change or, really, we can't be together anymore. I don't think they use us, rather, we let them use us." I told my dad all this and the talk got real heated. My dad was like, "where did you learn all that?" And I told him, "Morelia! In Morelia!"

Marbe is even surprised herself by how much she has changed. As she says, "*he aprendido tanto y me gusta mucho*" (I've learned so much and

I really like it). Her growth and independence delight her. Marbe is also aware that, as a college student living on her own, there are only certain things her father can tell her to do or not do.

Yola and Marbe's accounts speak to a difference between the urban and the rural that González-López distinguishes in relation to views on patriarchy and sexuality, noting that "patriarchy is not uniform or monolithic."[24] This is reflected in Yola's comments that, in Morelia, daughters are given a four a.m. curfew. Living in the city and getting an education may produce views that depart from those taught at home in Zinapécuaro. For Yola and Marbe, living in Morelia—the largest city in Michoacán, considered an urban setting—and receiving a higher education has exposed them to different forms of thinking that collide with the town's mentality of who young women should be. This, in Marbe's case, has led to heated debates with her traditional father.

No School Past the Sixth Grade

Three of the forty girls interviewed only completed elementary school: fourteen-year-old Luna, thirteen-year-old Mati, and sixteen-year-old Isabel. They each said it was their own choice. Mati was waiting to turn fifteen to attend adult school and complete her middle school in one year. But, in 2012, at only fifteen years old, Mati ran away with her twenty-seven-year-old boyfriend. He commutes to the U.S. for work and, upon his returns, lives with his maternal grandmother. Mati now lives there, too. It is unclear if her boyfriend will eventually take Mati to the U.S. Isabel refused to study in middle school. By 2012, she had a baby and was enrolled in adult school. She wanted to finish her middle school degree and then high school. As a single mother, she said: "I want to provide for my son." Luna did not pursue middle school because she wanted to stay at home and help her mother—a widow and domestic worker—with the house chores. There are no plans for Luna to return to school.

Mixed Messages and Schooling Practices

A recent documentary titled *De Panzazo* (2011) applies a neoliberal lens to public and private high schools in Mexico.[25] Lacking any consideration for the structural weaknesses that undermine the educational system, it proposes only personal solutions to what are in fact deeply political and structural problems. It appeals to Mexican society at large to work together to support the educational upbringing of Mexico's youth, but identifies no structural obstacles and proposes no actions other than by the individual. It presumes that, if students apply themselves, the possibilities are endless. The film, however, does provide some impressive statistics that suggest other outcomes. It reveals that, of every one hundred students enrolled in elementary school, eight will not show up for school on the first day, forty-five will complete middle school, twenty-seven will complete high school, thirteen will enroll in college, and only two will complete a post-graduate degree.[26] Thus, one hundred students need to enroll in school to produce two students with post-graduate degrees. The documentary does not account for the gender or sex of the dropouts, but the statistics conform to the life histories related by the girls in this study. When I returned in 2012, two years after the first set of interviews, I was able to track down twenty-six of the forty girls. Of those, six were either pregnant, young mothers, or had run off with a boyfriend; four were in college; six had dropped out of school; seven were still in high school; one had migrated to the U.S.; and one was working. By 2013, two were living in the U.S.

This pattern was found across the four groups of girls raised in varied familial formations. I wondered if their lack of access to higher education would then facilitate a move to the U.S. This is a difficult prediction to make. How did parents feel after their daughters dropping out of high school or even out of middle school and elementary school? I also wondered if the girls' lack of interest in pursuing higher education had to do with a discontent with the national discourse that surrounded them. I asked the girls for their thoughts on the Televisa ads as a way to further understand their schooling practices and connections to the nation. Seventeen-year-old Valeria said: "come on! Is that really Mexico?" Paloma observed that the things highlighted in them should build pride in being Mexican, but "the high levels of delinquency and crime make it difficult." When probed further, none of the girls felt they were really part of the nation in any meaningful way and were wary of the celebratory messages. The Televisa ads did not lure them into any nationalist identification. They think the ads are pretty, but nothing beyond that.

Many of the girls, particularly those who graduate from El CBTIS and *la prepa*, have already completed more years of schooling than their parents. But their future plans remain uncertain, for a variety of reasons. Jessica, for example, could not find a job after high school that related to her field of study, and college was out of the question because of her family's income level. Other girls receive mixed messages, or are discouraged from pursuing education, which influence their decision to attend college. They are at a crossroads, a place of limited and multiple mobilities. While growing up, they desire to become *personas realizadas*. As they finish high school, this desire is complicated by external pressures. Should they marry? Pursue a career? Work? Migrate to the U.S.? They hear voices in their town, their family, and their school that counsel them to carry themselves in a respectful manner—meaning not to hang out with boys, become sexually active, or get pregnant. As mentioned earlier, in the U.S. context, García describes this as performing a "sexual respectability," defined as the way Latina teenage girls in the U.S. negotiate contradictory messages about their sexuality.[27] Those who choose college are heavily criticized, those who are not married by the time they are eighteen years old are considered spinsters, and those who drop out are looked down upon. Girls then have to navigate a very thin line between options, desires, and respectability—all while operating under parents' expectations for them to do well.

Since *la secu*, girls begin to form opinions about one another shaped by the town's perception of proper behavior. They begin to judge and assign blame on girls who begin to deviate from ascribed and expected roles. When asked about why girls drop out of school, the following statements were typical responses:

> It depends on girls, if they are wild or not. There are some who want to achieve more and others who end up pregnant.
> —Laura, fourteen years old

> Girls who lack support from their parents usually drop out, others run away with the boyfriend.
> —Julia, thirteen years old

There are some girls who claim to be saints. I'm no saint. They call me *loca* [wild one] because I enjoy having boyfriends and chatting with boys.
—Carmen, sixteen years old

I'm no saint, but I'm not a wild one either. There are some wild girls who drink and hang out with boys. They're going down a wrong path! They're that way because they need their mom and dad. They need love. Instead of mentoring them, people criticize them.
—Sol, fifteen years old

Laura blames the girls, while Julia blames the parents. Parents, Julia believes, should protect and care for their daughters. Sol presents a more nuanced response holding girls, parents, and the town responsible for girls' choices or lack thereof. Carmen presents an intriguing response that points to a lack of space for girls her age to explore their sexuality, as she is automatically labeled a *loca* for hanging out with boys.

Similar narratives and opinions about one another are found among girls in high school. The following were typical comments from El CBTIS girls:

About 10% of the girls from my town want to study and 90% want to get married. They see me different because I still go to school.
—Caro, seventeen years old

Girls are not interested in school and either get married or work. They think marriage is the solution to life. We all need a career to secure our future.
—Dani, seventeen years old

There are no jobs, so hardly anyone studies. They work or get married. I don't really want to study. I want to get married.
—Marifer, seventeen years old

The girls receive mixed messages. Their responses often echo the view that girls can achieve anything, so long as they apply themselves. Yet, like Sol, sixteen-year-old Estrella presents a more nuanced response. She says: "there are many girls who drop out because they can't do it, others run off with the boyfriend, or get pregnant. Lately I've seen that a lot. I think it's because their parents do not look after them, or they themselves do not see life beyond a pregnancy or beyond a boyfriend. There is so much more to life! One has to learn how to balance between the personal, professional, and family. Before, pregnancies were rare. Now it's part of the quotidian life, it's the most normal thing." I asked Estrella where girls find balance and she assured me that it was at home.

Girls are expected to strike a balance, to do well in school but not too well. Even if they do find that balance, they can be sharply criticized. Marbe, who by 2012 was in her second year at La Michoacana, relates that her aunt told her the following while in high school:

> During this semester, I've been going to the Women's Hospital. My aunt sees that during the week I go to school, do my homework, I help out my parents. Holy Week just ended and there was a fair in town, a festival, and we needed to help my dad sell [pottery]. She sees that on weekends I go to Morelia, both days, for a shift and a half, about twelve hours per day and she tells me, "Oh Marbe, really, if I were you," she says, "I'd get married right now." Like, she thinks that it's easier to be married than to be in school. She says, "at the end, we all end up doing the same." She means married with kids. I started thinking and said: no!

Girls like Marbe are rare in her neighborhood. Her plans to complete her degree in nursing are well underway, regardless of what others think. In critiquing her aunt's words, she is exercising her agency and defending her decision to stay in school. Marbe also points to the assumption that, regardless of degrees, once married, all women will become stay-at-home housewives. The pressure to be young, married, and dependent in some ways comes from what girls at that age think they should do. In a follow-up interview in 2012, Jessica, then twenty-one, said that girls get married because they are looking for someone to support them:

> I think they do it so someone can take care of them. Either way the choice is always to get married, like, they can't see beyond that. "I don't have money to pay for college" or "if I start working, what if I get mistreated? Or, have a poor salary? I should just get married," they've told me. In fact, they've told me that I'm falling behind. They say: "you should already be

married." But no, no, like, I don't know. I have, like, another point of view about life. I know I still have a lot to learn. I still have a lot of growing up to do. I still have a lot of, like, things I want to accomplish. I don't know. For starters, I want to go to college, or even if I don't, I'd like a better job, move to the U.S., um, I don't know. I think differently. Obviously, I'd like to have a boyfriend or what have you, but not marriage, not now.

The girls' answers resonate with the findings of González-López. She describes the limited options women have in Mexico for economic stability. For women, marriage represents one of the few economic options for survival. Women, says González-López, have to protect their *capital femenino*, defined as a way to "explain how women and men assign a higher or lower value to a woman's premarital virginity depending on the socioeconomic context in which they grow to maturity."[28] The more virginity is protected, the higher the value and opportunities for economic stability. Girls then are told to do well, but this is fused with so many other meanings and expectations.

In some ways, the ads they see on the television portraying young women free and full of life may seem to provide them with options, choices, and different forms of mobilities. However, Zinapécuaro, their school, and the town, like the ads, also place limits on them. Girls like Yola, Marbe, and Jessica have learned to negotiate and balance the contradictory messages they receive, but not all girls share that experience. With such mixed messages, it is not difficult to imagine girls dropping out of school and not pursuing college. It is also not difficult to imagine that some of these girls will turn to the U.S. and become migrants.

After School Activities and Weekends

After school and during weekends is when girls seem to have most control over their lives. Aside from school, girls describe a world where there is little to do. Zinapécuaro, after all, is a small town and few travel outside it. When they do, it is usually to surrounding towns or to Morelia to run errands or purchase products only available in the city. Girls then have to develop creative ways to pass time. This usually involves activities in public spaces that include playing sports, being out on the town, and congregating on Sundays at *la plaza*. Such activities become performative acts that allow girls to see and be seen. These performative acts also become spaces to navigate that thin line between being sexually respectable and being labeled a *loca*.

For some girls, sports become an outlet. They play basketball, volleyball, or soccer, usually on a team from their local neighborhood. Sol belongs to a soccer team consisting of eighteen girls and two coaches called Las Chicas Heladas.[29] They practice every Thursday and Saturday ahead of the tournament game on Sunday. For Sol, winning tournament games is a badge of honor, particularly if her team plays against girls from their rival neighborhood called Las Hormigas. During the matches between Las Chicas Heladas and Las Hormigas, spectators cheer. They support one another and suspend the strong opinions about each other that frequently divide them.

Girls also enjoy being out on the town. After school, girls are hardly out by themselves. They walk downtown in pairs with arms locked, laughing and joking about the mundane. Boys tend to be the favorite topics of conversations. As sixteen-year-old Yuri said, "we chat about boys and love-related matters." Going to *la plaza* to run an errand is an opportunity to be out of the house, to socialize, and to be seen. It means a break from being home. Girls also enjoy riding four-wheel motorcycles called *cuatrimotos*. The franchise Elektra, a store that specializes in electronics and household products, opened a local branch downtown that sells *cuatrimotos* on credit. Teenagers pile up to four on the *cuatrimoto*, play loud popular music—banda, reggaeton, hip hop, Mexican pop— and cruise up and down the main streets. Such behavior also points to the performative act of being seen but also the wish to be desired, to be cool. It allows them to express themselves.

The highlight of the week is Sunday when the youth take over downtown. Sunday's routine is to attend evening mass at seven o'clock and then walk to downtown. For Jessica, Sundays are the highlight of her week: "I go to *la plaza* to walk around. I spend almost all day there. In the morning, I go to the market with my mom, then at night, I go to church and then to walk around again." Jessica works Monday through Saturday. Sunday is her day to relax and enjoy the town. She walks down the street with pep in her step, greeting everyone who walks by, eager to see what she missed on her brisk walks to work during the week. Wearing her long, blond, curly hair down, with skinny jeans and sandals, Jessica spends Sundays at El Café—a coffee shop owned by a once migrant to the U.S. who most likely learned how to make iced coffee while working at a café there—and tops it off with a slice of pizza. Nadia follows a similar routine: "on Sundays I go to *la plaza* with my friends. We usually talk about boys, who's dating who, who is cheating on who, things like that."

Girls walk in pairs down the narrow sidewalks as they circle *la plaza*. They walk down Hidalgo Street and 20 de Noviembre. After a few turns, they decide if they should walk once more or grab a bite to eat. If it is a bite to eat, it includes a frappuccino, soda, or an alcoholic beverage from El Café, a small space with chairs, tables, and a massive flat screen television that airs Los Monarcas soccer matches. Popular music plays on the speakers. The girls who go strategically sit by the door to see who walks in and with whom. Afterwards, they walk around the plaza a few more times before heading home. By ten in the evening, the town is once again quiet and teenagers will eagerly wait until next Sunday to perform the same ritual.

Future Plans: Dreaming of Mexico, Dreaming of the Modern

The girls' future plans include either dreaming of an imagined future in Zinapécuaro—college, a career, a home, a husband, and children—or their own migration to the U.S. With exceptions like Jessica, girls who express a desire to remain in Mexico are usually those raised in a seemingly heteronormative appearing families with no immediate family members in the U.S. Alternatively, and with exceptions like Camila, girls who expressed a desire to move to the U.S. are usually those raised in father-away transnational families with a father present. An obvious conclusion would be that girls who come from families with histories of migration are the ones who most likely want to move and vice versa. This is true to some extent, but an uncertainty surrounding their possible migration challenges this conclusion (see chapter 4). In this last section, I examine girls' attitudes toward choosing either to remain in Mexico or to migrate to the U.S.

Girls Who Want to Stay in Mexico

Girls who have little or no interest in moving to the U.S. tend to be those raised in a seemingly heteronormative appearing families or once transnational families. They derive impressions of life in the U.S. from what they see and what they imagine. From witnessing the return of the diaspora or their cousins and other relatives, girls hear that those who move to the U.S. work very hard. Eighteen-year-old Yola relates: "[in the U.S.] parents are never home. They are always working and never spend time with children." Eighteen-year-old Jackie has heard that in the U.S. people change their personalities and values, while eighteen-year-old Adi has heard that kids do not pay much attention to their parents. Most point to the good school system in the U.S. that would perhaps allow them to have a better education, but feel they could receive similar opportunities in Mexico. The stories they hear allow them to imagine the U.S. as a modern and urban place. Eighteen-year-old Luz says: "I've heard it's pretty. You can go shopping but you also spend a lot of time indoors. There isn't much to do there either." Adi adds: "I've heard it's pretty and safe, but it does not catch my attention." These girls are not seduced by modernity. When I asked the girls if they ever thought about moving, some said they imagine it would be difficult because of the language barrier. Valentina would like to go to Disneyland and imagines what would be like to go to school in the U.S.: "I'd like to go to Disneyland, but only to visit, not to stay. I really don't know what life would be like over there. I like the idea of high school. They have lockers over there where you can leave your books. I like that so I won't have to carry all my books around! It'd be cool to do high school in the U.S."

Girls that want to stay in Mexico hope to finish high school, attend college in Morelia, Guadalajara, or surrounding cities, and become *personas realizadas*. Estrella, who already has siblings attending college in Morelia, said that she is seeking independence, explaining: "I would like to be able to make my own decisions. I do not want to depend on anyone. It is not necessarily bad to depend on people, but it's good to find a balance." Similarly, Yuri has always wanted to go to law school. She recalls watching what she describes as conferences on the television as a little girl and telling her mother: "I want to go to those conferences and show the politicians that there is more to words. [Politicians] should not make promises they cannot deliver. There are so many innocent people in prison. I would like to help them." Law school, she feels, is one of the avenues where words and action can be coupled. She added that, "in Mexico, you can achieve success as long as you try." Camila hopes to enroll in the Military Medical School. As the youngest of eight siblings who reside in Utah and California, she has witnessed firsthand how her brothers and sisters have changed: "they have become too materialistic and I don't want that to happen to me." Instead, she hopes to meet the requirements to gain entrance and become an independent and successful doctor in Mexico.

It is unclear how many of the girls will complete their degree and become *personas realizadas*. As mentioned earlier, González-López found that women in rural areas in Mexico have few options due to limited opportunities. By 2012, Yuri was in her last year of high school. She had run off with her much older boyfriend. Her parents arranged a quick marriage to salvage her sexual respectability.[30] Although she persisted in completing high school, there were no plans for law school or to attend conferences where she could challenge politicians. In the evenings, Yuri helps her husband's family run their cake business. At fourteen, Valentina gave birth after dropping out of middle school. By 2014, there were still no plans to return to school, leaving her with an eighth-grade education. Camila did not meet the height requirements to enter the Military Medical School. Since she had no backup plan, she did a one-year nursing residency. The following year, she failed the entrance exam that would have assured her a spot at La Michoacana's medical school. Unwilling to skip a second year of school, Camila opted for a spot at La Michoacana's nursing school, which Marbe also attends. By 2014, Camila was in her last semester of nursing training. She was pregnant, which she felt could put her at risk in finding employment.

Perhaps none of these girls will migrate to the U.S. Some still share the desire to become a *persona realizada* in Mexico, but they will have to negotiate the limited and multiple mobilities within which they live there.

Girls Who Hope to Migrate

Many of the girls imagine a future in the U.S. They tend to present more detailed accounts of what they have heard about life there and of their own imagined future there living near relatives. Marifer has heard that life in the U.S. is better, while for fourteen-year-old Esme, migrating to the U.S. would allow her a fresh start. When she was thirteen, Esme's parents were on the brink of divorce, which she did not take well. She began drinking heavily on a daily basis and got caught at *la secu* with a bottle of wine inside her backpack. Esme wanted out and the U.S. offered an escape. For Mati, the U.S. "calls my attention. I don't know, ever since I was little, I wanted to go and see what everyone was talking about. They say it's very pretty! I'd really like to go." For Sol, the U.S. is a place that will allow her to build a home, own a car, and improve her economic situation. Some girls, including Yola, Sara, Jessica, and Marifer, were born in the U.S. and are citizens. Jessica and Marifer are hoping to get their U.S. passports so they can return legally to their birthplace.

Marbe hopes to migrate to the U.S. once she completes her degree in order to make more money and help support her family. She has heard of the low supply and high demand for nurses in the U.S., which may facilitate her chance of getting a work visa. The income she could make, coupled with her father Sixto's salary, would allow the family to repay all debts and live better in Zinapécuaro.

Girls' desires for migration speak to the limited possibilities they see in Mexico compared to the endless ones they imagine in the U.S. There is an underlying assumption that living in a modern nation will provide access to opportunities. Most girls have heard about how poorly Mexicans are treated in the U.S. (chapter 4), but their romanticized notions are much stronger.

Analysis and Conclusion

High expectations are placed on the girls, yet few feel the support needed to complete school and go on to college. Instead, they receive mixed messages that limit their multiple options. The television ads for Mexico's centennial and bicentennial celebrations highlight poignant discontent between the perceptions and expectations of young women as the face of the nation, and their far more complex lived experience as captured in these study's interviews. These women, particularly teenage girls, were not the intended audience of the ads. They were on display for the pleasure of men. Against a backdrop of transnational migration and the return of the diaspora, the dropout rates and the mixed messages the girls receive throughout their adolescence point to deep structural and patriarchal barriers in their lives. The choice—between achieving it all in Mexico or subscribing to the dream of endless possibilities in the U.S.—speaks to a dominating, hegemonic discourse of neoliberalism that has infiltrated these girls' world.

4

Migration Marks

Time, Waiting, and Desires for Migration

We urgently need more systematic comparative studies of how cultural mobilities are generated in everyday life and facilitated as well as constrained by specific circuits and institutions. The mobility of cultures is brought about not only by past and contemporary diasporic and migratory movements of people, but also by the technological innovations that have made possible travel of the imagination, thus enabling people who are stuck in one place to be influenced by ongoing political, economic and cultural transformations elsewhere. Migratory movements have created new avenues for the transnational flow of identities, ideas and practices. An anthropology of mobility imaginaries–narratives and ideas that depend on the creation of the otherness of one's own identity as well as of the Other–reveals how mobile local lifeworlds are always negotiated and contested, and constantly under transformation.
—Noel Salazar, "Towards an Anthropology of Cultural Mobilities," 64

It happened by accident. The year was 2006. Her parents' *compadres* were over for *cafecito* and *pan*. As usual, then fifteen-year-old Jessica avoided the kitchen during their visits. She found adult conversations uninteresting. Without meaning to, she overheard her mother's *compadre* raving about her last trip to the United States and her ears perked up. Ever since she was twelve years old, Jessica had been bitten by the migration bug and had imagined her own journey north. The U.S. was the place that would offer her opportunities to study, to work, to secure a better life. She grew up dreaming of the cities, skyscrapers, and the hustle and bustle of what she imagined to be the modern world. That night, her mother mentioned that Jessica had been born in the U.S. and had *una acta de nacimiento Americana* (a U.S. birth certificate). Jessica froze. All along she had thought of herself as Mexican. At fifteen, she suddenly suspended her future plans that had long been in place—plans for high school and trying to figure out how to pay for university in Morelia on her family's limited income. That evening, her dream of moving became more tangible, even possible. In her imagination, she began to envision a present of planning and a future of success. She just needed to figure out the process to achieve her goals.

Jessica was unsure about the steps she needed to take to return to the country where she was born. She felt more American than Mexican after finding out her citizenship status. She requested assistance from her aunt, a U.S. citizen who had lived in Illinois for more than twenty years, to mail her a copy of her birth certificate and social security card. The former was mailed immediately and the latter took two years. None of her relatives claimed to know where they had placed the social security card until a family member finally came forward and mailed it to her. By 2010, and now nineteen years old, she hired a lawyer to formalize her dual citizenship. After two years and hefty legal fees, she had everything in order. But, in 2012, her plans almost reached a complete stop. She had visited different organizations around Zinapécuaro familiar with the case of U.S.-born children and youth living in Mexico, with no passport but aspirations to return to their birth country. Some told her that she needed photos of her life in the U.S. as proof of her citizenship, the bracelet that was placed on her wrist at the hospital immediately after she was born, and her baby footprints, none of which she had. Others informed her that, if someone had worked on her social security card, she would be in trouble. Some opined that, since she was nearing twenty-one years of age and had not lived on American soil, she had effectively renounced her American citizenship.[1] All of this frightened Jessica. In May of 2012, she went to the U.S. embassy in Guadalajara carrying what she described as "her truth." She had passport-size photos taken and carried her birth certificate, social security card, and proof of dual citizenship. On January 28, 2013, seven years after the process began and eight months after her visit to the embassy, Jessica finally hopped on a plane en route to the U.S. eager to begin her new life.

From the moment Jessica found out about her place of birth in 2006 to her actual departure date in 2013, she experienced moments of uncertainty, ambiguity, and much anxiety. She experienced a time lag between learning about her citizenship status, desiring her own migration, and the actual move.[2] This is an experience characteristic of Mexican teenage girls like Jessica where desire and a possible journey of migration spread out over time, suspending the present.[3] During this lapse, what mattered most to Jessica was always the next step she needed to get closer to her move. She gave up trying to figure out how to pay for college and zoomed in on her future. In many ways, Jessica balanced different temporalities, inhabiting a present saturated with future plans that placed her life on hold. She still lived in Mexico, in the town of Zinapécuaro, had an active social life, and enjoyed Sundays at *la plaza*, but her future elsewhere was always looming.

I open this chapter with Jessica's experience as a point of entry into the stories of other Mexican teenage girls who express a desire for migration. Like Jessica, other girls I interviewed experienced a time lag between their expressed desire to move and the actual move. They shared Jessica's dreams of migration, of the modern, of city life, and of assumed opportunities in the U.S. What separates Jessica from other girls, however, is the unconditional support—emotional and financial—that she received from her parents. Girls with similar dreams, particularly those raised in father-away transnational families, did not necessarily find the same support at home. In fact, in most cases, their desire for migration was opposed and thwarted by their fathers, because they were young and because they were girls.

It is unclear how many of the girls I interviewed in Zinapécuaro will actually migrate, and it is not my intention to predict their future. My intent and purpose within this chapter is to examine that temporality of uncertainty, ambiguity, and anxiety. Of particular interest to this study are girls raised in father-away transnational families who I argue are placed on a migrant path as a result of their father's migration patterns, making them migrants in waiting. As such, they negotiate multiple temporal locations that include their daily practices, the returns and departures of the diaspora and their own fathers, and their own desires for migration. The temporal location they inhabit then includes their father's commutes and the temporal rhythms of the place in which they live, all of which provide girls with a unique subjectivity of time.

The stories of girls in this chapter point to a trend in migration scholarship—whether transnational or translocal—which argues that, within transnational social fields, locals do not have to move to physically experience migration.[4] What does it feel like to be caught in processes of migration without moving? Or to live in a place of movement that surrounds the local without physical movement? As migrants in waiting, their experiences force us to reconsider the meaning of migrants en route and to question when this stage begins, including the moment when dreams of modernity enter their lives and entice them to desire migration.

Temporalities of a Nation, Temporalities of Migration

Linear time and the constant forward movement has been central to capitalist development and progress. According to Edward Soja (1989), time has been seen as more important than space because it connotes "richness, fecundity, life, dialectic."[5] Time became central to capitalist development as the main means of disciplining the labor force.[6] In the conquest of the Americas, for example, the first invaders imposed a new time discipline as a major means of colonizing the minds of the indigenous populations. In southwestern North America, missionaries used bells to indicate to the indigenous labor force when to wake up, when to go to their assigned work, when to eat, and when they were allowed to rest.[7] Bells functioned as a way to discipline the time needed to maximize labor production. The time of the bells supplanted the previous sense of time regulated by the movements of the sun and the changes in seasons.

As linear time became privileged, so did ideas of progress. Developed nations came to see themselves as embodying progress and imagined themselves to be at the cutting edge of knowledge and its production. Occupying this space placed them in the present as current and contemporary. The nations that they conquered and exploited were relegated to a previous era of history and designated as primitive and rationally and ontologically deficient. These so-called pre-modern nations, which included Mexico, were placed in a different temporal location, and presumed unable to provide knowledge up to par with that of modern states. This is reflected in studies of the pre-modern world wherein the

Other is anthropologically constructed as an object trapped in a previous, static time frame.[8] Because European time is presented as linear, the placing of Others in a timeless past, as peoples without history, denies the reality of their existence in the same time frame. The anthropologist Fabian defines this denial of coevalness as *"a persistent and systematic tendency to place the referent(s) of anthropology in a Time other than the present of the producer of anthropological discourse,"*[9] which negates the presence and time of the Other, and her status as a modern subject.[10]

In the indigenous worlds of the Americas, time was experienced quite differently. Bonfil Batalla speaks of time in Mesoamerican civilization as cyclical, non-linear, and non-sequential.[11] Once the invaders arrived, this system was denied and negated. As languages and ceremonial practices were distorted or erased by armed force, Western notions of civilization—including time—began to transform life in Mesoamerica. Bonfil Batalla argues that this process, however, remains incomplete. He describes a process by which the arrival of the West in Mesoamerica actually created two Mexicos: an imaginary Mexico (that imagined by the West) and a Mexico *profundo*. The imaginary retains the West's hegemony over the *profundo*, constantly and actively denying the continued existence of the other Mexico, rooted in Mesoamerican civilization.[12] In the long history of Spanish America and Mexico, anything and everything Indian became portrayed as an obstacle, in the way of the imaginary Mexico's progress leaving it always on the brink of modernity, waiting, anticipating, trapped in a state of suspended animation.[13] The imaginary constantly looked to the West as a model to advance toward (what scholars used to refer to as) "First World" status. Denying Indianness was an essential aspect of this project.

Mexico encompasses the imaginary and the *profundo*. Each comes with their own notions of time. As Carlos Fuentes (1997) concludes, in Mexico, "there is not and never [has] been one single time, one central tradition, as in the West. In Mexico, all times are living, all pasts are present."[14] This is similar to what García Canclini refers to as multitemporal heterogeneities used to explain how, in Latin America, "modernization rarely operated through the substitution of the traditional and the ancient," but instead both co-exist.[15] As stated earlier, Amuchástegui Herrera cautions about the inequalities inscribed in distinctions between "tradition and modernities."[16] The multiple temporalities of the

Mexican nation highlight the conflicting and contradictory character of a nation described by its dominant ideology as almost always on the brink of modernity.

Within Mexico and its multi-temporal heterogeneities lie the temporalities of migration and of the diaspora. Within migratory practices, the temporal is circular and transnational. The circular includes departures, arrivals, and separations that cause families to live apart. They are always temporary but always continuous. Hondagneu-Sotelo found that the average migrant family separation lasts twelve years, although some families live apart for up to thirty years.[17] The migrant departs for the U.S. and returns home to enjoy the hard-earned money.[18] Those who remain behind wait for the departed to visit, to call, for remittances, or to be asked to join the absent party in the U.S. Those who leave mark the lives of those who stay through a circular practice of migration. This circular pattern moves forward in a manner that resembles rolling circles meeting at the time of departure and of arrival. This circular approach to migration, however, only measures the temporary departure of the migrant, and largely ignores the continuous state of waiting of those who remain behind.

Transnational migration scholarship tends to underscore how families across geographic locations remain in contact. Ethnographies, for example, have yielded fascinating accounts of the reproduction of Mexican customs and traditions in the U.S.[19] Culture flows in the other direction as revealed in research showing that migrants to the U.S. shape cultural practices in even the most remote villages in Mexico by returning home with cars, music, and clothing that then become part of the local culture.[20] The transnational flow of tradition and culture is a two-way street, virtually all in both location take part in transnational life in some way. In defining social fields within transnational migration, Levitt and Glick Schiller argue that "ideas, practices, and resources are unequally exchanged."[21] Similarly, Nowotny notes that the discovery of worldwide simultaneity "feigned a sense of time according to which the individual could be in any place at any time and participate in everything happening elsewhere."[22] Despite this, "simultaneity does not automatically translate into equality. In this respect, it is an illusion."[23] Simultaneity is an illusion in the sense that people experience events, time, separation, and borders differently because of a temporal inequality with unequal consequences for differently situated participants.

Those who migrate to the U.S., including the girls' fathers, inhabit a new temporality that requires them to negotiate Western hegemonic time.[24] Diasporic communities in the U.S., Michel Laguerre (2003) writes, must adapt the various temporal rhythms of their communities, including those from back home, to that of the mainstream U.S.[25] Dreby (2010) captures an important aspect of time and waiting within transnational families by identifying a temporal "mismatch" between parents in the U.S. and their children in Mexico.[26] She found that "families divided by borders lack . . . 'temporal coordination.' Parents' time in the United States is structured around irregular work schedules of forty to sixty hours per week . . . Parents do not want to give up their goals, because they want their sacrifices to be worthwhile; in the meantime, periods of separation grow longer."[27] Family members who remain behind, including Mexican teenage girls in this study, have to negotiate the temporalities of migration, of the diaspora. From circular patterns of migration, to inequalities produced in transnational migratory practices, differing time zones and a lack of temporal coordination, families of the diaspora experience a timing mismatch between fathers' lives in the U.S. and their own.

In Comes the Diaspora

The diaspora, traditionally silenced in hegemonic Mexican political and cultural discourses, has started to enter the national narrative. Whereas once the general view was that migrants to the U.S. were "deserters, turncoats, or weaklings unable or unwilling to stick it out back home," today national and local governments have noted the importance of their economic contributions to the nation.[28] Since the presidency of Vicente Fox (2000–2006), Mexicans in the U.S. have become visible in the national rhetoric. Castañeda (2009), for example, analyzes migration from Mexico to the U.S. from a Mexican perspective. In his view, immigrants are forming what he calls a "new middle class" that is beginning to reflect the actual population of Mexico. Their economic contributions to the country's economic survival have become more obvious.[29] They are sometimes described as heroes.[30]

Remittances sent back to Mexico from the U.S. have supported a local home-building industry and helped to pay for town improvements including new pavements, churches, and even local baseball stadiums. These material contributions make them visible. As Castañeda writes, they are "one of the country's best kept secrets and most sacred treasures."[31] Martínez, in turn, describing this same group of remittance-sending Mexican migrants, notes how the new realities produce a circular movement of migrants where "you meet your future by moving out, render tribute to the past by coming back home to visit and spend your hard earned dollars."[32] By spending their money, these migrants thus enjoy a middle-class status for a couple of weeks a year. At the same time, they add to the prosperity of their hometowns and thus become the sacred treasures Castañeda describes. Moreover, their celebration by political leaders like former presidents Fox and Felipe Calderón (20006–2012) does not indicate only admiration. Indeed, Mexican officials recognize that those who leave, and who travel back and forth over a period of time, are effectively removed from the roster of potential disaffected critics of Mexico's many problems. Thus, in their praise, Fox and Calderón might be celebrating the fact that they are no longer responsible for those citizens who have left because of their own failures of governance.

The lives and departures of migrants have also entered popular culture via *telenovelas* and reality shows. In 2011, the popular Televisa *telenovela La Fuerza del Destino* briefly addressed the lives of emigrants in the U.S. via Iván, the main character, who migrates to Los Angeles, California.[33] He is a handsome, smart, studious, and dedicated young man who finds work at a restaurant. Because he speaks a bit of English, he moves up quickly from dishwasher to waiter causing resentment among his Mexican American co-workers who think he is being rewarded too quickly without having paid his dues. This is similar to the scenario depicted in Gregory Nava's *El Norte* wherein Enrique, the Guatemalan refugee who works in a restaurant as a busser, is pitted against his Chicano co-worker who calls the then INS to have him deported.[34] This trope continues to be recycled on Mexican national television, vilifying the Mexican American and victimizing the Mexican migrant. *Telenovela* viewers are exposed to the same tropes where they form opinions of Mexican Americans in the U.S. that are usually not positive.

The lives of Mexican migrants are also on display in reality shows. *La Academia*, Mexico's version of *American Idol*, is a singing competition reality show on TV Azteca where participants compete to win a record deal. *La Academia* also holds auditions in the U.S. and usually has at least two participants that represent the Mexican diaspora. In 2011, there were two diasporic participants: Carmen from San Francisco and Gustavo from Chicago.[35] Brief snapshots of their lives were shown as though to represent all Mexicans who live in the U.S. They are spoken of as if they are strange and unique beings who choose to risk it all for a chance at a better life, dismissing or forgetting the long history of Mexican emigration to the U.S.[36]

In Zinapécuaro, Mexican teenage girls see the U.S. through the return of the diaspora in their city. This allows them to continuously form their own opinions that may or may not conform with what is presented to them on television. For some of the girls in this study, the return of the diaspora produces dislike and concern arising from a limited understanding of life in the U.S. and from exposure to U.S. racial hierarchies. These reactions contain resonances of broader conversations about Mexicans in the U.S., some of which date as far back as Octavio Paz's (1994) assessment of the Pachuco in *The Labyrinth of Solitude*.[37] Some of the girls, for example, are not very fond of the return of the diaspora, particularly of the girls their age who they feel return with an attitude and air of superiority to Zinapécuaro locals. When asked about the return of the diaspora, the following comments were common:

They pretend to be all that just because they speak English.
—Yola, eighteen years old

They only return to show off *lo material* and make others feel bad.
—Toñita, thirteen years old

[It's] illogical that they return speaking English, aren't they Mexican?
—Gisela, sixteen years old

They think they are all that, but, they left because they needed to and are there for a reason. Why do they think they are better?
—Estrella, sixteen years old

There are some girls who come and hang out. When you walk by them, they start speaking English. I mean, what's that [all about]? Anyone can learn English.
—Yuri, sixteen years old

Yola, Gisela, and Yuri critique girls who return speaking English. Unfamiliar with anti-bilingual measures and anti-immigrant sentiment, and different historical periods in the U.S. that have chastised those who speak Spanish, they assume an ultimate betrayal in purposely denying the mother tongue and rejecting their Mexicanness. In their statements, they reveal misconceptions of life in the U.S. that in some ways are supported by what they see on television and the news. Estrella makes sure to underscore that Mexican migrants left because they had to, pointing to their working class background whereas she feels part of an imagined middle class that places her atop the diaspora. As members of the working class, Estrella wonders why they think they are better. I want to suggest that these types of resentments are in large part because the diaspora possesses what girls perceive as embodied sensations of modernity that Mexican teenage girls like Toñita desire. Their ability to speak English, to travel regardless of their class status in the U.S., is what girls like Estrella resent. In some ways, the shift in attitude that Castañeda proclaims has not reached the girls in Zinapécuaro.

Girls' reactions towards the diaspora also express concern. When friends or relatives return, they bring stories of how badly Mexicans are treated in the U.S. Such stories include tales of relatives' encounters with U.S. racist practices in the workplace or on the streets. The national media also contributes to such narratives via the stories they highlight on *telenovelas* or Adela Micha's *Las Noticias por Adela*. Iván's experience, as previously mentioned, is but one example. When asked about their awareness of Mexicans in the U.S., the following responses were offered:

Mexicans leave knowing they may be discriminated, but they risk it anyway for their family.
—Carmen, sixteen years old

Gringos mistreat Mexicans. They humiliate them. I'm afraid of going.
—Sol, fifteen years old

Mexicans are exploited in the U.S., they are humiliated because they are Mexican.

—Jackie, eighteen years old

Often it is Mexicans discriminating against Mexicans, not *gringos*.

—Yola, eighteen years old

[I've heard that] Arnold, the one with the weird last name, is in favor of building the fence and all that. They shouldn't treat us as if we were criminals.

—Lali, seventeen years old

The statements above are almost in complete opposition to the previous set. Rather than resenting the diaspora, they feel solidarity with it. The girls seem to feel the plight of Mexican immigrants and their poor treatment in the U.S. personally. Yet they also fall in line with the familiar trope of vilifying the Mexican American and victimizing the Mexican immigrant, as highlighted by Yola.[38] At the same time, they also communicate an understanding of how and why Mexicans leave despite knowing they will be racialized. They understand that, in some way, the Mexican body is already racialized long before crossing the border.[39] Lali and Jackie point to the nightly news as the source that informs their opinions of how Mexicans are treated in the U.S. These comments also reflect the findings of Zavella, who noted in her research that the Mexicans she interviewed in Mexico were well aware of events that happen in the U.S.[40]

These girls fail to make connections between stories they hear about the treatment of Mexicans in the U.S. and the need for the diaspora to return to Mexico and regain part of their humanity lost during the months or years of arduous labor in the U.S. Part of that humanity means displaying what they have worked so hard to attain. Oftentimes, it is the material that is the most tangible. After all, that is the reason why they left. The girls are quick to assign blame on how the U.S. mistreats their fellow citizens, yet they themselves express resentment towards the diaspora. As previously mentioned, this is part of a larger narrative of how Mexicans view the diaspora from home.

The girls' contradictory feelings, coupled with witnessing their fathers' commutes, cause them to develop complex notions of life in the

U.S. Those who live in transnational families are also eyewitnesses to the possible success and higher quality of life they are able to have precisely because of migration. Their exposure to the diaspora teaches them who to be and what to avoid if they migrate to the U.S. What is precarious about their attitude is the fact that they may never know who they may become until they themselves migrate.

The return of the diaspora also exposes girls—especially those who hope for migration—to a particular type of migratory journey. As noted in chapter 2, La Entrada del Señor de Araro and the Christmas holidays are when the diaspora returns. Most girls who expressed a desire for migration said they would model their journeys after the diaspora and return for La Entrada and Christmas, as these are holidays they would certainly hate to miss. They note the dates and times migrants return and, if they were to leave, they intend to return during the same periods of time. Migration, in their eyes, does not mean a permanent move; it does not mean a "one-way ticket."[41]

Migrants in Waiting

Those who desire a future in the U.S. have to wait. As discussed in the introduction, the literature on youth captures the elongated waiting they experience to enter adulthood. In this section, I examine desires for migration via the stories of Jessica, Marbe, Paloma, Toñita, and Carmen, and their varied forms of waiting they experience. These girls' stories reveal the interruptions to their daily lives caused by growing up within transnational social fields, for some, and a father-away transnational family, for others, which make them unable to plan long-term. I examine how their desires for, and denials of, migration place them in a temporal location where they experience uncertainty, ambiguity, and anxiety—all temporal experiences—about their present in Mexico and possible future in the U.S. I analyze their experiences as examples of how, in some ways, the progress of time is removed from their immediate realities in waiting.

Interruptions to Routines

Growing up in a transnational family and within transnational social fields interrupts girls' daily routines. Deborah Boehm et al. (2011)

describes how "migration can be both a rupture and a continuation of social life."[42] For girls raised in transnational families, their daily lives include regular phone calls, waiting for remittances, and physical visits and departures of their fathers. Fathers' returns once or twice per year alter household dynamics. When he returns, the mothers and daughters may have to work since the husband/father is no longer sending remittances. In some cases, fathers resume their pre-migration activities when the money he brings runs out. Fathers may return to work in their pottery business, others become construction workers, some work in the *campo* as *campesinos* or farm workers, as cab drivers, or delivering products, all of which seem temporary. Usually within months of his arrival, his next departure looms.

It was rare to find a girl who preferred her father's arrivals. In fact, most girls raised in transnational familial arrangements said they prefer his absences.[43] Growing up in a transnational family where the father is the migrant from birth made girls used to their living arrangement. They did not know their father too well as they only spent time with him upon his return. The normalcy of growing up without their fathers makes his presence feel strange. Upon his return, if the dynamics at home were altered too much, then girls anticipated his departure. Such was the case with sixteen-year-old Carmen.[44] Of her father's visits, she said:

> C: Well, things change a lot because, like, he likes to drink a lot and I don't feel comfortable. Things change, like we all go out like a family, but when we go out, he likes to drink. He's at home and he's drinking. Like, when he gets here, he drinks one day and skips the other, just like that . . . He likes to take us out. Wherever we want to go, he takes us. We are always out and about and are hardly home when he is here, but the thing I don't like is that when we go out, he always drinks. He never, well, there's only been one time that I vividly remember when he did not drink. I don't like to go with him anymore because I'm afraid we'll crash or something . . .
>
> LS: Does he usually drive?
>
> C: Yes. We used to get into a lot of accidents when we went out. I'd get really scared and now I hardly go with him. Sometimes he is not that drunk, but when he gets like that, like, too much, I don't like to go with him. That's why I don't like him to come because he drinks

too much and over there [in the U.S.] he hardly drinks, that's why I
prefer that he does not come.

What perhaps could have been happy times for Carmen become dangerous and even abusive moments. She actually prefers his absences
when he has only a ghost-like presence. While her father is away, however, he sends money on a monthly basis and calls regularly. Carmen
does not have to worry about food, clothing, or shelter, as her father's
remittances are enough to cover all expenses. During his weekly phone
calls, Carmen speaks with him. He is genuinely interested in Carmen's
feelings, school, and friends. This behavior makes Carmen wish for his
return. However, when he does return, he becomes a different father, a
different person. Once her father returned to Zinapécuaro after losing
his job in Virginia and stayed for almost one year. Carmen had just completed middle school and had no desire to enroll in high school. There
was no income flowing in. Both Carmen and her younger sister Paula
were expected to work and contribute to the household. They found
work at a local bakery. The months he was there reminded Carmen of
why she wishes him gone. She describes his routine: "from the moment
he returns until he leaves, all he does is drink. When he is not drinking,
he lays in bed, watching TV, or asleep, that's the only thing he does."
His brothers who live in the U.S. were urging him to return to Virginia.
They sent him money for his plane ticket but he spent it on alcohol. It
is difficult for Carmen to assess the reasons for her father's contradictory behavior. On the one hand, he is a responsible father who is doing
what a migrant father agreed to do—send remittances and offer his family a better chance at life. On the other hand, there are issues beyond
Carmen's comprehension that make her wish him gone. Perhaps there
are reasons for his behavior that Carmen is unaware of which make it
difficult for her to feel comfortable with his presence.[45] We could imagine that Carmen feels joyous to have her father around, that she might
like them to live how she imagines a heteronormative family should do,
but the complications of life, of her father's character, get in the way.

Fifteen-year-old Paloma shares a similar discomfort during her father's returns.[46] As the youngest and with most of her siblings in the
U.S., she feels close to her mother and her siblings' children whom she
lives with. As mentioned in chapter 2, Paloma was born into a transna-

tional family. Her father Pablo began commuting to California for work long before she was born. When asked to describe her feelings about her father's commutes, Paloma said:

> Now I'm a tad used to it, but, from what I remember, it's what he's always done. I didn't like it at first because, I don't know, I liked having him around, for him to be here. He would leave and I'd say, 'come back!' And now, as I got older, it's the complete opposite. I like it when he's gone because my mom is more flexible and lets me go out, so, when he is not here, I can go out more, be out and about. When he is here, I can't go out anywhere because he hardly gives us permission to go out, so, after a while, I realized that I like it more when he is not here because I feel more free, more free to go out with friends, to the park, or anywhere. And now, I don't know. Now, there are times when I wish he were here, and I want him to be around. I like it when he is here because, I don't know, there is more order in the house when he is here and when he's gone, things feel a bit out of control. Everyone does whatever they want, that's when I wish he were here. But then I say, no, if he is here, I won't be able to go out, he won't give me permission to go out. I like it when he is here, I like him to be here but when he leaves, I don't know. I don't feel the same as when I was younger. When my dad is here, I don't go out. I don't see my friends.

In one long answer, Paloma reveals all of the mixed feelings and contradictory emotions towards her father. Part of it has to do with his refusals to grant her permission to go out freely. These feelings also have to do with her questioning the authoritative role he adopts with such ease upon his returns, despite knowing little about the household's dynamics. It is in these moments when girls like Paloma express their agency, albeit a fragile one.[47] His behavior as the man of the house is precisely what Paloma critiques and questions. Since he is her father, however, Paloma feels obligated to comply. Within her analysis, Paloma is also able to discern some of the benefits of having him around. The household feels more organized for the couple of months he is present, and her family feels like a seemingly heteronormative appearing one. Like Carmen, however, Paloma mentions experiencing a lack of freedom when her father is around.

Other girls like seventeen-year-old Marbe feel added responsibility at home while her father is away. Marbe is the oldest of six children.[48] Our first interview took place in 2010. We sat in the living room, where she began talking about her responsibilities when her father Sixto is away. She confides:

> As the oldest, I am responsible for the youngest. I have to get good grades and be a role model for my *hermanitas* and *hermanitos*. Emilia, for example, is not doing too well in school. I have to encourage her. I tell her, "come on girl, if I can do it, so can you." No one put me in charge . . . Like, my parents never told me directly, no one told me, but um, I think that it has always been the case, ever since I was little. For example, when my dad was in the U.S. and my mom needed to run errands—because he has always gone to the U.S. long before I was born, even before [that], my mom would stay home with us, alone. My grandparents were usually working, and um, my mom would tell me, "Marbe, please stay here to look after your little sister." My little sister was only two months old, a newborn, and my mom left her in charge of me. "I'll leave her here." She'd put her in between pillows and I'd sit there, next to her and she'd say, "I'll leave her here with you, but don't touch her. If she pulls the blanket over her face, bring it down so she won't suffocate." And my mom says that when she'd return a bit later, because she never took too long, that I was still sitting in the same position she had left me. I hadn't moved! I was there taking care of my little sister, and ever since I was little, I felt that responsibility. I didn't know what it was then, that I was being responsible, but you feel it. She's younger than you so you need to protect her. Then my mom had two more daughters. There are four of us, four older sisters and two little brothers, six and eight. I had to look after all of them too.

The responsibility Marbe describes is not only because she is the older sister, but also because her father is gone. While Sixto is away, her mother relies on her for help around the house. Marbe became the caretaker whenever Poncia, her mother, needed to run errands. The cleaning, assistance in disciplining the younger ones, and chores around the house fell to Marbe's care. This routine changes, however, when Sixto returns. For Toñita, Marbe's thirteen-year-old younger sister, her father's returns mean she does not have to work in the family business. The family business is a shop in downtown Zinapécuaro where they sell pottery, including mugs, plates, and *molcajetes* (mortar). When her father is gone, she has to go downtown on the weekend to sell pottery: "sometimes I only go on weekends, usually on Saturdays. When my dad is here, we don't even need to go on weekends because he takes one of my little brothers. He also tells us that we don't have to go because he is here to handle the business. When he is not here and I'm in school, I usually don't have time during the week, but I do have to go on weekends." Her father returns and handles the business. Toñita's work and school routine change depending on whether her father is in the U.S. or in Zinapécuaro. By 2011, with their older sister Marbe in college and living in Morelia, Toñita and Emilia were the two who had to help around the house and in the family business.

These snapshots of their lives show alterations in the girls' routines. The lives of Carmen, Paloma, Marbe, and Toñita changed when their respective fathers returned to Zinapécuaro. The normalcy of their lives, of their routines, become altered. Permissions and outings no longer depend on girls' desires to be out and to be seen. For Carmen, family outings are common but unpleasant. Her father's drinking and behavior makes her wish for his return to the U.S. Paloma is able to experience living in a heteronormative appearing family for the months her father is present, but also wishes him to return to the U.S. She feels *encerrada,* or locked in, when he is around. As a fifteen-year-old, she is beginning to enjoy being out of the house and spending Sundays at *la plaza,* which is off limits when her father is around. For both Marbe and Toñita, household responsibilities change. As the older sister, Marbe needs to help her mother raise her younger siblings, a duty she describes above. Toñita's routine is also altered as her father's returns and absences dictate whether or not she must help her family at work.

What is notable about their answers is the lack of desire to function as a seemingly heteronormative appearing family with their father present throughout the year. They are not overwhelmed by loss or consumed with desires for wholeness. As young teenagers, their desires and concerns are to enjoy school, dating, and outings to *la plaza.* With a father present, there are limits to the activities in which they can engage. This complicates their young lives. Some girls like Paloma express a need and a desire to have her father present, and the reverse when he is around.

Carmen, Paloma, Marbe, and Toñita know exactly when to expect their father to visit or call. In Marbe's and Toñita's case, their father leaves in June and returns by December. This means they need to get used to his schedule—they know their duties and responsibilities when he is away and when he returns. They know to prepare and figure out ways to hide their relationships with their boyfriends when he is home (chapter 2). Carmen knows very well when her father will call. She can then choose to be around the home on Saturdays when she is certain he will call or leave the home if she does not feel like talking to him. Almost all the girls know what to expect and arrange their routine and behavior accordingly. But this re-arrangement means that the normalcy they are able to develop when their fathers are away is subverted. This is all part of growing up in a transnational family.

Waiting for Migration

Girls raised in transnational families are perhaps the most touched by migration, as they are witnesses to their fathers' yearly commutes. They are not the only ones who express a desire for migration, but their closeness to the U.S. and to migratory practices make it plausible to migrate. These girls see their father once per year and are able to ask if they can join him north. But they are also recipients of the dated but consistent sexist and patriarchal beliefs about women's roles within the family. Scholars have rightly challenged the portrayal of Mexican men as *machistas* as oversimplified and one-dimensional, yet sexism indeed persists in Mexico as it does in other countries.[49]

The responses that the girls receive from their fathers regarding desires for migration reflect the persistence of gendered and sexist practices in processes of migration where sex and age intersect and place limits on migration. I asked Paloma if her father had ever thought of taking her and her siblings to the U.S. As a U.S. resident, he could have submitted documents to legally take them north. Paloma said no:

> P: Well, actually for us, folks have always asked, "hey, why don't you fix them [their papers]?" Like, he has papers, "why don't you fix their papers to take them all over there?" And he says, "what are they gonna do over there?" He says no. Then he says, he said it once, I'm not sure if he meant it or if it was just a comment. He said, "if you want to go to the U.S. one day, well you can go once you marry and

your husband can take you. If not, I won't take you." He has never wanted to fix my mom's papers either. He always says no, "what business does she have going to the U.S.?" He doesn't want to. He's always said he won't because . . . I don't know. He has a really strong personality and is very moody. He says that, over there, kids our age are very rebellious and we'd become like them. Over there, you can't yell at your kids or discipline them because right away they call the cops and they'll throw you in jail, so my dad says no. "Why do you want to go over there for? For work?" he says, "that's why I'm here, to support you." He always says no, that he won't fix our papers and has only fixed my brothers', my three brothers who live over there.

LS: What do you think about that?

P: Well, the truth is, I think it's unfair. Like, the fact that we are women does not mean that we don't have the right to come and go or to the same thing he wants to give my brothers . . . Though I don't agree with him, I can't throw it on his face because that's how he is and I'm used to it.

Her father feels like he is very much the provider, the breadwinner. If he takes his family to the U.S., it would be a sign of his inability to take care of his family. His masculinity is defined by his ability to provide for his family in Mexico from the U.S. A house, a wife, and well-dressed children display his success. As such, he fails to see any desires held by the women in his family about moving to the U.S. As he says, "that's why I'm here, to support you." It is what is expected. Paloma's father seems to take pride in not having to take his family to the U.S. as he is able to display his success in Zinapécuaro via his children and his home.

Carmen shares a similar story to Paloma's. I asked Carmen if there were any plans for the family to move to the U.S. Just like Paloma's father, Carmen's father also refuses to take any of his daughters there:

C: The thing is, my father says they cannot fix my papers because then I'll get married and there won't be much time . . . I'm not even sure.

LS: Does your dad have papers?

C: Yes, and I just think, well, if one day I do get married, it's likely I'll go, but I don't know. I don't know if I'll stay or if I'll go. But I would like to go over there.

LS: Has your dad fixed your mom's papers?

C: The thing is, he says he doesn't want to take us because life is too
hard and doesn't want to take my mom or any of us. He says, "what if
you get married over there and I don't ever see you again?"

LS: Would you like him to fix your papers?

C: Of course, I'd like to go, but he says we've run out of time, we don't
qualify anymore, and that he can't. And like I say, what if I get married? The papers will still work for something. I always say, if I get
married, what's it gonna matter if I have papers or not? He says life in
the U.S. is hard, and well, I don't know. I just don't get it. It's hard to
understand. I don't get his reasons. If it were up to me, I'd go.

Carmen sounds confused in trying to explain what seems to be a sense-
less reason her father provides. He, however, will take her younger
brother when he is old enough and Carmen finds this quite confusing.
"Why my brother and not me?" she wonders. As in Paloma's case, and as
will be discussed below, Carmen's father does not want to fix her papers
because he feels that, once she marries, her husband will benefit from
her social capital. Her father does not want to share what is his with a
man he may not approve of, therefore Carmen's possible migration will
have to wait. Access to social networks and social capital are conditioned
by age and sex. For fathers, legal residency or U.S. citizenship become
investments they must protect and are therefore not easily shared. There
is also his fear of never seeing Carmen again. If Paloma and Carmen
want to go to the U.S., they must find a different way to do so, as they do
not have access to their father's social capital.

The three sisters—Emilia, Toñita, and Marbe—also said their father
does not want to take them to the U.S. They have each asked him various times, but each time he refuses. Sixto, their father, usually tells them
that, "*en El Norte*, children fail, they lead ugly lives and become *vagos*
[troublemakers]." Sixto shuts down any talks of a possible move to the
U.S.; he immediately says families there are not united and, if they were
to migrate, theirs would disintegrate. He concludes by asking rhetori-
cally: "is that what you all want?" Emilia said: "we used [to ask him] to
before, but my dad doesn't want to . . . He says that those who go usually stay and so he doesn't want us to go. I've talked to my sisters about
this and I tell them I'd like to go and that it'd be easier for us to go while

we are still young." Marbe is almost eighteen. I asked her if her parents wanted her to move to the U.S., she said:

> No, and actually my dad's older brothers, one of them is a U.S. resident and he fixed his children's papers and now they all live in Chicago. He offered to help my dad with the fees so that he could fix our papers. Also, some of my dad's really good friends told him to fix them before I turned eighteen. They would always tell him, but my dad doesn't like to go. He doesn't like it over there. I also don't see my mom too excited with the idea. She'd like to go but only to keep him company but not to stay. My dad says he thinks we are better off here, that maybe our lives would be a tad more glamorous over there, but no . . .

By 2010, her father had submitted the paperwork to become a U.S. citizen with the goal of fixing the younger brothers' documents. I asked Toñita, the youngest of the three, how she felt about that, to which she replied: "well, why doesn't he fix mine? I want to go, too!" She added:

> The truth is, I don't know. I think that there is a bit of *machismo*, right? Even if one does not want to think it, it is there. The truth is, like, *machismo* still exists and they say more so in Mexico. And it's true, um, he says that maybe they [her little brothers] will be able to get them [the papers] faster and need them more than us. But that's not true, you never know. Like, for example, my dad knows what it feels like to have to go [to the U.S.] and leave your wife and family. So, like, for example, if one of us gets married to someone who has papers, we won't have ours. I would want him to think how hard it would be for us. He says: "when you date, choose wisely. Make sure he has a stable job here and won't have the need to go to the U.S., or if he does, make sure he has papers so he can fix yours."

Toñita's father also refuses, at least for now, to fix his daughter's papers. That responsibility, he feels, should be on her future husband. Toñita's narrative also points to her father's perception of her brothers needing legal status more than Toñita and her sisters because they are men. This resonates with Carmen's father also wanting to fix her little brother's papers and Paloma's father only fixing those of her older brothers. The belief that the brothers—the boys—may need it more than the girls has to do with the assumption that, as men in the making (and assuming their heterosexuality), they will be the sole provider of a future family. The U.S. may be an option for them, therefore having *papeles* will facilitate their future duties.[50]

Girls like Toñita do not passively accept their fathers' responses. They exert fragile agency.[51] Paloma thinks it is unfair that her bothers have more privilege because they are men, while Carmen questions her father's stated reasons. Toñita characterizes her father's actions as displays of *machista* behavior. In their narratives, girls critique their fathers and challenge sexist attitudes, but fully understand there are limits to what they can do about it.

I share these long quotes and accounts above to point to the workings of age, gender, sex, and sexuality that limit the desires for migration of the girls in this study. Immigration scholarship has shown that women have in fact always migrated. In *Gendered Transitions*, for example, Hondagneu-Sotelo documents how single women who left by themselves developed their own social networks. There are also cases of Central American teenage girls who leave on their own for the U.S., crossing the dreadful Chiapas-Guatemala border and riding La Bestia (the beast) or the freight train from the Chiapas-Guatemala border that rides along Mexico en route to the U.S.-Mexico border.[52] This transnational journey, however, remains viewed as primarily masculine and extremely dangerous. The girls in this study are *hijas de familia* from very traditional households, meaning they still fully rely on their mothers and fathers. It is difficult for them to break ground like the adult women in Hondagneu-Sotelo's study due to their age and gender, even though some of them are over eighteen. They are still growing up in a family and town where traditional migratory practices remain. They have yet to reach adulthood and are still under the care of their parents. Unlike boys, there is no rite of passage and no access to social networks awaiting them. Their sex and sexuality are also used to deny them access to migration. According to the girls, fathers usually cite their fear of life in the U.S. as the reason for not taking them. Fathers fear their daughters will become *vagas* (troublemakers) who will call the police and turn on them if fathers try to discipline them, including controlling their sexuality. González-López defines this as the U.S. sexual threat that for fathers becomes "[a] culture of sexual fear permeating the everyday lives of immigrants who settle in inner-city and marginalized barrios that begins to shape their views of a daughter's virginity and premarital sex."[53] González-López states that such attitudes are more common among fathers and/or men who come from rural areas in Mexico. In her research, she examines patriarchy as a regional phenomenon, characterizing its urban expression as more liberal than the rural one. Her approach guards against the tendency to generalize and acknowledges regional specificities. For the Mexican men in her study, protecting their daughter's sexuality or virginity is not the priority. Instead, fathers hope to protect them for their own safety. Men, according to González-López, perceive the U.S. as unsafe and therefore prefer to keep their daughters in Mexico. Safety also means protecting their daughters from the racialized and gendered hierarchies in the U.S. If daughters lack documents, they may experience violence en route. Furthermore, within her study, González-López also found that men refused to bring their wives because in the U.S. "their claws come out." This becomes a threat to male power within the home and within the U.S. Men fear becoming powerless and the inevitable changes that would come with migration if they were to bring their wives.[54]

I certainly do not want to reproduce old debates and narrow views of sexuality. Chapters 5 and 6 examine girls raised in a similar familial arrangement whose fathers decided to take them to the U.S. In Carmen, Paloma, and Marbe's case, perhaps their father simply did not wish to remain in the U.S. and was working to return to Zinapécuaro. But there is, however, an obvious persistence of sexist practices experienced by the girls in this study that cannot be overlooked. Paloma's father essentially told her that her husband can take her to the U.S. once she marries, assuming her heterosexuality and denying her access to his social capital. Carmen's father tells her he cannot fix her documents because, what will happen if she gets married? Unclear on what marriage has to do with the U.S., Carmen feels it is difficult to understand the reasons he gives her as they do not make much sense to her. Because her father remains an authority figure, Carmen cannot do much else as he holds the power to become a U.S. citizen and submit the documents if he so chooses. For Emilia, Toñita, and Marbe, their father's concern is family unity and the well-being of their daughters, but what about wanting to fix his sons' documents? Fathers' answers fall very much in line with González-

López's findings—that of fear of the U.S. as a sexualized threat. But it also seems quite apparent that more so than protecting their daughters from what they perceive as the U.S. sexual threat, fathers' concerns are also about control and power over social capital. This is evident when Paloma's father tells her he does not want to share his social capital with her future husband whenever that happens.

For González-López, sexuality is a "malleable process in constant flux."[55] In "Virginity in Mexico," Amuchástegui Herrera defines sexuality as hybrid, and therefore fluid and changing.[56] Like González-López, Amuchástegui Herrera cites critical differences between rural and urban patriarchies. Both authors speak of sexuality in relation to virginity and a woman's right to her sexuality. The fathers of the girls in this study practice a rural patriarchy. In so doing, they feel they will hand over their daughters to another man, so, why fix their documents? Why worry about their future? Girls, at least the ones in this study, are still seen as the responsibility of a man, be it their father or husband. This points to the persistence of sexist and patriarchal practices in rural Mexico.

In an attempt to move away from binaries, I would like to highlight that fathers' sexist practices do not lead the girls to vilify them. Marbe's father, for example, is actually a very loving man who deeply misses his family while he is in the U.S. working hard to support his six children, ailing parents, and older sister. Perhaps what may help us analyze and move away from reproducing a dominant perspective is to also understand fathers' complex personhood. As Gordon states, "complex personhood means that people suffer graciously and selfishly too, get stuck in the symptoms of their troubles, and also transform themselves . . . [it] means that the stories people tell about themselves, about their troubles, about their social worlds, and about their society's problems are entangled and weave between what is immediately available as a story and what their imaginations are reaching toward."[57] Carmen's father is stuck in the symptoms of his troubles. Only he knows why he drinks in Mexico and not the U.S. His altering personality indicates that he is a troubled, but largely responsible father. Fathers may be concerned about the gendered, raced, and classed hierarchies in the U.S. and want to spare their daughters such dehumanizing treatment should they bring them to the U.S. They may want to spare their daughters the trauma that comes with migration while en route. Fathers may be aware of daughters' romanticized notions of life in the U.S. and the possible disillusionment they would experience if they were to bring them. However, we cannot ignore fathers' desires to fix their son's papers.

Though I did not interview fathers, the girls' narratives of growing up transnationally present a story of how age, gender, sex, and sexuality shape not only their lives but also migratory practices. If Paloma, Marbe, Carmen, Emilia, or Toñita were boys, access to social networks and social capital would be at their disposal and they would not be waiting for migration.

Uncertainties, Ambiguities, Anxiety

Girls waiting to migrate are hindered from making long-term plans. This produces uncertainties, ambiguities, and anxieties in girls' lives. Toñita has always dreamt of moving to the U.S. In 2012, she was about to complete her first year of high school at *la prepa* in Queréndaro.[58] At *la prepa*, students are required to choose a field of study during their second year. The fields of study include humanities, computer science, and chemistry. The goal of selecting a track is for students to gain an introduction to the area of study they may want to purse at the university. As the end of her first year nears, Toñita wavers between selecting the humanities that will allow her to enroll at La Normal in Morelia, and chemistry, which would allow her to study engineering, her real passion. Studying humanities and attending La Normal is a safer route because schools are always in need of teachers, while the competitive nature of engineering makes Toñita doubt the possibility of finding work after college. "After all," she says, "who hires engineers in Mexico?" If she went to the U.S., however, engineering might prove to be a lucrative field. Having to choose one area of study now makes her anxious. She has told her father repeatedly to take her to the U.S: "I've told my dad that I would like to and, if it's possible, to do high school [there]. Well, long before high school I wanted to go to the U.S. and study over there so I could do engineering. I have cousins there that are in college studying engineering and are doing well! They say that often you come out of college with job offers. I would like that. I told my dad that I'd like to follow my passion and it seems safer to do engineering over there." The decision Toñita needs to make is one that may impact her future.

In Mexico, she faces a choice between being practical and following her dream. Because Toñita holds out hope and expresses a desire to move to the U.S., uncertainty surrounds her. After her father became a citizen, I asked her if he had a list of whose papers he would fix first. She said: "he would fix my mother's papers first, he said that then the youngest ones [the boys], and I'm like, why not me?" Toñita's desire to go to the U.S., coupled with the decision she needs to make during her second year of high school, produces much anxiety.

The uncertainty, ambiguity, and anxiety produced by migration become central parts of girls' lives. Jessica, whose story opens the chapter, was not raised in an immediate transnational family but waited a long time to get her U.S. passport to return to the place where she was born. Her experience displays the same anxiety of migration. As discussed earlier Jessica requested a copy of her birth certificate and social security card, which took two full years. During the next two years, she hired a lawyer to get her dual citizenship in order. Once her dual citizenship was in place, she visited La Casa del Migrante—an office staffed by people who answer questions about migration. La Casa del Migrante is located in downtown Zinapécuaro (Figure 4.1). It is a room with a desk in the middle, two filing cabinets, and three chairs for the clients to sit. Flyers are taped to the wall with information about the rules of La Casa. When Jessica visited La Casa, she was given a list of items she needed for her passport—birth certificate, pictures, social security card, baby footprints, and the bracelet with her name on it, which was assumed to have been placed on her wrist immediately after she was born. All she had at that time, however, was her birth certificate and her social security card. With the items she had, she took a trip to San Miguel de Allende in the state of Guanajuato. She was told of an office there that would verify her documents, mail them to Mexico City and, if cleared, procure her passport in no time. Once Jessica arrived in San Miguel De Allende, however, they told her they could not help her because she lacked pictures that showed she had lived in the U.S., the baby footprints, and the wrist bracelet from the hospital. By May of 2012, she was awaiting confirmation for an appointment she made at the U.S. Embassy in the city of Guadalajara. The constant back and forth of this process caused Jessica tremendous anxiety. I asked her if she knew of

Figure 4.1. La Casa del Migrante in Zinapécuaro, Michoacán, Mexico. Photo taken by Lilia Soto.

other young people who were in the same situation who could maybe have assisted her. As she said:

> I know people who have experienced something similar, not the exact same situation of having been born in the U.S. and immediately brought over here, but they are very smart people that tell me, "well, I did it this way but we're not the same. You may not get the same results if you do what I did." Like, I've also bumped into people, not to make them look bad or anything, but to be quite honest with you, they don't help me and instead give me the run around. They say, "you know what? So and so can answer your questions." So I go to the places they recommend and I don't get any help there either. I don't know if they think I'm dumb or something. All confuses me! The options they give me make no sense. Then they say, "but why did you do that for? It was fine the way you had it." Or, "why do you need to go? What do you need that for?" I don't know. It's just too much sometimes that, to be quite honest with you, I can't handle it at times. I can't stand it. There are times when I say, "Oh God, I should just go straight to the embassy and have them tell me exactly what I need." Going to the offices in Morelia isn't really helping. They don't answer any of my questions. But, God willing, I'll go [to] the embassy. We'll see if they can issue the passport. But I've been told that if you do not have the right paperwork, which I don't, they won't even see you.

After receiving her birth certificate, social security card, and dual citizenship, she did not go straight to the embassy because she did not know that she could. Besides, she was told not to bother with the embassy if she did not have all the necessary paperwork. She went to the embassy after exhausting all of the resources she was aware of—La Casa del Migrante, the office in San Miguel De Allende, and multiple visits to immigration-related offices in Morelia. When that did not work, and with her aunt's assistance from Illinois, an appointment was made. I ran into Jessica a few days before her appointment and my own departure back to the U.S. She wanted me to help her translate the English instructions she had downloaded from the Internet from the U.S. embassy in Guadalajara regarding the necessary documents needed for a U.S. passport, all of which she already had. It seemed that Jessica, a U.S.-born citizen, was being denied her right to return to the country where she was born. Even before migration, Jessica's citizenship was already in question.

While Jessica waited, her plans to move to the U.S. consumed her present, and her imagination ran wild. The U.S. was her only plan. Jessica did not want to pursue college in Morelia because her family did not have the money, but also because her plans included migration. She said:

Financially speaking, well, we don't have much. Like, going to college is very expensive, but like, to be quite honest with you, my documents are not in order. Like, if I keep going higher and higher, it'll never end! I first need, well, when I found out at fifteen about all this, I said, "wait a minute, I need to slow down even if it takes years." Like I told you earlier, the lawyer took a long time to process the paperwork for my dual citizenship. He would add and delete paperwork. So I told myself, "No, I'd rather slow down, get all in order, everything fine and legal so that I can move forward." I can't move forward if legally something is not correct.

Part of pausing, as she says, included completing only high school and working to save money for the paperwork—the lawyer and the trips she made to San Miguel de Allende, to Morelia, and the pending trip to Guadalajara. Jessica truly feels the U.S. is the place she needs to be. Part of it is her mobility imaginary where she envisions greener pastures. Jessica is so enamored with the U.S. that she describes it as the perfect place. She said the following, "the thing is, well, it's just, I've imagined it for so long that in my mind it's perfect, the perfect place, pretty, clean, everything organized. I don't know! Very pretty, nothing like the town where I currently live, like Zinapécuaro. Um, I tell you, I'm not dissing this town but really, my goal is to return to the U.S. I don't know. It's always been my calling, especially when I see my relatives. When they return they just look so pretty! Like, it's a completely different way of life." Responses like Jessica's reflect the disillusionment she feels in Mexico. In the same vein, Toñita feels that studying engineering in Mexico is pointless because she will not be able to get a job thereafter. What makes it difficult for me as a writer, listener, and researcher is to see the illusion in their eyes and their hopeful tone of voice, and to contemplate how their idealizations of the U.S. will most likely lead to disappointment if they do in fact migrate. Jessica seems to be aware of this, but I am unsure as to what extent.

In the process of waiting for the future, parts of their present are denied, and it becomes difficult to make long-term plans. The girls continue to enjoy their daily lives of going to school and to *el jardín* on Sundays, they still look forward to their fathers' returns and possibly their own desired migration. But all this waiting forces them to also live in a permanent state of not now, not yet, where their hopes and dreams are suspended, while the progress of time is stopped.[59] Just like the Mexicans who suspended their present in hopes for a better future back in 1982, so do girls like Jessica[60] suspend their present for an abstract future in the U.S.

Conclusion

Girls' subjectivities of time alter understandings of migration. They point to a waiting aspect of migration that hitherto has not been explored fully. Migration is about moving, about searching for a better chance at life always produced by macro and micro forces. Individuals make decisions to migrate and choose which type of migrant they will be: permanent or circular. If permanent, the whole family may migrate; if circular, family members may remain behind. As shown in this chapter, when family members remain behind, they wait. Migration then is as much about waiting as it is about moving.

Girls' stories illuminate aspects of waiting for migration that have yet to be theorized within immigration scholarship. Fabian argues that the time of the Other is denied. In some ways, it feels like girls' time—their present and future—is also denied. Toñita is a telling example. Denial places Toñita's present on hold; she is uncertain of the present and of what the future will hold. A more nuanced understanding of time emerges from the experience of waiting for migration. The time lags and the in-betweenness they produce certainly do not mean people are simply waiting idly for something to happen, but it is important to acknowledge that migration processes begin long before nearing the border. Theoretical frameworks of migration should include a temporal analysis of migration to understand the unique experiences of those stuck in a time lag between multiple worlds.

5

The Telling Moment

Pre-Crossings of Mexican Teenage Girls and Their Journeys to the Border

Ya me voy, yo no quiero
sin dinero, tengo miedo pero voy;
para'l norte ya me voy
por el jale, ya me voy
no se a donde pero voy . . .

Gotta go, I don't wanna,
Got no money, I'm afraid but I'll go;
Going north, gotta go,
For work, gotta go,
Don't know where, but gotta go . . .
—Las Cafeteras, "Ya Me Voy," *It's Time* (Las Cafeteras Music, 2012) CD

"Mark my words," he said. "When you're a *teeneyer* it's like something
comes over you. Rock and roll sounds good. Believe
me." He laughed as if I knew what he was talking about. I
hadn't seen him this happy in a long time.
"Well, it's not going to happen to me." I pouted and ignored
his chuckles at my expense.
"Just wait," he said. "Once you're in New York, you'll be-
come a regular *teeneyer Americana.*"
"I'm not going to New York."
"Your mother's talking about moving there."
My stomach fell to my feet. "What?!"
—Esmeralda Santiago, *When I Was Puerto Rican*, 206

It is late October of 2006 and the working-class, predominantly Mexican neighborhood in Napa is getting ready for Halloween. Orange lights, carved pumpkins, and other Halloween decorations adorn the street. Martha and I are sitting on a sofa at her paternal grandmothers' house, originally a two-bedroom dwelling. The grandparents turned the garage and part of the backyard into rooms to accommodate Martha's parents, her younger brother, aunts, and uncles. Martha shares one long room furnished with a sofa, a desk with a computer, and three-twin size beds—one for her aunt, one for her younger brother, and one for her. A curtain divides her aunt's bed from the rest of the room and provides a bit of privacy.

We begin the interview. I notice Martha is soft-spoken, so I ask her if she could hold the microphone with one hand. This does not seem to bother her or make her feel uncomfortable. She is a tall, slim sixteen-year-old with long dark curly hair and a set of straight bangs framing her face. She wears her hair down and constantly plays with it with her other hand. Wearing dark blue jeans and a beige T-shirt, she starts the interview by saying: "My name is Martha and I am from La Piedad, Michoacán." Since I was interested in her pre-migration experience, I asked her if she remembered the day she was told of the move to the United States. She provides the following answer: "I don't remember what day it was but, um, it was at night and I was preparing to go to school the next day and she [her mother] told me, 'you are not going because we are leaving [to Napa].' It came as a surprise." Martha's weeknight routine changed immediately after being notified of the plans. She stopped organizing her books and school uniform and instead began to focus on her future. Although Martha had wanted to migrate to Napa to join her paternal grandparents and had heard her parents discuss a plausible move that included only her father's departure, she never imagined it would actually happen, let alone so suddenly. What was it about that evening and the sudden interruption to Martha's nightly practices that created such a shift in her life?

When asked about the telling moment, girls like Martha describe what they are told with such vivid detail that it is clear it has become a signature event in their lives.[1] Moreover their memories hold common patterns. In detailing that moment, girls place themselves back in time and re-tell, almost word by word, the conversations they had with their mothers and other relatives in the hours prior to their departure. They recall having to decide who to see, who to say goodbye to, what to pack, what to store away, and what to bring with them, all in a matter of days. Negotiating their departure required them to compartmentalize and re-arrange their world as they knew it.

Along with eighteen Mexican immigrant girls, Martha was inter-viewed in the fall of 2006 in Napa, California. These girls arrived from various cities and states in Mexico between 1998 and 2006. Each girl migrated to join fathers, mothers, siblings, or grandparents, and to chase the elusive idea of a better chance at life. Before migration, the girls were raised in some type of transnational family. They came from families already fractured and separated by borders and processes of migration.[2] Like the girls from Zinapécuaro whose stories are narrated in chapters 2 through 4, some had expressed desires for migration and had imagined who they would become in El Norte.

When they were told of the actual move, the majority of the girls expressed feeling surprised. Even if they had imagined the trip, the actual reality felt rushed and unexpected. This is a common response that Naomi Tyrell (2011) found among children who are not included in the decision-making process of migration.[3] Some girls even said they no longer wanted to leave.[4] The element of surprise was accompanied with astonishment and mixed feelings towards what felt like a sudden and urgent rupture in their lives. Their parents had arranged the move in advance, but had only told their daughters days and, in some cases, hours prior to their departure. Throughout the planning process, the girls were unaware of the behind-the-scenes conversations their parents had conducted.

In this chapter, I explore the telling moment followed by prepara-tions and the moment of departure. The sudden awareness of having to move almost immediately caused resentment and resistance. The girls reported melancholy about what they were leaving behind. Being left out of the decision-making process is not unique to the Mexican expe-rience. Tyrell found that it is not uncommon for immigrant parents to not include their children when making such decisions.[5] Sometimes, though not always, Tyrrell continues, age is a factor in whether or not parents consult with their children.[6] In this study, girls are left out of the decision-making process because they are young and because they are girls. Unlike its role in the lives of boys and men, migration is not a rite of passage for girls and women.[7] Though this may appear as a dated argument, particularly with the examples of Central American children and youth, including girls and young women, embarking on journeys on their own, a more traditional migration of Mexican girls remains in place.

I situate girls' stories of departures to highlight the powerful transition they experience. The moment of telling is one filled with uncertainty, of internal turmoil for the girls. There is uncertainty as they become what Susan Bibler Coutine (2005) describes as migrants in transit.[8]

The girls who moved to Napa already had fathers, mothers, or other relatives residing there. Most of the girls were aware that their families would eventually reunite in that place. But, until they formally learned of the news, they lived in a kind of limbo, not fully knowing they would one day move. Unsurprisingly, the moment when their parents told them they were leaving constituted a key experience in their young lives.

The Girls

It is the fall of 2006. H.R. 4437 and the subsequent spring marches are still present in the minds of Martha, Elena, Angela, Eliza, and Lorena.[9] A major Latino/a organization articulated the dire consequences the bill purported by making it "difficult for legal immigrants to become U.S. citizens": it would have disrupted "American communities and put all Americans at risk by broadening the definition of smuggling to include anyone who aids or transports an undocumented immigrant;" it would have made "everyone who comes to the U.S. to work subject not only to deportation but also imprisonment;" it would have disrupted the U.S. economy by creating an overly broad and retroactive employment verification system without creating legal channels for needed workers to work lawfully."[10] Many of the marchers and protestors were high school students from major urban centers, including Los Angeles, Chicago, San Francisco, and New York. I recall listening to students from Los Angeles's Garfield High School on National Public Radio who voiced their opposition to the racist measure and made a call to incite fellow high school students to join them in protest—a call reminiscent of the high school walkouts of the late 1960s during the Chicano movement.[11]

The spring of 2006 featured pro-immigration rallies, speeches, and marches. It also saw vile racialized anti-immigration discourses revolving around what Leo Chavez (2013) defines as the Latino Threat Narrative.[12] This is a discourse that includes unfounded beliefs such as:

Latinos are a reproductive threat, altering the demographic makeup of the nation. Latinos are unable or unwilling to learn English.
Latinos are unable and unwilling to integrate into the larger society; they live apart from the larger society, not integrating socially.
Latinos are unchanging and immutable; they are not subjects to history and the transforming social forces around them; they reproduce their own cultural world. Latinos, especially Americans of Mexican origin, are part of a conspiracy to reconquer the southwestern United States, returning the land to Mexico's control. This is why they remain apart and unintegrated into the larger society.[13]

These polarized views of immigration provided a space for girls to hear what others thought of immigrants like themselves, including both the support and the opposition.

In Napa, three marches—two in the spring and one in late summer—responded to H.R. 4437. Each was covered by the local newspaper, the *Napa Register*. The third march took place on September 2006, months after the spring marches, and was organized by a local group called Latinos Unidos del Valle de Napa. Once again, the *Napa Register* covered the march. Although this time there were no counter-protests, the article cited one Napan saying: "how can you get out there and demonstrate for something that's illegal. And if you haven't got the papers to prove you're here legally, you've got a lot of nerve getting out there and flaunting it."[14] This is an example of the continuous discourse surrounding the Latino Threat Narrative that Martha, Elena, Angela, Eliza, and Lorena were exposed to in Napa.

The marches gave the girls the time and space to respond to the anti-immigrant sentiment they felt. Martha, for example, took part in the spring marches. She said:

M: There were lots of people that supported us who had papers that said, "no, they don't deserve that [treatment]." But I also saw on the

news that there were some who were against us that said no, that we
did deserve it. Yes, it hurt me a lot because, um, from what I know
California was part of Mexico, no? Then I don't know why, um, there
are rules about papers if all people are worth the same . . . Though
there are mean people, not all should pay for that.

LS: Can you describe some more how you felt during the marches?

M: Well, almost like, I wanted the president to see us, for him to think
that a lot of Mexicans need lots of help because they risk a lot, [they
risk] their lives to cross the border or however they cross, to get here,
and for them to suffer as much as they do, like, no, it's not fair. And
yeah, I'd say, "I hope we can get help," wishing that the president
would just think a little about our demands.

The nineteen girls I interviewed were all recent immigrants like Martha.
Though they had been aware of anti-Mexican sentiment prior to their
arrival, the marches of 2006 provided them with firsthand exposure to
the tumult and spectacle that surrounds immigration.[15]

Martha, Elena, Angela, Eliza, and Lorena grew up in Mexico, all with
some family member(s) in the U.S. Much like the girls interviewed in
Zinapécuaro, prior to migration, they lived lives typical of Mexican
teenage girls. Some like Martha, Elena, Angela, and Lorena, went to
school, while others like Eliza helped around the house and held a seasonal job during the harvest season at a local asparagus plant. Much like
the girls in chapters 3 and 4, these girls expressed a desire early on to
migrate to the United States. However, unlike the girls from Zinapécuaro, their plans to migrate were not thwarted by their fathers. Instead,
their parents made the decision to move to the U.S. and bring them
along without consulting with them. Below, I provide a brief narrative
of the girls' lives.

Martha

Martha, a junior at Napa High School, arrived in Napa when she was
eleven years old. Of the nineteen girls interviewed, Martha is one of
three girls who migrated with her entire family. In fact, she was the only
one whose immediate family was never separated. Her paternal grandparents, with whom she is very close, had been living in Napa for over

twenty-five years. Each year, they returned to La Piedad bearing gifts that would fuel Martha's imagination about life in Napa. Her father's reasons for moving to Napa were complicated. When he was a child, he lived in Napa. He returned to Michoacán, married Martha's mother, and tried to raise a family of four on the salary he received from his work as a server at a local restaurant. Because his salary was not enough, he raised the possibility of commuting to Napa for work. Martha's mother resisted the idea of living apart as she felt their family was already fractured with grandparents in Napa. These conversations, however, coupled with her grandparents' yearly returns, allowed Martha to imagine that she, too, would eventually move north. This did not mean she did not enjoy her life in La Piedad. School, church, and afterschool activities shaped her days. Martha remembers activities, usually outside of her home, as sources of freedom. As would not be the case once the family moved to Napa, Martha was allowed to play outside with friends, often late into the evening without worrying her parents. She was very close to her aunt Lili, with whom she often went to church. Although her aunt Lili remained behind, Martha keeps in touch with her, communicating usually by telephone or email at least once per week. Leaving her aunt Lili behind exacerbated the feelings of rupture bred by migration.

When Martha and her family arrived to Napa, they moved into her grandparents' home and have lived there ever since. She speaks fluent English, but chose to do the interview in Spanish, carefully selecting her words. Martha remembers that the move to Napa happened too quickly. Her family told her on a weeknight as she was preparing for school. After hurried packing, they left two days later.

Elena

Elena, a tall seventeen-year-old with braces and short red hair, comes from San Marcos, Oaxaca.[16] She walked into the interview wearing a pink beanie to keep warm from the already late October chill of Napa. We sat down in an empty classroom after school. It was quiet, as the students had already gone home. I asked Elena to describe her life in Oaxaca. She spoke of the *solar* (cornfield) next to her house where corn once grew. Mandarin and *guayabo* trees had since taken over the field. During playtime, Elena used to hang from tree branches, often pretending that one of the tallest trees was a Ferris wheel like the one she rode at the fair. At other times, the branches became horses for her to ride. Such games speak to the imagination of a young child. Her grandparents and great grandparents, whom she was very close to, lived next to the cornfield. She spent a lot of time at their house and describes how each morning she ran across the *solar* to take their breakfast order. At times, she says, it became a race between her and her younger brothers to see who would be the first to ask and take the order. Since her mother had a minimart and a bakery, breakfast always included fresh bread from the oven. Martha used to play with her cousins *a la comidita y a la casita* (tea party or house), using empty crates from her mother's minimart as tables, doors, and TV stands. During the town's fairs, she eagerly purchased toy dishes and play phones to furnish her *casita*. She went to school every day and, thanks to the remittances her father sent home, was able to get a private school education during her seventh grade year—a sure sign of achieved Mexican middle-class status. When asked if she ever thought she would move to Napa, Elena responded:

> Ah, yes, yes, I thought. At times playing around I thought I'd be moving, but at times, I did think [so]. Because for me, what we have at the house is that we always sit down and talk. And then, when we decided to come over, I knew we'd be moving here, that we were going to fix our papers and come over here because my mom and dad, well, they had told us many times. We thought so because we would overhear their conversations with other people and we had an idea that one day we would all be here together . . .

She knew of a possible move to Napa as it was a constant topic of conversation, particularly upon her father's returns. Aunts, uncles, grandparents, and great grandparents often asked her father Silvio when he would take the whole family to Napa. Her San Marcos family did not agree with the transnational familial arrangements Elena's father had chosen to raise his family. She was used to her father's commutes as he had been commuting long before she was born. Elena would overhear these conversations, which in a way disrupted the routine of her family since she constantly thought of and overheard conversations about a possible move. Napa as a location, hundreds of miles from Oaxaca, became close proximity to Elena.

Angela

In the fall of 2006, Angela was a fourteen-year-old freshman at Napa High School. A tall brunette with long curly hair and freckles on her face, Angela looked much older than her age. She was eager to share her unique story, which indeed differed from other accounts I had heard. Angela was born in Napa and, as a newborn, moved to Ario de Rayón (Ario for short) in the state of Michoacán with her mother and older sister Pati. She stayed in Ario until she turned three years old. She completed kindergarten and first grade at a local elementary school in Napa. After two years in the U.S., her father felt he could provide them with a better life if they returned to Ario while he remained in Napa. Angela, her mother, and her older sister Pati returned. This time, Angela was enrolled at a local private Catholic school—it seemed her father had been right. For Angela, however, her return to Ario brought tremendous difficulty. Though she could speak Spanish, she found that she could neither read nor write. The nuns—infamous for their strict teaching methods—often shamed Angela in front of the class. To stop the shaming, every day after school, her mother worked with Angela to teach her skills to succeed in second grade. But Angela had other concerns. Her father's absences caused her tremendous pain. She had always had a close relationship with him. While we spoke, Angela began to cry as she described his absences. She does not remember phone calls, but does recall that his regular visits to the family were short. He always brought her Barbie dolls, which she kept hidden in a box. No one was allowed to play with them, because they were special gifts from her father—a unique connection she shared with him.

Angela ultimately became used to her life in Michoacán and in fact has fond memories of playing with friends after finishing her homework. Like many other girls, she formed a very close relationship with her grandmother. Despite her father's absence, Angela eventually settled in at home and did not want to return to Napa. They returned at the end of fifth grade when Angela was eleven years old. Her family has since returned to Ario, but only for visits. Angela does not think they will ever return to live in the place she now refers to as home.

Eliza

When I interviewed Eliza, she was seventeen years old and attended the eleventh grade at Napa High School. The interview took place at her house on a Thursday evening in late September. We were supposed to meet after school earlier in the week but Eliza did not show. She then called me and said we could talk at her home. I hopped in my car and drove north on Jefferson Street for ten minutes to get to her house. She had just woken up form a nap when I arrived. Wearing jeans, sneakers, and a white top, Eliza's long brown wavy hair was pulled back in a ponytail. Her petite frame carries a sense of wound caused by migration, which becomes more visible when she speaks of her life, of the troubles she had with her father and of the loving relationship she shared with her grandfather who remained behind. She began by telling me that she sleeps all day. After she arrives home from school, Eliza lies in bed and sleeps until seven p.m., at which time she wakes up, has dinner, takes a shower, and goes back to sleep. This has been her routine since she arrived in Napa in December of 2005.

La Purisima, Guanajuato, is the *rancho* Eliza left behind. Her father, who had been a commuter since he married her mother, had begun living mainly in Napa in the mid-1980s. Two of her older sisters moved to Napa five years before Eliza and the rest of the family arrived. As the years of commuting continued, Eliza's father found the commute back to La Purisima more difficult and his visits decreased. Eliza and her family endured long months of isolation. During her time in Mexico, Eliza completed sixth grade, then quit school. Although there were middle schools near her town in Guanajuato, she opted to work instead. One of the last jobs she held before moving was packing asparagus at a local factory from July through October. When she was not working, her routine changed depending on the day of the week. On sunny days, Eliza would sit under a tree outside her house to draw and write her thoughts down on a notebook. On weekdays, she enjoyed going to the *tianguis* (flea market) to buy household needs. Sundays included visits to her grandparents' home in the nearby town of La Calera. Eliza, her mother, and younger sister would spend the whole afternoon there and did not return home until the late evening. She had a very close relationship with her grandparents, particularly her *abuelito* (grandfather) or *belito,* as she called him: "my grandpa, he's a bit older than my grandma. I miss him a lot. Though at times he was strict with me, he'd make me laugh. He was always happy. Sometimes I'd be hanging outside, chatting with friends, and he'd get there and hug me. He'd call me *muchacha* or *hija.* When we'd leave his house, I'd tell him, 'I'm going *belito,*' and he'd say, 'Yes, *hija,* I'll stop by later to see you.'" There were always plans for Eliza's family to migrate to Napa. Eliza in fact had told her mother she had wanted to move, particularly after her boyfriend migrated there. Initially, the plan was for Eliza's mother to leave first. Her mother, however, did not want to leave her children or her parents behind. There were also plans to send for Eliza, but these never materialized. Finally, for reasons unknown to Eliza, her father called one Sunday evening with the news that they had to leave immediately. They left for Napa the very next day.

Lorena

Lorena is a fourteen-year-old freshman at Napa High School. She came into the room wearing her reddish straight hair down and played with the tips during the interview. "I like to dye my hair," she said. "It used to be black." Lorena came to Napa in 2006 from Sayula, a town in the state of Jalisco, to join her mother after living apart for four years—three years in the U.S. and one year in Guadalajara, the state capital of Jalisco. Her mother first moved to Guadalajara after separating from Lorena's father. She worked in the state capital for one year leaving Lorena and her younger brother under the care of their maternal grandmother. Not being able to make ends meet, Lorena's mother tried her luck in El Norte. The plan was for Lorena and her younger brother to follow her. Her brother left six months later. Lorena was supposed to leave with him, but she feared the border too much and stayed behind. When her mother moved to Napa, Lorena was forced to move in to her father's home. She did not enjoy living with her father, but expected it to be temporary, only until Lorena followed her mother to Napa. Despite disliking her father's home, however, Lorena was hesitant about moving north and leaving him. She felt conflicted. On the one hand, Lorena felt her father neglected her. He spent most of his time with his much younger girlfriend, paid her little attention, and never offered Lorena words of encouragement. In fact, no one in her father's house ever bothered to check that she went to school or did her homework. Nor did he provide money. Her mother's remittances, sent directly to her, provided Lorena with the only money for clothes and daily expenses. On the other hand, he was her father. He did not want Lorena to move north; indeed, he had "forbidden" it. Her mother, however, had repeatedly told Lorena that the decision to move was hers to make. Lorena was, in fact, well equipped to make such a decision on her own since she took care of herself, went to school every day, and spent her free time with her cousins, friends, and her boyfriend.

On Saturdays, her father's family got together for dinner and Lorena was expected to participate. Sundays were reserved for her maternal grandmother. Lorena warmly recalled how the day began with church. They then passed the whole afternoon sitting on a bench, talking. There, she told her *abuela* about her struggles with her father. They also discussed her possible move to Napa. At night, they went out to the town square—the *plaza*—where they ate dinner at a local *taco* stand. In the end, her mother made the decision for Lorena to move. Lorena left quickly on a Monday morning just four days after her mother had sent her a one-way ticket to Tijuana.

These quick snapshots of the girls' experiences are very similar to the ones introduced in chapter 2. Even though the girls are not from Zinapécuaro, they come from very similar towns, familial arrangements, and shared desires for migration. The lives of girls in this study—both those interviewed in Zinapécuaro and in Napa—are lived on the brink of migration.

Migration Journeys

Scholars of immigration have approached immigration journeys from three perspectives. The first framework focuses on when an emigrant crosses an international border, becomes an immigrant, and adapts to life in the U.S. The second emphasizes how physical migration and the act of crossing are no longer exclusive to the experience of migration because of transnational circuits, networks, and modes of communication.[17] This approach illuminates how transnational communities are intricately connected, how the penetration of U.S. popular culture in local communities alters peoples' lives in Mexico, and how the continuous movement of people, ideas, and culture is lived on both sides of the border. The third perspective zeroes in on the journey of migrants—mostly from Central America—to the U.S.[18] All of these frames compel us to rethink the nature of crossing and what it entails.

In *Pedagogies of Crossing*, M. Jacqui Alexander (2005) describes the act of crossing as a moment that "might instruct us in the urgent task of configuring new ways of being and knowing."[19] For Alexander, crossing implies inevitable change in the crosser. Alexander defines crossing as an event that is "meant to evoke/invoke the crossroads, the space of convergence and endless possibility; the place where we put down and discard the unnecessary in order to pick up that which is necessary. It is that imaginary from which we dream the craft of a new compass"[20] Once the other side is reached, the crosser begins to get rid of the unnecessary as a survival mechanism. There is also a physical and emotional transition or, as Gloria Anzaldúa (1987) described, "a constant state of transition."[21]

For migrants who cross an international border, there is the illusion that crossing may provide endless possibilities. As Leo R. Chavez explained in 1992:

> More often than not, crossing the border illegally is a monumental event in the lives of Mexicans and other undocumented immigrants. A potential migrant usually has to gather some resources from family and friends, since for most getting to the border and finding someone to help them cross is an expensive undertaking. After the preparations have been completed and only the actual crossing remains, the moment of truth arrives; a successful crossing can only be hoped for, not guaranteed. For undocumented migrants, crossing the border is a territorial passage that marks the transition from one way of life to another. No matter how similar it may seem to the way of life left behind, or how many relatives and friends await the new arrival, life in the United States is different for the undocumented immigrant.[22]

The resources and preparations seem minimal compared to the "moment of truth" that is crossing. Will the migrant be able to cross? Will crossing bring the imagined endless possibilities? For Chavez, crossing the border will lead to a "territorial passage, [which,] like more conventional rites of passage, can be divided into three important phases: *separation* from the known social group or society, *transition* (the "liminal" phase), and *incorporation* into the new social group or society. These phases are not always of equal weight or importance in a particular territorial passage."[23] The focus here remains on crossing and not as much, for example, on the preparation. As Chavez states, preparations happen before any of the other phases take place, but: what exactly do those preparations entail? When do they start? How long do they last? How do pre-migrants prepare for the actual act of crossing?

As mentioned above, transnational migration scholarship argues that a physical movement does not need to happen for migration to take place. This is an argument first made by Levitt in *The Transnational Villagers*.[24] When discussing migration journeys, recent studies follow the same pattern.[25] In *Transborder Lives*, Stephen finds that "[i]n everyone's testimonies about migrating to the United States, the narrative about actually crossing the border is an important event. Often crossings are traumatic and repeated, and they remain difficult secrets migrants carry with them."[26] Zavella argues that "migration entails a social death, particularly if one crosses the border without documentation through dangerous routes."[27] Finally, in the words of Maria Luisa De La Garza (2011), "one who decides to emigrate leaves *what s/he has*, annuls *what s/he can* and almost stops *being*, if not actually *existing*."[28] The words and phrases that stand out include: social death, annuls, being, not existing—all of which in some way relate to what is left behind, to the being who is left before crossing. How does the migrant decide what to leave behind and what to bring with them?

Chavez, Stephen, Zavella, and De La Garza are but four examples that are meant to illustrate the centrality of the physical act of crossing to the act of migration. Coutin found that, for Salvadorans migrants, the preparation begins at two separate moments: that of making the decision to migrate, and that of securing the means to do so.[29] Below I examine the moments of telling and the moment of leaving in order to highlight the powerful transformation and reorganization that migrants experience long before nearing the border.

The Telling Moment

In Esmeralda Santiago's (1993) memoir, *When I Was Puerto Rican,* the character of Negi is caught by surprise when her father tells her she is leaving Puerto Rico for New York with Mami and some of her siblings. Mami, her father says, has made up her mind to move the whole family in stages to New York. Negi, Santiago's central character, is part of the first stage. "My stomach fell to my feet," Negi recalls.[30] Negi's experience—of discovering she is suddenly moving, and then of leaving home, without understanding the reasons why—mirrors that of Martha, Elena, Angela, Eliza, and Lorena in my interviews. They were all unaware of the reasons for their migration. The decision to move was made by parents who may have taken months, perhaps even years, to plan and prepare. For the girls, however, it felt like a sudden decision with immediate consequences.

Growing up in a transnational family makes migration seem familiar and possible. The girls' stories, however, underscore the substantial difference between an abstract knowing and an actual physical move. When asked about the moment of telling, each girl remembered her surprise, shock, and even initial denial when she first heard the news of the physical move. Martha's story illustrates the point.

At first, Martha said she remembered nothing about the telling moment. Only when I probed further did she begin to recall details:

LS: Do you remember what day it was, what you were doing?

M: I don't remember what day it was, but, um, it was at night and I was preparing to go to school the next day and she [her mother] told me, "you are not going anymore because we are leaving." It came as a surprise.

Of course Martha was quite young then, only eleven years-old when she left La Piedad, Michoacán. Understandably, she had trouble reliving that evening. She remembered that it was in the evening because she was gathering her school materials for the next day. The fact that she was getting ready for school underscores her total ignorance of her parents' plans to move. In fact, she says, that evening felt like any other until her mother told her not to bother getting ready for school. The way that Martha was informed of the decision left little room for her to ask questions or respond.

> LS: Do you know why they decided to move that day? Do you know what made your daddy [say], "we are leaving, we leave now"?
>
> M: They had some problems . . . They were going to separate, but decided it would be best to move and start a different life.

Martha's first explanation for the move was that her parents were having marital problems and that the start of a new life in Napa would allow them to iron out the wrinkles in their marriage. As I turned off the recorder and began gathering my equipment to leave, however, Martha suddenly said that her father had been involved in a fight at his workplace. This, it turned out, was the real reason for the departure and for its suddenness. Apparently, the fight made leaving immediately so urgent that relatives and friends from Napa had to help facilitate the quick departure. Martha's memory of that evening appeared at first foggy because she was uncertain of the main reason. Was it her parents' marital troubles? Her father's fight? Or a combination of both? The uncertainty surrounding their departure contributed to Martha's confusion. In only two days, the family was gone.

For Elena, the telling moment was a bit different. While out and about in San Marcos with her mother, she recalls overhearing adult conversations that included questions about if or when they would be moving to Napa to join Silvio, her father. Though she was not part of the conversations, her ears always perked up when Napa was mentioned.

> E: We'd get an idea, when they would talk to other people, we knew we would all be here one day, all of us together, but I didn't think it'd be after my first year of middle school. I thought, I did think I'd be moving, that we would all move over here. I just didn't know when, and then, like half way into my first year of middle school, that's when they told us that we'd be moving. My mom is the one who told us, that we'd be coming over here with my dad.
>
> LS: Do you remember what you were doing when she told you? Why that day?
>
> E: No, I don't remember. . . .

LS: Was it a weekday?

E: I think so. I think it was a weekday when she told us. More so because I would see so much movement because my dad would call her
to tell her what we had to do, what to bring and things like that, and
what not to. Like, three months before we left, she hired an English
tutor so that she could teach us a bit of English, or at least for us to
be able to say, "hi, my name is," or, "my last name," or "my age," or
something like that. And so yes, we sort of knew, especially after they
hired the tutor, that was probably the best clue and so I think that
was that.

Elena looked for clues and noticed a change: an English tutor, more
regular phone calls from her father, and lots of movement that included
organizing and packing, all of which Elena took as signs that signaled a
nearing departure to Napa. We continued:

LS: And so your daddy did not want English to be a barrier once you
arrived to your new school in Napa?

E: Yes, yes, that was the reason. I think that's why they hired the tutor so
that she could teach us. In middle school, I had an English teacher,
but it wasn't just, like, she'd arrive and would tell you to open our
book and turn to a page, "this book and this page." She'd say what it
said on the page. She would not go over it the next day. That next day,
we were expected to know what each word meant and how to pronounce it. She wouldn't tell us anymore, she would just, she would
dictate the words out loud, we'd have to write the words down. If you
wrote the word well, you'd do good. If you didn't, too bad! "That,"
she'd say, "is no longer my problem." It just felt like a one-day review.
We'd study the verbs one day, and the next day the nouns, and things
like that. We wouldn't go over the material like we do here [in Napa]
where we go over what we learned the previous day, and over there
[in Oaxaca] it wasn't like that.

LS: You mentioned you noticed that something was different at home?

E: Yes, because we already had . . . Well, we'd get home from school. I
remember my mom told me that we were going to start taking English lessons, that a girl would be teaching us, that she was going to be
our tutor. I think her name was Karina, and my mom told us that she

would give us English lessons, and so we went each day in the early evening, like at five to her house so she would teach us English like the colors, um, how we pronounce our names and little things like that which would later become handy.

In Elena's case, it was not so much that she did not know. Being incredibly perceptive, she knew something was going to happen as she felt a change. Despite expressing desires to move and noticing the movement around her, she was still surprised when her mother told her that weekday.

For Angela, the news came suddenly in the middle of one afternoon as she hung out with her friends outside her house. She and her friends were making plans to participate in a pilgrimage to the nearby town of Zamora:

Yes, I remember. I was with my friends, planning the day when [we would] all walk to church, the big one, without shoes, thinking of how we'd get there without wearing any shoes. It's a church in a nearby town. I don't remember the name of the church . . . but the thing is, you walk without your shoes until you get to the church. My friends and I were planning the time of departure and all that, and then my mom got there and told me, "Angela, come here I need to talk to you," and I said, "okay, I'll be right there." And I told my friends, "keep making plans and fill me in when I get back," and um, I told them, "I'll be right back." And I went to see my mom and she said, "we're going to take a trip," and I said, "where?" And she didn't want to answer me. She just said we were going to see my dad . . . [starts crying]

As the children talked about their plans, her mother called her inside and altered them. They were going to take a trip, her mother told her. After much inquiring, her mother told Angela they would meet her father at Disneyland. Angela felt there was more to the trip, but her mother would not tell her. In fact, Angela learned that her mother had arranged the trip and completed all of the preparations needed for their visit. Still unsure of where she would meet her father, she was not sure if Disneyland was in Mexico or in the U.S. Angela did not understand why her parents had suddenly made the decision. It all felt rushed, almost mysterious. As she remembered this moment, Angela began to cry and I stopped recording so she could feel free to release her painful memories. When we resumed the interview, Angela told me that she had had no time to do much of anything before they left. Life, as she knew it, drastically changed.

Eliza describes the telling moment in a similar way. It began with an unexpected phone call from her father to her mother one Sunday evening, letting her mother know of the plans. It was December of 2005. Months prior to the phone call, Eliza had expressed desires for migration. There were plans to send for her but these never materialized. In an act of defiance, Eliza said, "it's fine. I didn't want to move anyway." But then one Sunday evening, the phone rang:

> E: But then in December, that was when they decided that we would now come. On that day, I did not want to come. My mom told me, "well, don't come. If you don't want to leave, don't, and stay here," and I told her, "yes, I'll stay here." [My mom said], "how can you think I'll ever leave you here?" [I replied], "well, why do you offer then if you don't mean it?"
>
> LS: Who called that evening?
>
> E: My dad. I don't remember. Well, actually I do. It was on a Sunday. It was at night. We had just returned from my grandparents' home. I was lying down on the bed, watching TV in the room when all of a sudden, out of nowhere, my dad calls. My mom answered and she didn't believe him until he told her, "it's true!" and she says, "let me go tell my mom and my dad," and he said, "I'll call you back again to tell you what you need to do." She hung up and so we went back to my grandparents' home . . . and we told them we were leaving
>
> LS: Do you know why your dad made that decision so suddenly?
>
> E: Well, I think he did it because of my mom. He had already told her that he wanted her to join him but my mom didn't want to. She didn't want to leave her parents, that's why she didn't want to leave. They told her to leave, to follow him. I was used to it and said, "I don't want to go."

Eliza's evening was completely turned upside down. A typical Sunday turned into her last Sunday in La Purisima. A quotidian evening lying in bed in her room watching TV was interrupted by a life-changing phone call and a one-way trip to Napa. Her uncertainty began. For a second, Eliza thought she had a choice to remain behind after expressing her discontent with the decision. Her mother, however, would not allow it.

In Lorena's case, she spoke on the telephone with her mother almost daily. Only on rare occasions when their school and work schedules conflicted did the two fail to connect. During these phone conversations, Lorena's pending move to Napa always came up. Her mother continued insisting that Lorena could make the decision on her own whenever she felt ready. As Lorena's relationship with her father worsened, however, her mother stepped in and decided for her: "yes, my mom told me, and told me about four days before that. Like, well, she told me she had bought the ticket and said, 'you know what? You have to leave on such a day,' and I, well, I felt bad because, well, I didn't want to leave, but, whatever, I had to." In the end, Lorena did not have a choice.

> Well, she made it [the decision] because she was desperate for . . . Like, because we weren't together and also because I would tell her all that [was] happen[ing], all the problems, everything my dad did to me, I would tell her. And she, of course, got angry, right? Um, then my uncles were also rude to me at times. They would say things about my mom, things that were not true, things that were not true that I knew were not true and I didn't care. But they would make me feel bad, then, my mom got frustrated and told me, "you know what? You are leaving such day, I already bought you the ticket."

Despite her frustrations with her father and his family, Lorena cried when she learned she was leaving. But she also recalls having contradictory feelings of sadness and happiness. She said: "the moment she told me, I felt really sad and well, I, I don't know, I felt like crying, maybe of happiness because I was finally going to see her and my brother." Not surprisingly, Lorena was frightened to move. It was not only the move itself but also her father's possible reaction that scared her. What if she got caught? Would he allow her to go? He had, in fact, threatened her, warning her not to leave. But now she had a ticket with only four days remaining before her departure. Those last days were filled not only with fear but also preparation.

These stories concern decisions to migrate that were made without the input of the girls involved. In fact, the majority of the girls interviewed were not asked if they wanted to migrate to the U.S. Only fourteen-year-old Sofia was asked if she wanted to migrate to Napa with her parents or remain in Tlazazalca, Michoacán, with her grandparents. She chose the former. Here, the intersections of age and gender in the decision-making process are apparent in the telling moment: Martha's father made the decision because his life was in potential danger and he needed to protect his family; Elena's father finally felt ready to bring his family to Napa; Angela is still not clear why her parents made the decision; Eliza's father was ready to reunite with the family in Napa; and Lorena's mother sent for her to protect her from her father. These are all genuine and loving reasons parents gave to protect their children, yet there is pain involved, particularly for the children. There is no ideal way to make a decision and transmit that to children, but the pain of being excluded in the decision-making process adds a shock and suddenness that further exacerbates what already feels like a hectic journey. That moment shifts life as they know it and suspends their daily activities, which plunges them into a state of limbo. Upon hearing the news, they experience a moment of turmoil and uncertainty.

Preparation

After the telling moment, Martha, Elena, Angela, Eliza, and Lorena began to prepare. It would be a trip without a known return date. What would they pack? What would they carry with them? How would they prepare? They had certainly heard stories about the U.S. and life in Napa, but there is a difference between an abstract possibility and an actual physical move. Some of the girls had only a few days and thus preparations were rushed.

For Martha, the whole experience unfolded much too quickly. Her mother informed her they were going to leave and had only two days before their departure:

LS: So she told you one night and you left two days later?
M: Aha. I didn't go to school [the next day]. I felt sad because I couldn't, I didn't have a chance to say goodbye to my friends. I told her,

"please, we aren't leaving until the evening!" Since I used to go to
school at night [the evening shift], that's why I had time to see them.

LS: What did you do the last few hours you were there?

M: Packing clothes, and I was happy [to move], but uh, what I wanted
was to talk on the phone but my friends were all in school and so I
didn't have a chance to do much.

Martha's narrative shows some ambivalence. She felt both excited and a
bit sad because there was no time to do much more than pack clothes
and toys. There was much confusion during the next few hours. Martha
negotiated that confusion by packing and controlling what she could,
what mattered at that moment. Amid that confusion, she was able to
pack her favorite doll and a few items of clothing. What she had to leave
behind, however, continued to hurt. She still misses her family, especially her aunt Lili. After her departure, her family continued to live as a
transnational family, a fact that complicated extended family relations.

Towards the end of my interview with Martha, however, I suddenly
learned a new fact about the family's move. We had then been talking
for more than an hour. As we prepared to wind up the interview, I asked
her if there was anything else she wanted to tell me about Michoacán,
migration, or Napa. She said yes and a startling tale suddenly emerged:
"yes, um, the, how we came was with some, someone else's papers, mine
belonged to a man [a young boy], so they had to cut my hair really short,
from having it really long, and yes, I felt really sad when it was . . . it took
us two days. One day I did my first communion and we left in a rush
the next day. The day I did my first communion that was when I didn't
go to school. I got my hair cut [the] morning that we were, that morning of the day we left." All of a sudden, it made sense why Martha liked
to play with her hair and why she always wears it down. Before they
cut her hair, Martha did her first communion. The next day, her long
hair was cut short and she was gone. Martha needed to look like a boy
because she had a boy's passport. Cutting her long curly hair was meant
to make her appear convincingly male. If the family had waited longer
to migrate, the plan—which hinged on Martha passing as a boy—might
have been compromised. That her parents had procured the passport
suggests that they had been planning the move for some time. All of
these plans were unknown to Martha. They never explained either their

reasons for moving or their plans. All Martha knew was that her parents were having marital problems and that a fight had happened between her father and his co-worker. Decisions were made and the family left in a matter of days.

I asked Elena what she had been able to pack and bring with her to Napa. She had mentioned earlier that her father continued to call her mother to give her specifics of dos and don'ts. Below is what Elena was able to bring with her:

> I brought pictures of my grandparents. I brought a Virgin of Guadalupe. I am a devout Catholic and a follower of her. I have faith in her. I think it was one of the first things I packed. I also wanted to bring all my clothes. I didn't want to leave it, but my mom told us to only pack five outfits. I didn't want to leave any outfits behind. Out of all of us, I packed the most. I threw in like six pairs of pants, six or seven, and the same number of tops. I think my brothers only threw in five and I, I don't know, I didn't want to leave my things behind. It was hard for me. Then, when we got here [to Napa], they bought us clothes more fitting for school because here at school, you cannot wear the color blue or red.[31] So, it was khakis, white, well, you could wear blue but not all blue. Nor could you wear blue belts or bandanas. And so they bought us clothes that were appropriate for school.

Though Elena seemed to have more time to prepare, she was still only allowed to take very few items with her. As she states, it was hard for her to decide what to pack, as she did not want to leave anything behind. Upon her arrival, she was confronted with a new reality that included school rules about the colors and styles of clothing that she could wear.

Angela had no time to prepare much as she did not even know where they were going. Because her mother prepared her luggage, Angela did not even get a chance to choose what to bring:

> The only thing I brought with me was a little coin that a friend of mine [gave me], we've been good friends ever since, ever since I can remember, since before I left [to Napa] the first few times. It's a gold coin with the Virgin of Guadalupe and she has one too. That was the only thing I brought . . . and I remember that the next day she [her mother] told me,

"let's go, we're going to see your dad," and my mom already had packed all my stuff. That same day, I didn't have a chance to be with my friends, I just left them, I didn't tell them anything.

So a perplexed Angela left. Perhaps her mother had sensed how Angela would react, and therefore avoided telling her. Her mother packed lightly because she knew they could purchase clothes and material goods in the U.S. There was no need to carry anything. Angela left behind her Barbie dolls, her friendships, her daily activities, her school, and her plans for the pilgrimage. Who would care for her Barbie dolls? Would they remain hidden in the same box where she left them? What would happen to her friends? Would they still participate in the pilgrimage without her? Angela was not looking forward to her return to Napa.

Eliza also only had a few hours to prepare as it was already evening when she found out that they were leaving the next day. I asked her if she was able to bring something special, perhaps a stuffed animal. She said "there was no time to do any of that. All we did was pay off any pending debt my mom owed, organize the home, go to the city, come back, and then leave." Would they have time to put plastic covers over their furniture? How would the dishes be stored? The appliances? Would they put their clothes inside suitcases or in boxes? Or would they remain hanging in the closets? Would their possessions gather dust? Should they disconnect the phone, cancel cable, water, and electricity services? What would happen to their home? In the hours that Eliza had that Monday morning, she stored her life away. Life at La Purisima had already changed. Eliza was already changing even though she was nowhere near the border.

Lorena had only four days to plan her move. She used the time to prepare carefully. That Saturday night before she left, the customary family dinner was held at her father's house. Fearful of their anger if they found out about her one-way ticket, she said nothing to anyone except her maternal grandmother, an aunt and her husband, and a friend. They were the four people who helped Lorena slip away that Monday morning:

LS: Did you spend the night at your grandma's?
L: No, what happened is that, well, it was like, I would always, like, in the morning, I would leave.

LS: As if you were going to school?

L: Aha, no one would wake me up, I woke myself up, like, with the alarm on my cell phone and well, I left, and like, no one, on a week-day, no one comes out [of their room], and well, I would only say to no one in particular, "I'm leaving" and I'd leave, and like, they didn't know anything, like, they didn't care if I went to school or not. Then, I would just, that day I remember I left, and one of my aunts who lives in a *rancho* nearby, like, over there [motioning with her hand], she spent the night, then I thought, "maybe it'll be harder for me to leave in the morning, no?" But no.

At first, the plan seemed to be compromised. The family had the party on Saturday, as usual, but an aunt ended up staying through Monday. Lorena's comments here also underscore her reasons for leaving. No one ever cared whether she got to school on time, so she was able to sneak away, pretending it was a school day like any other. Despite her aunt's unexpected decision to spend the night prior to her departure, her leaving in the end went smoothly:

That night I went to sleep with, with the clothes I was wearing, I just wore the uniform, I um, well, the P.E. uniform were sweat pants. I wore it and like that, I left like nothing. But a friend had already done me the favor of, that Saturday, she stopped by and took some of my clothes, she took it and did the same on Sunday. On Monday, I just had like, I just threw a notebook and other things, and well, I left but no one found out. Then I left, but instead of going to the bus stop, I went to my grandma's and no one, like, well, I, the plan was that no one had to see that I had gone to my grandma's house because I didn't want to get them all in trouble. I didn't want to do that.

Her friend and her grandmother assisted Lorena. As she told me, one friend was able to smuggle clothes and shoes, pictures of her friends, stuffed animals, hairpins, earrings, make up, and perfume of her own choosing out of her house. Thus, on the morning she left, she needed only a small backpack. Although Lorena feared for her grandmother, who had already been threatened by her father, her departure went smoothly.

These narratives offer insights into the complexities of sudden departures illustrating the pangs the girls felt from having to leave friends and familiar things behind. Martha, Elena, Angela, Eliza, and Lorena all tell disturbing stories. I originally hesitated to include the details of Martha's departure. However, because immigrant teenage girls are so absent from the dominant discourses about migration, I chose to present the stories that they shared. As the interviewer, I witnessed their tears and the various moments when their tone of voice cracked.

The move also shows the various ways that the border affected them even before they physically crossed it. For Martha, the preparations included a haircut and passing as a boy. Elena had more time to select the material things she wanted to take with her. Angela had no choice. In Eliza's case, the preparations were so quick that she did not have the time to do much. For Lorena, the border had long been a haunting presence in her imagination. Their fragile agency in motion allowed the girls to negotiate the last few hours or days they had in Mexico. Martha, Elena, and Lorena selected what they could carry with them, while Eliza returned to her grandparents' home one more time that evening and helped organize her home. Lorena and Eliza expressed concerns, while Martha hoped to talk to her friends. It is within these negotiations where they were able to exert some control.

These narratives also show that the difficult border-crossing meant that most of the girls could not carry much with them. How then, without most of the material world that meant home, would they reconstruct a home in Napa? Almost everything non-material that was familiar to them also remained behind. All of the girls left grandparents, knowing that these older people were unlikely to ever move to Napa. They left friends and a familiar place. Their family's migration thus disrupted not only their ties to other girls of their own generation but also to older women—and men—across generations. Worse, perhaps, was the fact that few parents explained the reasons for moving. Thus the girls were uprooted from everything they knew without knowing why. Even when parents made some attempt to explain, they were apparently quite vague. The transition to the Napa Valley thus began.

The Moment of Leaving

This last section addresses the actual moments prior to leaving as described by the five young women. I deliberately asked no questions about how each crossed or whether they had *papeles* to do so. I wanted to avoid creating any connection to *la migra* or the work of the Border Patrol or Homeland Security. Thus I have similarly avoided any categorization of people as legal, illegal, or undocumented. In the case of Elena and Angela, though, it is clear that they had U.S. permission to move north.

Even though I did not ask leading questions, many of the girls told me stories that suggested a clandestine trip across the border. Martha's story, for example, of having to cut her hair so that she would match a boy's passport, suggests one version of the "undocumented" border story. There was no other such evidence in the other stories and I avoided probing. Because she offered it willingly, I begin here with Martha's story:

I didn't know how, I thought we were going to cross like by the river or the desert. I didn't know anything, just that I was supposed to pass as a man, but, I said, "I guess I have to behave like this." I just didn't think. We came on a bus. We took it in Tijuana to Los Angeles and, yeah, a man, he wanted to smile at me and my mom said, "don't laugh because they'll know you are a [girl]! They'll be able to tell." And yeah, when you, when you cross, they put the passport or whatever next to you and they didn't notice they weren't ours, even though we didn't look like the photo. I think God did something there . . . and then something really funny happened because we didn't look like the [passport] photos, so we went to the bus, and what are those people called? An immigration agent helped us with our bags. And my mom began to wonder, "where is *la migra*?" And my dad would tell her, "shush! They are the ones helping us!" And we were like nothing. We weren't thinking. We knew many people die [crossing] but we didn't know any of that and so thank God that was our experience. Thank God we didn't have to suffer. But either way, we did risk a lot just like the people who let us borrow the papers. Because while we were there, the people in front of us were caught with fake documents that weren't theirs, but I didn't feel anything, I felt calm. I believe in God and we prayed a lot.

This is the immigrant story that Stephen found so common about crossing.[32] Clearly, Martha feared the crossing. She describes her faith in God, born in her religious upbringing, as crucial during that moment at the border. In addition to finding strength in faith, Martha's family was also helped by the plight of the family in front of hers. This family was caught with false documents. This may have distracted ICE (the new post-Homeland Security name for *la migra*) agents as they inspected Martha and her family. Whatever the case, Martha is certain that God and her hair saved them. Right before they left Michoacán, her mother took her cut-off long hair and donated it to the Virgin. In her own words, "it was a very sad experience when they cut my hair, but they took it to the virgin. I think that's what helped us." Her hair and her prayers, she believes, are ultimately what allowed them to get to Napa safely.

I asked Elena what she did last before the move. Although her mother had already done most of the packing, based on her father's tips and suggestions, Elena still needed to say goodbye to her family:

> I said farewells to my family. I said goodbye to my grandparents, my uncles, my cousins. The toughest part was saying goodbye to my great grandfather José because when we went to see him, my dad went in first and told him we were there to say goodbye. After my brothers [went in], well, after my brother José [named after his great grandfather José], the next one, he is younger, after him I went in. He [great grandfather José] gave me his blessing and I remember he made me cry. I remember he was the only one who made me cry because I was happy that I would be moving to be with my family. At the same time, it felt bad to leave my town, my house, my things, my friends, my grandparents. But more than anything, I was happy and I was like, "I'm going to be with my family." And so yes, I knew that once we got to Napa, I would be sitting on the table every day and I would get to see them. I'd get home from school and see my dad. Or at least know that he would be coming home late from work, but that he'd be coming home. I would get to see him that day. I knew that at night he would be in the room he shares with my mom. When I said goodbye to my great grandfather, the last thing he said was, "this will probably be the last time we see each other," and like, before, I had told him that I would be leaving, but that I'd come back, that I would come back and see him again. He said no, that, that [voice quivers and

breaks], that this would probably be the last time we'd see each other. We left in August and he began to get real sick in November and then, on November 20th, he died. The year he died, I came back. He died and we returned in December. And it was, when we arrived to my dad's house, I went to my great grandfather's room and he wasn't there. His bed was gone. Instead, there were candles outlining the shape of a cross. It really hurt not to see him because my parents, when we didn't have school or on weekends, they would tell us each morning, "go ask your great grandpa what he wants, if he wants his shake." He injured his back and didn't really like to be out. And so my dad would tell us to take him a shake. Or my grandma liked *pipian*, the *chile atole* that's made out of corn. And *boleras*. At our house, at the minimart, we also had a bakery. My grandpa, my mom's father, was the baker. When the *boleras* were ready, we would take them to my great grandpa so he could eat a *bolera*. So, because of my parents, we were used to running across the *solar* and go ask my great grandpa José if he wanted yogurt, jello, a shake, or when we had *pipian*, if he wanted *pipian*, things like that. We were always with him so when I returned, I wanted to see him. But more than anything, I wasn't fifteen yet and for my *quince*, I did not want a big party. The only thing I wanted was to be with my family and for my great grandparents to be there. I never met my dad's mom and so I always hung out with my grandpa Refugio and my great grandpa [José]. I had another great grandma who was my grandma's mom, my dad's mom. She was still alive, so it really hurt because that's all I ever wanted, I felt bad at times. At times, I'd say that all I wanted was to return and be with them for my *quince* . . . I think that for many [girls], turning *quince* is very important, more so if you are Mexican because it is celebrated. So for me, my *quince* was very important and I wanted to spend it with my whole family. I knew it would not be possible, but at least with those whom I shared the past thirteen years of my life, my grandparents, great grandparents, some uncles, my dad, and so when I turned fifteen, my great grandpa José was gone. That really hurt.

Here, we see precisely the way migration disrupts lives. Elena was happy about leaving because she would finally be with her immediate family. She described that, once in Napa, she knew her father would be coming home at the end of the workday and she would get to see him every day. The way she describes the yearning for her parents to be together in Napa also meant separating from the family that would remain behind. The disruption of ties across generations is clear from Elena's story. It would not be possible for her great-grandfather José to join them in Napa. He then remained behind and the fracturing of Elena's family continued.

As Angela rode with her family in the cab en route to the airport, she was still a bit puzzled as to where exactly she was going to see her father. Was it in Disneyland as her mother had said? If so, where was Disneyland? She describes the last hours before leaving:

> When we were in the cab, my mom told us, as I saw my friends go by, she told me that my dad was taking us to Disneyland, and well, I didn't know where that was and I thought, "oh, it's probably here, right? In Mexico." But I didn't even know that it was in Los Angeles, here in the United States. I was happy, right? Because I was about to go to Disneyland but when I found out, when I read the sign that said, "Welcome to the United States," and all, I was like, I started to cry.

Although she figured they would probably be heading north, Angela was not fully certain until she read the sign that read: "Welcome to the United States." At that point, she realized they were moving to Napa yet again. This time, she did not think they would ever return to Michoacán. Even as they rode away in the cab, Angela's mother was still not telling her where exactly they were heading, prolonging the uncertainty she already felt.

I asked Eliza about her move and the last things she did:

> E: Well, I was very surprised. I was shocked and didn't want to leave. Then we went to my grandparents' house and I started to cry. I cried even more on the Monday we left my *rancho*. I was very emotional. Everyone was crying and so I started to cry, too, especially when I didn't see my grandpa. He didn't come to say goodbye.
> LS: Where was your grandpa?
> E: He didn't want to come. He took off to the *campo*. He could not bear to see us leave.

In Eliza's case, the departure felt so emotional because they did not know if or when they would return. Her *belito* knew this and therefore chose to distance himself so as not to witness their departure. The suddenness of the decision and the uncertainty of the return made it difficult for Eliza. Who would she become? Would she be able to see her *belito* again? Would she remain the girl who liked to chat with her friends? At that moment, Eliza did not yet know she would become depressed in Napa, sleeping all day to numb the sadness.

Lorena had the most secretive move, all accomplished behind her father's back. Lorena first went to her grandmother's house where her aunt and uncle picked her up and drove her to the airport in Guadalajara. She flew alone to Tijuana. Once there, another uncle met her and together they crossed the border, traveling north to Napa: "[my aunt] and her husband did me the favor of taking me to Guadalajara. From there, like, well, I went to the airport and from there I went to Tijuana and in Tijuana, my uncle, one of my uncles was there and we crossed." In Napa, she reunited with her mother after three long years of separation. With her mother were her one-year-old half-sister, her mother's new partner, and her younger brother.

By the time Martha, Elena, Angela, Eliza, and Lorena neared the border, multiple decisions, packing, farewells, family separations, and transitions had already taken place. A transformation had already unfolded. This is the fracturing and disruption they experienced after the moment of telling, as preparation and departure followed. The moment of leaving felt like the last step needed to reach the border. From there, a new transition, a new crossing, would take place. The "monumental event," as Chavez describes it, would begin.[33] The moment to "discard the unnecessary in order to pick up, which is necessary," would also begin.[34] But, by the time they arrived, they had already annulled part of who they were.[35] The journey did not start at the border. The border, and crossing it, would become a continuation of a journey that had already begun.

Conclusion

The pre-crossing planning and preparation reveal the extended temporality shaping the seemingly sudden event of border-crossing. Due to complex processes of migration and transnational familial formations, Mexican teenage girls have already had to make life-changing decisions even before nearing the border; they are already missing who they will no longer be after crossing.[36] As De La Garza states, via Zavella, they have almost already stopped being.[37]

Each story the girls shared challenges the customary perceptions of migration. Although none of the girls took part in planning the trip, they each articulated a fragile agency about their families' choices and migration in general.[38] Such articulation points to the workings of age and gender that have a bearing on girls' migration. Girls' voices and fragile moments of agency point to the limited access they have to the decision-making process of migration, which will inevitably affect them. They have no say if or when they will migrate. As firsthand witnesses, they provide keen insights of how decisions are made and the role family members play. Girls in this study become the recipients of quick decisions about migration and movement that are made by their parents. They have to respond quickly and adjust to a plan that may have been in place for a while. Unbeknownst to them, they have to respond and act quickly before the opportunity evaporates. Through their stories, we can see they have paid a high price materially, emotionally, and psychologically for these moves.

6

Imaginaries and Realities

Encountering the Napa Valley

If we want to study social life well, and if in addition we too want to contribute, in however small measure, to changing it, we must learn to identify hauntings and reckon with ghosts, must learn to make contact with what is without doubt often painful, difficult, and unsettling.
—Avery F. Gordon, *Ghostly Matters: Haunting and the Sociological Imagination*, 23

Mexicans have always had an uncanny instinct for finding the soft spots of the American labor economy. Where there are jobs to be had in low-skill, low-wage industries, sooner or later the Mexicans will be there. The difference now is that many are settling now in places where Mexicans have never settled before, beyond the border states of the Southwest.
—Rubén Martínez, *Crossing Over: A Mexican Family on the Migrant Trail*, 232

Sixteen-year-old Olivia grew up hearing about Napa. While living in Atacheo, a town in the state of Michoacán, her connection to Napa developed as she witnessed her father Heladio's yearly commutes. Heladio lived in Napa during most of the year and returned to Atacheo for two months with stories of the labor he did at the *winerias* and *el fil* (wineries and the fields). Olivia never knew what that meant, but she imagined Napa, part of El Norte, as a modern city with skyscrapers, paved roads, and freeways—what Salazar describes as the cosmopolitan world "out there."[1] As we sat on the carpeted floor of the three-bedroom apartment in Napa where she currently lives, Olivia recalls hearing stories of Napa's beauty while she lived in Atacheo. She was no longer going to school, but knew that, upon migration, she would resume her education and eventually become a nurse. For Olivia, Napa was the place that allowed her to dream of a better life.[2] Upon arrival, she found herself in an unfamiliar place, spending most of her time looking after her little brothers and in charge of the household's reproductive labor at home. Outside of home, her life remained on the margins of a thriving wine and tourist industry. A new routine, the responsibilities she had at home, the unfamiliarity of the town, and her inability to speak English made the realities of her arrival question what she had once imagined.

Salazar finds that, nowadays, scholars are aware that the spaces of marginality pre-migrants may occupy before migration may re-appear after migration.[3] Understanding marginality and migration then opens up the space to question the imaginary, where the idea that everything is better and more modern on the other side of the border. Olivia's contrast between her ideas before migration and the reality she encountered after it allow for a broader examination of the migrant imaginary.

This chapter examines the initial experience of girls like Olivia who arrive in Napa after having lived in a transnational family since birth. Upon arrival, these girls not only need to get used to a new town, school, and language, but also a new family life and a new routine dictated by the marginal place their families occupy in the local economy. They arrive in a town with particular demands for the kinds of workers needed to produce an ambiance appealing to tourists. Napa, after all, is the second most visited place in California. I situate girls' arrivals within this place by examining why girls' fathers migrated to Napa. I explore how the imaginings of the U.S. as "greener pastures"—as expressed by Olivia, Dulce, Silvia, Leti, and Lucy—contrasted with their immediate realities upon arrival.[4] I discuss the immediate changes they encounter in the forms of new temporalities and spatialities shaped by their new routines, household chores and responsibilities, limited outings, and endless hours of loneliness and waiting. Using Tim Cresswell's (2004) definition of place as a focal point of investigating how the girls understand their world, I situate girls' arrivals in Napa in a place that has already written them out of its narrative and placed them on the margins.[5]

Mexican Migrants in Napa

Olivia's pre-migration story is very similar to the ones told by sisters Marbe, Emilia, and Toñita. She grew up in a transnational family from birth witnessing her father's commutes. Much like Elena (chapter 5), Olivia always knew she would move to Napa, but was unaware of the exact date. Napa was a place very familiar to her ears and imagination. Heladio, her father, made the decision to bring his wife Petra, Olivia, and the two young boys, Juancho and Pepillo, to the city in November of 2005. They had been living as a transnational family then for fifteen years. He placed the phone call on a Monday and the family left the following Thursday. Petra felt relieved to leave as her two young boys were starting to get older. She had witnessed how men in her town were prone to migrate to the U.S. and Petra figured her boys would one day, too. The older they were, thought Petra, the more difficult it would be for them to learn English, do well in school, and get better jobs. As discussed in chapter 4, fathers are more willing to send for their sons than for their daughters. This is rooted in patriarchal assumptions that daughters, upon marriage, will become the "property" of another man and therefore do not need to migrate. The boys' future, not her daughter's, was Petra's main concern. Olivia was fifteen years old when she left Atacheo. She completed only the eighth grade and was no longer going to school. According to her mother, her future as a young woman was not as important as that of her little brothers. Petra assumed Olivia would soon marry and that her husband would take care of her, therefore the possibility of her having a better chance at life was tied to heterosexuality and *capital femenino*.[6] Taking for granted their heterosexuality and desires for heteronormative families, Petra thought that, once Juancho and Pepillo grew up and married, they would be able to support their own family from the U.S. Olivia did not mind having only completed the eighth grade as she had other plans. Once she arrived in Napa, she figured she would have the opportunity to return to school and finally work towards becoming a nurse.

After fifteen years of living in a transnational family, Heladio finally had the resources, stability, and desire to bring his family north: he lived in a three-bedroom furnished apartment and had a year-round job in *el fil*; the boys were getting older; the commute was getting harder; and he wanted his family to be with him.

As a migrant product of the post-peso devaluation and economic crisis of the 1980s and 1990s (chapter 1), Heladio had left for Napa as a teenager to work. There were plenty of jobs in Napa's newfound wine and tourist industries. With relatives—cousins and uncles—already living there, he viewed the move as a challenge and rite of passage into adulthood.

Although migration from Mexico to Napa had been continuous since the 1940s, it intensified as Napa itself changed radically from the 1970s onwards.[7] The flourishing wine and tourism industries were the main impetus behind this change. Dozens of studies track the transformation of this small, seemingly rural, town in Northern California into a major center for wine, food, and tourism. As this industry grew, so did the population of Mexican immigrants in the Napa Valley.

Wine and winemaking have a long history in Napa. Since the arrival of the first Spanish missionaries, the building of the first mission, and the construction of local presidios housing Spanish soldiers and officials, wine has been an important part of the Valley's economy. It all began when a priest, José Altamira, accompanied by a group of soldiers, stumbled upon Napa while looking for a site for what became the last mission in the Sonoma Valley in 1821.[8] The colonizers immediately recognized the fertility of the Valley's soil and began to grow grapes to produce wine, both for drinking and for use in religious activities.[9] This is considered the origin moment for local winemaking.[10]

George Yount, considered the first non-Mexican to settle in the Valley during California's Mexican period, is credited with planting the first vines.[11] The arrival of Charles Krug and other Germans in the 1850s during the U.S. period marked the beginning of the commercialization of winemaking.[12] Krug is credited as the person who first made wine for consumption and production purposes. The prolific production of the 1880s was halted by the 1906 earthquake and the Prohibition, and resumed only in the 1940s with the arrival of the Italians—including the Trincheros and the Mondavis in the Napa area and the Gallos in Modesto.

The Mondavis became one of the "most prominent families in the Valley."[13] The family patriarch, Cesare Mondavi, arrived in 1906, first to the state of Minnesota to stay with relatives. The boosterist literature that surrounds his life omits mention of the anti-Southern and Eastern

European migration of this period, culminating with the Immigration Act of 1924. Instead, Cesare Mondavi is presented as a hard-working businessman who returned to Italy in 1908 to marry his sweetheart Rosa Grassi and brought her back with him to Minnesota shortly after. As a winemaker at his home in Minnesota, and as a member of the Italian American Wine of Virginia, he was sent to California in 1919 to purchase grapes. This was during the Prohibition years and the grape business was profitable. By 1923, he relocated his family to Lodi, California, and Cesare Mondavi began his grape-growing business. His two older sons, Robert and Peter, were working in the family business; together, they purchased the Charles Krug Winery in 1943 for $75,000—the same winery that had once belonged to Charles Krug himself. Upon Krug's death, the winery had become property of James K. Moffit, who sold it to Cesare Mondavi and to this day, the winery still belongs to his family. The purchase of the Krug winery cemented the business marriage between two of the most well-known names in winemaking in the Valley.

The emergence of the Mondavis coincided with the bracero program, which brought a wave of Mexican immigrants to the Valley. Hired mostly to labor in the fields, Mexican men from Michoacán and Zacatecas began working in family-run wineries. Sandra Nichols (2002) traces the story of four men from Los Haro and Jeréz, Zacatecas who arrived in Napa as braceros to work in the Charles Krug Winery.[14]

Until 1976, Napa's wine remained little known outside California. This year, however, proved a watershed year for the Valley's winemakers. A blind wine tasting contest in France, known as the Paris Wine Tasting of 1976, awarded the Napa Valley's 1973 Cabernet Sauvignon from Stag's Leap Wine Cellars the top prize in the red wine category, with the Chateau Montelena's 1973 Chardonnay winning the white wine competition.[15] French consternation was intense, but Napa Valley was now on the map. The tasting proved what California's winemakers had been contending for years: locally produced wine could compete with and even beat French wines from Bordeaux and Burgundy. Not surprisingly, wineries proliferated across the 30-mile length of the Valley. Wine tasting facilities, restaurants, wine auctions, and an endless list of wine-related activities soon followed. New wineries attracted more people, both visitors and residents, to the Valley. Today, five to six million visitors per year have made Napa Valley a "Disneyland for adults."[16] Books, articles, and even whole magazines devoted to Napa all display a boosterism that continues to draw people to crowd the two-lane highway that runs Up Valley.

The city of Napa itself is separate from this place called Up Valley, a scenic drive north from the city on highway 29. It includes a series of what were once sleepy small towns: Yountville, Oakville, Rutherford, St. Helena, and Calistoga. This Up Valley area is what tourists imagine when they plan their journeys, a place where the wineries, fine restaurants and spas for tourist consumption are located. Unlike Up Valley, however, the city of Napa was not a tourist destination until very recently. In the past few years, however, entrepreneurs have figured out that the city can be recreated to rival Up Valley destinations. Fine restaurants have opened along the Napa River in downtown with the aim of attracting tourists there too. Arguably, it began with COPIA: the American Center for Wine, Food, and the Arts with its famous Julia's Kitchen, Cinema, and other sorts of shopping and entertainment venues. COPIA has since closed but boutique hotels and restaurants permeate the city.[17]

The Paris Wine Tasting of 1976 changed wine, winemaking, and tourism in the Napa Valley. This contest put the Napa Valley on the map as a place able to produce superb wine and enabled it to become a favored tourist destination.[18] This key moment is widely discussed in the literature, but the cheap labor needed to tend and pick the grapes that make the wine is not. The event of 1976, and its ramifications in Napa, coincided with Mexico's economic crises of the late 70s and *la crisis* of 1982. Mexican migration to the Valley has been relatively constant, albeit circular, since at least the 1940s, and, with work available, it became a preferred destination especially for Mexicans from Zacatecas, Jalisco, and Michoacán. The "push" from Mexico and the "pull" from Napa were synchronized to produce this flow of migrants. In the 1970s, however, few families were actually settling in Napa. The Mexican presence increased during the harvest or crush, as it is known, when the grapes are ready to be picked and wine is in the production process, but the population declined when seasonal labor drew workers elsewhere, including back home to Mexico.

The 1980s brought more Mexicans to the Valley. The economic crisis in Mexico pushed migrants to Napa and their increased visibility, not only in the Valley, but also in the U.S. as a whole, led to a limited amnesty under the Immigration Reform and Control Act of 1986. As mentioned in chapter 1, IRCA sought to legalize immigrants who had resided in the U.S. before January 1, 1982, to penalize employers who knowingly hired undocumented workers, and to allow agricultural workers to legalize their status through the SAW program.[19] Under IRCA, over three million Mexicans were able to legalize their status and apply for family reunification.[20]

The year 1986 became a landmark in the Napa Valley for another reason. A massive flood, not uncommon in Napa,[21] led authorities to decide that "something [needed] to be done."[22] A flood control plan implemented in 1998, more than ten years after the 1986 flood, brought major changes to the city of Napa. With the flood protection plan, Napa City's downtown also began a revitalization process. The downtown area is now a "must stop" for tourists en route to the wineries. Napa began to need more service workers. Bussers, dishwashers, valet parking attendants, and hotel workers were hired to cater to and pamper the tourists. Mexican immigrants fill many of these positions.

These developments led to the continuous arrival of Mexican men, and later their families, including girls like Olivia. Workers like Heladio, a product of the 1980s exodus from Mexico, heard of the year-round labor opportunities. What started as a seasonal and circular migratory journey for many men became a permanent move, and they decided in turn to bring their families north to settle in Napa.

Constructed Images and Realities

For Olivia, Napa was the place where her father worked and lived most of the year. It was the place—the marker—that allowed her to cognitively map her father's absences.[23] All the girls interviewed in Napa had imagined moving there at some point in their lives. Their imaginations were fueled by stories they had heard from their parents and fellow migrants who returned to Mexico after a stay in Napa.[24]

For Salazar, imaginaries always imply movement, whether or not one moves, and "play a predominant role in envisioning both the 'greener pastures' and the (often mythologized) memory of the 'homeland.'"[25] For Schmidt Camacho, "the imaginary represents a symbolic field in which people come to understand and describe their social being."[26]

Napa played an interesting role in the imagination of girls like Olivia. They felt seduced by life there. It was a way for Olivia and other Mexican teenage girls to imagine their participation and perhaps "to reach the same material benefits" as those who live in Western countries.[27] The girls imagined that a better life would be possible in the United States, a place where they would become modern subjects and perhaps resemble what they saw on the television set.

I couple the approaches of Salazar and Schmidt Camacho here to examine this concept of imaginaries. On one hand, Salazar questions the accuracy of the idealized images of "greener pastures" in the U.S. and cautions against reliance on the assumption that "better" automatically unfolds upon crossing the border. On the other hand, Schmidt Camacho emphasizes the fragile agency that can emerge from imaginings of a better chance at life. Upon arrival, the girls discover that they have come to a place that has already marginalized them.

Imagining Napa

When Dulce arrived in Napa from Irapuato, Guanajuato, she was fifteen years old. Dulce had lived in a transnational family since birth. While her father commuted to Napa for work, she remained in Mexico with her mother, younger brothers, and older sister. No longer going to school, she had strong desires to migrate to Napa, particularly after her sister left for New York. Finally, her father sent for the family in October of 2005. A year later, I found myself talking with her about her immigrant experience in the two-story townhouse she shared with her father, mother, and younger brothers. Her older sister, who lived in New York, would soon be moving to Napa and the family would finally reunite. A now slender sixteen-year-old with very tanned skin, Dulce remembers always wanting to move to Napa since she was little. She grew up witnessing her father's yearly commutes. Hearing stories whet her appetite for El Norte, the place she wanted to go "*pa' conocer*" (to get to know).

> D: I heard that it was very pretty and that there, that here it was very
> pretty and everyone would say, "oh my, Napa is so pretty!" [said
> mockingly.] And that it was "such a pretty city!" And, well, that's how
> I imagined it.

LS: Pretty, like, how?

D: Well, that you could go anywhere, you could go wherever you
wanted, and, if not, that, that there was more freedom here and all.

Dulce's mocking tone comes from her disappointment with Napa. However, this notion of "pretty" came up in more than one interview. "Pretty" signifies in this context a modern aesthetic available arguably in the West. Shoes, dress style, and homes were all markers of a "better" and "prettier" Napa, a "better" and "prettier" life in the U.S. unavailable and inaccessible in the Mexico the girls inhabited before migration. Dulce's descriptions also include ideas of freedom and modernity that she believes are only possible in a modern nation-state such as the U.S. In describing Napa as a place where freedom abounds, Dulce alludes to features attributed to modern nations. Irapuato then becomes the place of lacked freedom and mobility. These ideas reflect Salazar's notions of "greener pastures" in the West that pre-migrants imagine, but they also resonate with long histories of discourses about modernization by political leaders and social scientists on both sides of the border.

Silvia is a seventeen-year-old migrant from a small town in Michoacán called La Estancia de Amezcua (La Estancia, for short). She arrived in Napa in January of 2006 after having lived in a transnational family since birth. From a young age, she knew her move to Napa was simply a matter of time. Her father gained his U.S. residency under IRCA's amnesty. As soon as his children were born, he filed the paperwork to bring them to Napa. In November of 2005, Silvia's mother Lola received a letter requesting her to appear before the U.S. Consulate in Tijuana. By January of 2006, the family entered the United States legally. Because Lola knew they would be moving to Napa, she only allowed Silvia to finish the sixth grade. There were no middle schools or high schools in La Estancia, therefore a daily commute to Zamora, the nearest city, would have been necessary. Lola did not see the point in this schooling as their move to Napa was around the corner. She thought: why should Silvia start a new school if she would be pulled out at any time's notice? Overall, Silvia missed four years of schooling. As in Olivia's case, for Silvia, Napa was the place where she would continue with her schooling. I asked Silvia how she imagined Napa and she shared a similar vision: "when I imagined it, it was big, like, streets all over, buildings like in Los

Angeles, because I always imagined it. But, later on, people began to tell me *historias* [stories] that it was more like a ranch, a ranch with lots of fields, so I started imagining it differently. I always imagined it as in a dream." The *historias* she heard about Napa molded her vision of the place she would soon move to. Her response differs from Dulce's in that there is no mention of freedom. Their answers, however, do overlap in terms of imagining Napa as a modern city, although Silvia's imaginaries adjusted as she heard other stories.

Seventeen-year-old Leti also imagined Napa as a modern city. She arrived at the age of nine with her mother and older brother on September 12, 1999. They came from a small town in the state of Michoacán called Indaparapeo. Like Olivia, Dulce, and Silvia, she was raised in a transnational family from birth. Her father Ramón had been commuting to Napa for work since he was a teenager. Ramón visited Leti and the rest of the family once, sometimes twice, per year. He kept in touch with her through letters. When she was little and unable to read, her mother would read them over and over until she memorized his words. Once she learned how to read, Leti not only memorized the letters but re-read them each night before going to bed. His words of love and encouragement kept Leti strong. She always felt she would move to Napa: "I can't explain how I knew, I just did." Like other girls, she, too, grew up hearing that El Norte was a place where wine was made. She explains: "I did not think there would be so many trees. I thought it would be different, more like a city with tons of buildings, many, many buildings. I did not think there would be too many Mexicans, only Americans." For Leti, El Norte meant skyscrapers, concrete, steel, and modern machinery. These ideas of modernity perhaps came from Hollywood films delivered to her television set before her migration.

Fifteen-year-old Lucy imagined Napa quite differently. She came from La Purisima, Guanajuato, at the age of fourteen and is Eliza's (chapter 5) younger sister.[28] We met in a classroom after class at Napa High School. She walked in with her dark curly hair pulled back, wearing a white sweater and jeans. A set of glasses kept her hair tucked behind her ears. Her father, she said, had warned her not to pay much attention to *historias* about Napa. He assured her that she would visit one day and witness for herself the beauty and the roughness of life in the U.S.: "whenever people would get there [to La Purisima], they'd say that it was pretty over here [in Napa]. But my dad would say, 'don't believe them. One day you guys will come and will see on your own how things are here.'" Following her father's advice, she tried not to wonder too much about Napa, but was not always successful. She imagined Napa as a clean city, "without any trash on the streets." More significantly, in her imagination, Napa represented the place where her family would once again be together. She had lived in a transnational household since birth, first because of her father's commutes and then because of her older sisters' departures. She yearned for her family to be together again as one unit and imagined Napa would be the place where that dream would materialize.

For these girls, Napa meant something "pretty" and "better," an urban environment that would bring a welcome change in their lives. What is peculiar about their answers is not so much what was said, but what was not. They did not imagine vineyards or wine when they thought about Napa, which means that Napa is not a place for them to visit but to work in. They had heard stories of Napa as a place for work, not leisure. Yet, in being consistent with ideas of "greener pastures," Napa would become the place to return to school and become professionals, or the place where their family would reunite. Based on their answers, these desires for schooling or for the family to be together seemed impossible in Mexico. Napa, then, became a place that would bring fruition into their young lives.

Realities of Napa

Living far south of the U.S.-Mexico border, the girls stretched their imaginations and envisioned the place where their fathers and mothers worked, the Napa where they might one day live. When they finally arrived, they were forced to confront both their constructed images of the Valley and its realities. All of their memories of those early days suggest that those were highly emotional times for each of the girls. Below I explore the realities they encountered upon arrival.

Olivia arrived on a Friday in October of 2005. She had begun that week just like any other in Atacheo. On Monday, her mother received the phone call from her father with instructions. By Friday, Olivia found herself in Napa. One week after they received the call, she was sitting at a desk at Napa High School on her first day of class trying to learn

English. I asked her how she felt those first few days:"I felt like, it felt like . . . I didn't feel anything. I didn't feel. I didn't feel myself. I couldn't, I couldn't talk." Reality sunk in: "the town is not ugly, but um, I imagined it differently. Either way I live here . . . I'm not sure for how long, so it's okay . . . But I miss my grandparents, my aunt. We have a lot of family here [in Napa] and, for that reason, I got very close to them [grandparents] and my aunt [in Atacheo]. I got along really well with her [aunt], with my grandparents, with my grandpa. But I feel I miss my aunt the most." Olivia had developed close relationships with the relatives that remained behind in Atacheo. Her departure severed those relationships.

Because everything around her felt unfamiliar, Olivia did not feel connected to anything. She spent her first few days in a kind of limbo. By the time I interviewed her, she had been living in Napa for almost a year and had found a routine. Imagining modernity and living in a modern city no longer factored into her answers. Instead, the reality of having to navigate life on the margins, of not feeling like herself, became the focus of her life.

When Dulce arrived in Napa, she found herself questioning her initial ideas of freedom. She confessed she did not feel free: "over there in Mexico, you could be out and about, but not here because, well, it's dangerous for one to be out late at night and so here, you don't go anywhere. If you don't go out with a boyfriend or friends, you don't go anywhere and so it's very different." With Dulce's answer, we begin to see what Salazar describes as the mythologized memory of the homeland when, at a personal level, everything in Irapuato was better. This is also an instance of Zavella's "peripheral vision,"[29] whereby everything in the former home is better than the new one. Dulce begins to romanticize Guanajuato and what life was like before migration. Her response about losing her sense of freedom is common. In her case, her parents work all day and Dulce is in charge of the reproductive labor at home. Her free time feels limited. When she arrived, she also had other concerns:

D: When I got here, I didn't know anything. I didn't know a word of English. What if someone asked me a question? What am I going to say? Are they going to turn their back on me because I don't speak English? I was afraid of that, that people would think less of me.

LS: When you first arrived, what did you think? How did you see Napa?

D: That, no, that it wasn't pretty, that's what I thought. It all looked different from what I had heard. It just wasn't pretty and that was it. The day I got here, I wanted to turn around and go back and I said, "why are we here? We were doing so well in Mexico, how did we end up here?" My mom said the same thing too. I just wasn't comfortable.

Dulce was unaware of the marginal space Mexican immigrants occupy in the U.S. This was not the case for Zinapécuaro girls. Here, the difference may be that, since the mid-2000s, a wave of anti-immigrant and anti-Mexican sentiment has been felt all over the U.S.—and it is not receding. Girls in Zinapécuaro were well aware of this. Because girls from Napa migrated prior to the current wave of anti-Mexican sentiment, they may not have been aware. For Dulce, all of a sudden, she found herself there and began to question what she had heard and imagined. Perhaps she was unaware of the marginal place she occupied in Guanajuato that had pushed her father to migrate, or perhaps that did not matter because she lived among the comfort of the familiar. Napa did not seem like the place where Dulce could reinvent herself or a place of modernity.

In Silvia's case, she had paid close attention to the ways in which Napa was described. She said she always imagined Napa as in a dream. Upon her arrival, however, she described the dream turning into a nightmare:

It turned into a nightmare because I felt so terrible. I, when we got here, I felt resentful. I wanted to share my feelings with someone. When I first got here, I got real skinny, skinny, skinny! And my mother got very scared. She was so surprised I had lost so much weight in five days, three days on the bus and then two days after we got here. I was very chubby before. From one day to the next, I was skinny, skinny, skinny, and my mom got scared. She worried that I had gotten sick. Then, when we got here, I don't really remember the day . . . I think it was a Saturday, yes, a Saturday. I think it was on a Saturday morning. No, wait, it was a Thursday, now I remember, it was Thursday! We got off the bus in Vallejo. My dad called my uncle so that he could pick us up. While we waited, we saw all these kids walking by with their backpacks on their way to school.

The nightmare Silvia recalls has to do with her weight loss and feelings. Lola, her mother, has had heart problems and feared Silvia would develop them, too. Her family moved into a wooden shack built in the back of a house where it got cold at night. It was a room with three beds: one for her parents, one for her little brother, and one for Silvia. With no closets or room for dressers, Silvia's clothes were folded on a pile next to her bed. The nightmare Silvia described also included her reaction to the room. Back at La Estancia, she had her own room with closets and dressers where she could store her clothes. When migrants in waiting imagine life in the U.S., it is difficult to envision the initial changes they will inevitably encounter.

Leti arrived on the evening of Sunday, September 12, 1999. Though it was a bit difficult to see the town at night, Leti recalls:

> We got here at night and, um, when we got here, everything seemed so different. At times, I was like, I was afraid, afraid that an American would come out, like I had seen on movies, and attack us because we were Mexicans, and so I was afraid they'd do something to me. I remember that, when we got here, here to Napa, um, we got to my uncle's house and my dad asked us if we were hungry and we said no. We got to his house and slept in the garage that was turned into a bedroom. My dad rented the room for the four of us. The next morning my aunt invited us to the store. I went and saw all the huge stores! They were so pretty.

For Leti, arriving in Napa meant confronting what she had been exposed to before migration. The U.S. popular culture delivered via the television set in her house in Michoacán included anti-Mexican immigration films that made Leti fear *los Americanos*. Leti's initial feelings also point to confusion. Her response shows the strangeness of arriving to a place that she had imagined for so long, a place where she now would live for an indefinite period of time.

Lucy was also disappointed after arriving in Napa. As mentioned earlier, she imagined Napa to be the place where her family would be together. This was not ultimately the case. Instead, she found a family that continued to be fractured. One of her older sisters was married, and Lucy found herself living with a new member, a brother-in-law, who was a stranger. While waiting to move, Lucy had imagined she would spend time with her father and siblings, and, for her first few weeks in Napa, she did. She arrived in December when frequent rain kept most of the family together indoors. But, when the rains stopped, everyone, including her mother, went off to work: "[I didn't think] it would be as frustrating, that it'd be from work to home and from home to work. I didn't imagine it'd be like that, but I guess that's how it is." This was the U.S. that Yola describes in chapter 2. Yola lived in California for a few years and recalled how family life revolved around work schedules. For Lucy, even on weekends when the family was together, many outings were cut short because someone—one of her sisters or her father—had to return home to get ready for work. Lucy found herself spending most of her time on her own.

Despite the fact that Napa was in some ways a familiar place for them, the place where their family members lived and worked, it was at the same time completely foreign. They found themselves living in a place very different from what they knew. This new Napa was thus shrouded with fear, disillusion, and depression. Although they eventually settled into lives of their own and made friends—some from their hometowns and others from other places in Latin America—the "*no me sentía*" ("I did not feel like myself") that Olivia described is echoed across all of the girls' stories.

Napa

What is interesting about the girls' answers in the previous section is that the place into which they arrived has been portrayed in the official tourist literature as a romantic and idyllic tourist destination. Writers in travel guides, boosterist literature, and historical accounts have portrayed Napa as a place evoking a quaint country atmosphere, possibly a villa in Italy or a small town on the outskirts of Paris.[30] For most recipients of these messages, Napa connotes a little piece of Europe north of San Francisco, which in recent decades has become a popular weekend destination for those seeking prize-winning wine and food in a rural atmosphere, or an escape from the crowded urban life of the Bay Area. Napa's booming wine economy, luxury shopping, and cultural events together provide abundant leisure activities for a flourishing tourist industry. All this growth has one origin: wine.

Since the 1970s, tourism has modified the landscape of both the Up Valley region and downtown,[31] producing a space where tourists arrive to consume bottles of rare wine only available in the Valley and to purchase wine paraphernalia. As Don Mitchell (2000) states, a landscape "provides a context, a stage, within and upon which humans continue to work, and it provides the boundaries, quite complexly, within which people remake themselves."[32] Tourists arrive to remake themselves by indulging in the experiences the Valley offers: wine tasting, restaurants, mud baths, shopping, and an endless list of festivals offered throughout the year. Many believe what Paul Lukacs (2000) says of wine, that it is the civilizing drink.[33] Tourists from all over the U.S. and from many foreign countries (particularly European ones) flock to Napa. The yearly Napa Valley Wine Auction brings *la crème de la crème* of high society to the area. Tickets sell for $2000 per couple, a price that automatically attracts a crowd of particular wealth.[34] At the auction, those in attendance display their affluence and status through bidding. In the year 2000, a 1992 wine bottle from Screaming Eagle Winery sold for $500,000.[35] According to Alan Deutschman (2003), Chase Bailey, the man behind the bid, hoped to remake himself in the landscapes of the Napa Valley.[36]

Traditionally, tourist sites were concentrated Up Valley. Tourists split their visits between highway 29 and the Silverado Trail, two roads that run parallel to each other connected by charming perpendicular streets filled with trees and vineyards. On highway 29, the attractions include the wineries Robert Mondavi, Beringer, Niebaum-Coppola, Opus One and Charles Krug. The Silverado Trail, often called, "the Napa Valley road less traveled," is a thirty-mile road that runs from the entrance of Napa all the way to the city of Calistoga.[37] The famous Mumm Winery is located on the Trail.

Since 2000, downtown Napa has been added to the list of tourist meccas, a featured attraction on the wine tasting trail. Napa's local officials worked hard to help transform the town. Lauren Coodley (2003) traces the beginnings of the transformation to the catastrophic flood of 1986. Because of recurrent floods, the land along the river had long offered cheap homes and low rents for those looking for affordable housing, usually poor and working-class Mexicans. In the aftermath of that devastating event, outside officials promulgated a flood control plan.[38] Its implementation began to displace the working-class people living near the river.[39] By the mid-1990s, a redevelopment plan had been put into effect. This flood control plan coincided with the vision of Robert Mondavi and Margrit Biever Mondavi, who had long championed a food and wine center in downtown Napa. The Mondavis donated $20 million and raised funds to construct COPIA: The American Center for Wine, Food, and the Arts that opened its doors to the public in November of 2001.[40] The Center's mission statement declared: "COPIA: The American Center for Wine, Food & the Arts was created to educate adults and children to the joys of living well. At COPIA we expose the positive roles that wine, food and the arts have played in our lives, from the most primitive civilization to the present and into the future. We have something for every interested person—wine and food lovers to professionals—and offer a full spectrum of programs from art exhibitions and outdoor performances to food tastings and accredited courses on winemaking."[41] As stated earlier, COPIA went bankrupt in 2008, but it was only the beginning of a wave of changes that altered downtown Napa (Figure 6.1). The *San Francisco Chronicle* constantly publishes articles highlighting the proliferation of new wine bars and restaurants opening in Napa.[42] Paul Franson (2003) terms this a "rebirth" of downtown,[43] which includes the renovation of the Napa Valley Opera House and many restaurants around the Napa River—from Bounty Hunter Rare Wine and Provision, to Celadon, Angéle Restaurant and Bar, and Cole's Chop House. With COPIA, the development of the "up and coming"[44] Oxbow District continued to undergo transformation and now includes the Oxbow Public Market, opened on February of 2008.[45] As the local newspaper *Napa Register* reported: "The Oxbow District is rapidly acquiring the amenities to attract well-heeled tourists, including those who want to spend a portion of each year."[46] Napa, therefore, "has been transformed into a service sector economy, jobs in hotels and restaurants as well as wineries have become plentiful."[47] Needless to say, the value of the property around the river has increased markedly.[48]

As with any revitalization project—a process that inevitably entails gentrification by investors and buyers seeking housing in a tourist hot spot—property values skyrocket, subsequently increasing the costs of homes, including rentals, for locals in the area (Figure 6.2).

Figure 6.1. Promotional ad for the new downtown Napa. Photo taken by Lilia Soto.

Figure 6.2. Promotional ad for the new downtown Napa. Photo taken by Lilia Soto.

Wite-ing out Mexicans

The lure of jobs at tourist venues pulled the girls' fathers to migrate there, first as cyclical workers during the crush season and then as permanent workers in the service industry or *el fil*. Yet, very few historical, journalistic, or boosterist accounts mention Mexicans. In fact, they are largely left out of the historic narrative of the Napa Valley. As mentioned earlier, the girls then arrive into a place that has already excluded them; a place that has already deemed their presence not part of the constructed romantic image. If or when Mexicans are mentioned, it is at best as a sidenote about the labor they provide, and, at worse, in a racist and stereotypical manner that portrays them as unwanted and unproductive intruders.

Three examples highlight the dominant discursive portrayal of Mexicans as workers. Jonathan Swinchatt and David Howell (2004) explain that, "[i]n Napa, where the focus is on quality rather than volume, handpicking is underwritten by the low cost of predominantly Mexican labor and the high price of Napa wine, boosted by the booming 1990s"[49]—mentioning Mexicans purely in relation to the labor they provide. A second example comes from Kate Heyhoe and Stanley Hock (2004) who, in the course of documenting the Trinchero family's philanthropy, mention Mexicans only as the objects of charity benefitting from the family's construction of a day labor center designed to hide laborers from view and create orderly recruitment of low wage workers for contractors and individuals:

> Day laborers looking for work once hung around the parking lot of St. Helena's Sunshine Market. It was not the ideal situation especially for picturesque Napa Valley. The Trincheros joined forces with The Work Connection, a day laborer work resource for both employers and employees, and volunteered office space and a location on their property as a central hiring site, open to all valley laborers and hirers. It's well organized and includes Spanish-language translators to assist both workers and employers.[50]

Mexicans clearly are not situated within the idealized visions of the picturesque Napa Valley and, as workers, are ever present but shunted away from tourists. Finally, Deutschman quotes Jean Phillips, the vintner who made a bottle of wine that was auctioned for $500,000,[51] who states that Mexicans prefer to drink tequila over wine at the end of the harvest.[52] Defining wine as a civilizing drink and noting that Mexicans eschew it leads Phillips to embrace a racialized and classed hierarchy that places Mexican tequila drinkers at the bottom.[53]

Two further examples portray Mexicans in a negative light. Cheryll Barron (1995) includes a chapter entitled "The Mexicans" in her book *The Dreamers of the Valley of Plenty*, a book that received celebratory reviews.[54] She uses a woman named Aileen Flanagan as a guide and translator who willingly explains her own knowledge of the Mexican immigrant community. It seems Flanagan, who lives with a Mexican farm worker and their son, has the authority to speak for and translate for Barron what Mexicans think and feel about their promiscuity, infidelity, and sexuality: "I ask Aileen if there is much infidelity in Mexico. 'Yea, in Mexico they are allowed to screw around. So you have some guys who will have a woman in each town!'"[55] Who made Flanagan a Mexican spokesperson and why is Barron writing about this in 1995? Barron's project purports to understand why there are few Mexican vineyard/winery owners in Napa. Her conclusion is simply that "they stubbornly resist assimilation,"[56] as if assimilation will lead to owning a winery. This is the Latino Narrative Threat that Chavez examines.[57] As in most accounts on and about Napa, there is no structural analysis of race and class. Barron ignores the fact that property values in Napa escalated exponentially and that *The Dreamers of the Valley of Plenty* excludes the dreams of Mexicans. In 1980, land in the Up Valley sold at $13,000 per acre.[58] By 2007, an acre of land in the Up Valley sold for $275,000.[59] The market costs for houses and condominiums also soared. In the city of Napa, average home prices went from $362,000 to $443,000 between 2002 and 2004.[60] A winery sold in 1964 for $1.2 million was bought for $2.5 million in 1976.[61] Who has the accumulated capital to purchase and run a winery that in 1976 sold for $2.5 million? Is this not the question that Barron should be asking instead? Should we assume that this, too, is the 'dream' of Mexicans? Racism permeates the epistemic approach of some writers who have produced the dominant narrative of the Napa Valley.

Similarly, James Conoway (1990) uses Rafaél Rodríguez, one of the early workers in John Daniel's Inglenook winery, as his "native informant."[62] Daniel was forced to sell Inglenook in the 1960s and Rodrí-guez left to work on other projects. The Daniel family kept the Niebaum estate. Shortly after John Daniel died in 1976, his wife Betty Daniel sold the estate to Francis Ford Coppola who changed the name to The Niebaum-Coppola Winery. Coppola hired Rafaél Rodríguez back as the supervisor of the winery.[63] Conaway traces how the founders of the wine industry and their descendants were forced to sell their family-owned winery and vineyards to more highly capitalized conglomerates that caused tremendous changes in the Valley.[64] Rafaél Rodriguez, for Conaway, provides the only continuity: In Napa, something had basi-cally changed in the two decades, "One person not marked, one person whose existence proved that the valley could have unqualified good ef-fects on people, was Rafaél Rodríguez."[65] Everything changed but the quaint Mexican.

Those who write about the Napa Valley thus produce an Eden, a Euro-phile's ideological construction to compete with France and its popular and prestigious wines. It is what attracts them to write about the Napa Valley. Coodley cites the frustration with this narrative as expressed by council member Cindy Watter: "I was elected to the Napa City Council, and I found myself up to my eyeballs in problems: evaporating value tax, gang violence, and a working class about to get slammed by the closure of Mare Island . . . If I had to read one more paragraph about someone cracking open a bottle of cool crisp Chardonnay as he surveyed his acres from his receda, I would have to start a class war. Because of my experi-ence I can no longer read with composure anything about the romance of the Wine Country."[66] A romance it is. The celebratory narrative about the lives of the wine-makers of the Napa Valley continues. A 2003 *New York Times* article highlighted events, must-see places, and where to stay and eat.[67] Fall and winter are now also considered the best seasons to visit the Valley. The *San Francisco Chronicle*'s wine section regularly features articles about wine and food in the Napa Valley. Linda Mur-phy in "Judgment Day: Part Deux," for example, featured the thirty-year anniversary of the famous "Paris Wine Tasting of 1976."[68] But the *San Francisco Chronicle* does not only feature contests. On June 19, 2007, the Mondavi Family graced the cover of the *Chronicle* because of the pub-lication of a new book, *The House of Mondavi*,[69] which celebrated the family.[70] On April 7, 2005, the *Chronicle* featured Carl Doumani, a win-

ery owner who sold his Stags' Leap Winery, but kept some land to produce wine on a much smaller scale.[71] On December of 2005, the Davies
family and the history of Schramsberg Vineyards were highlighted.[72]
And there have been many more.

While these many writers aiming at the popular market are per-
suaded by what is actually a faux-European ambiance in the Up Valley,
and produce the expected history focused on the lives of the wealthy,
two historians—Coodley and Linda Heidenreich—are more skeptical. In
their respective projects, they are concerned with examining the lives of
Napa's own citizens.[73] Coodley has written a local history about how a
blue-collar town became a place that is "inseparable from an image of
luxury and easy-living."[74] She traces the transition from the old Napa, a
town where people worked in local industries, to the new city, where most
employment lies in the service sector catering to tourists.[75] Heidenreich
ties a local history to the violent construction of the U.S. nation-state
where U.S. expansionism, colonization, domination, and an ideology of
manifest destiny assisted in the making of the U.S. empire and its subsequent impact on "a very local town."[76] Both Coodley and Heidenreich's
work are examples of "the new local history," tied into the global world.
According to Stephen J. Pitti (2003), such work requires a search for the
unseen and the unheard.[77] Coodley and Heidenreich offer a resounding
counter voice to the nearly constant chorus of Napa boosterism.

It is very unusual to see articles like the one from December 19, 2004,
in the *SF Chronicle Magazine* entitled "Grapes of Wrath Revisited,"
which focuses on the workers who pick the grapes that make the wine
that bring tourists and wealth to the Valley.[78] The piece focused on the
fieldworkers, their housing and wages, and the central role they play in
the wine industry. Yet, the history of the new Mexican migration to the
Valley since the 1970s has been largely ignored.

There is one dissertation on the topic. Sandra Nichols has explored
the lives of some of these Mexican workers in the wineries.[79] She traces
the lives of four men—Pascual De Haro, Feliciano De Haro, Enrique
Segura, and José Manuel Saldívar—who came from Los Haro and Jeréz,
Zacatecas, to the Napa Valley. They came during the bracero program
in the 1950s when the Modavi family requested four workers for their
Charles Krug Winery.[80] Once chosen, the four began their migration to
and from Los Haro/Jeréz and Napa.[81] According to Nichols, when the

four arrived in the Valley, they decided that Napa reminded them of Los Haro/Jeréz, because, in Nichols' words, it had an agricultural feel familiar to them.[82] As an agricultural town, Napa's employment was heavily seasonal. Men came to work during the late summer and early fall, picking and crushing the grapes. They then returned home to Mexico where they tended to their own lands. That ability to move between Napa and Mexico for what is called "the crush" became more difficult in the 1990s when higher levels of border enforcement and a plethora of anti-immigrant laws and regulations severely restricted movements from south to north and back.

Employment in the wine industry, however fraught with regulation, has changed Napa's demographics. Today, the city is home to many Mexicans and Central Americans. According to the census, the Latino population of the city of Napa has grown from 3.1 percent in 1970, to 8.7 percent in 1980, to 14.2 percent by 1990, 23.7 percent by 2000, and 32.2 percent by 2010. By 2016, demographers estimated a Latino population in Napa at 37.6 percent of the town.[83]

Their Napa: *El Remate, Las Winerias,* Walmart

The girls in this study arrived in Napa at a time when the city was marketing its legacy of winemaking as part of its present identity. They came to a city that sold itself as a facsimile of a European village. Mexican immigrant girls were not the target audience for these tourist temporalities and spatialities. They did not frequent the fine restaurants or live in the upscale redevelopment areas. The celebrated entrepreneur growers and winemakers were the employers and often exploiters of Mexicans like them and their families. The Mediterranean towns evoked by the architecture of Napa were far removed from the Mexican villages and cities where they grew up. Yet, just as tourists inhabit imagined identities and remake themselves in the Napa Valley, these girls moved through space and negotiated time to craft new identities of their own therein. The girls quickly claimed spaces in Napa outside of school. On weekends and after school, they went to places very different from the city's celebrated tourist destinations. For them, the iconic places in Napa were not wineries, restaurants, or high-end shopping venues, but rather the church, the flea market, and Walmart.

On Sundays, highway 29, which runs along north and south through Napa, fills with cars moving in both directions. In the northbound lanes, tourists rush to reach the wineries in Up Valley, while the southbound lanes are filled with Mexicans en route to the flea market.[84] Anglos and Mexicans share the same road, but they are moving in different directions. After the Spanish-language mass at noon, migrants pile into cars and pickup trucks and drive off toward the flea market, which they call *el remate.* The northbound cars hold tourists and *bon vivants,* most of them white and all eager to indulge in the pleasures of tasting and purchasing fine wine. The southbound lanes are filled with working-class people, most of them with brown bodies, going shopping in search of cheaper prices on food, clothing, and electronics. Mexican immigrant workers and tourists thus inhabit the same Valley, but they rarely see each other *en masse.* These contrasting streams of highway traffic, each heading toward completely different destinations, reveal the racial and class fissures that fracture the Napa Valley. Only on these Sundays, when they can catch brief glimpses of each other across the median, do the sides meet.

Though it may be pure coincidence that the wineries are at the opposite end of the county from the flea market, the distance between the two attractions underscores how the very different worlds that Napans inhabit relegate different races to different spaces. People with wealth and power seem to like this segregation. On the rare occasions when interactions occur, immediate actions are taken to ensure that such encounters are not repeated. Around 1998, for example, Spanish-language mass at St. John the Baptist Catholic Church in downtown Napa was conducted on Saturday nights and again on Sunday mornings at nine o'clock.[85] This mass usually ended at about ten-thirty in the morning. The next Sunday mass celebration in English did not begin until eleven o'clock. But Spanish-speaking churchgoers gathered outside the church after their mass, lingering and socializing. From there they made their way to local restaurants for breakfast, and then set off for their weekly trip to *el remate.* Their presence and visibility disturbed Anglophone churchgoers coming for mass at eleven, who complained that the lingering congregants were disrupting their turn in the church. They claimed that they could not find parking spaces, that they had trouble entering the church because of the "massive" number of people gathered outside. Soon, church officials, responsive to these parishioners, moved the Spanish language mass from nine o'clock to noon. This disrupted Mexicans' Sunday routines. It did, however, save the English-speaking worshippers from having to see or interact with their Spanish-speaking "brethren in Christ."[86]

When I asked the girls about their cognitive mappings of Napa and about the places they regularly visited, the wineries, spas with mud baths, and luxurious shopping centers were not part of their answers. Everyone, however, mentioned *el remate*. Of course these girls are all teenagers who are underage and thus excluded from the wine-tasting offered for a fee at the wineries. So, even if their families went to these events, they could not participate. But these girls' replies to my questions make it quite clear that even those in their community who are old enough to drink do not go to the wineries. In fact, the celebrated attractions and amenities of the Napa Valley play little role in their lives on a leisurely level.

The girls then develop a different routine. They are generally left in charge of the reproductive labor at home that leaves them little time to explore Napa. Scholars have previously found that gender determines which children will help around the home, and it is usually the girls.[87] Olivia and Dulce are not only friends, but also neighbors. They walk to and from school together. On Fridays, they get together after dinner and take their little brothers to the park. While the brothers run around the park, Olivia and Dulce usually talk about the places they have left behind, Atacheo and Irapuato, respectively. Their conversations about Mexico usually focus on old friends they left behind, the routines, boyfriends, celebrations, and parties that they recall.

When not at home or the park with Dulce, Olivia sometimes goes to Mexican dances organized by the local church group, as well as to weddings and *quinceañeras*. Other than that, she is usually home keeping up with her obligations to housework and childcare. I asked:

LS: On any given day, what do you do?
O: Well, my mom works. At times she does not have time to clean up, so I do it. Or I go to the park with my friend. She usually stops by [on Fridays] between 6:30–7:00 p.m. and we go. Then, we get back at 8 p.m. and so I take a shower and go to bed.

L: How about a Saturday or Sunday? What do you do?

O: My dad usually works on Saturdays and so I get up and we clean the house. Sometimes we go to the store in the afternoon and things like that. On Sundays, if my mom does not work, we go to the stores or take trips . . . sometimes we go to Target or Walmart. Sometimes we go all the way to Vallejo or Fairfield, or to visit my aunt who lives in Calistoga.

When she lived in Atacheo, Olivia had a very active life. She belonged to a dance club. Rehearsals and performances took up most of her evenings and weekends. Although she helped her mother around the house, she did not feel it was her primary responsibility. In Napa, however, it was her duty to look after her little brothers, Juancho and Pepillo, and the house. Because her parents are always working, she usually finds herself home alone.

When I asked Dulce the same question, she shared a similar routine of housework, babysitting, and lots of time on her own.

D: Well, um, when school's out, I take the bus. It drops me off over there by Old Sonoma [Road]. I walk home with a friend [Olivia]. Then after I get home, I start making dinner, usually something my mom told me to cook, so I do that. Then, I clean the house. We eat, I take a shower, then I do my homework and go to sleep.

LS: Is it your responsibility to clean the house?

D: Well, no. I think it's my mom's, but, like, she gets home tired and so I have to help her cook or help her clean up. We just clean on the surface because we do a more thorough clean on Saturdays. That's the day when we usually clean.

LS: How about on a Friday night? What do you do?

D: Well, sometimes at night, like, when I get out of the shower, I watch *telenovelas* or just whatever is on TV. Sometimes I listen to music and I go to sleep. Other times I snack.

LS: Saturday or Sunday?

D: Well, on Saturdays I clean the house. I take a shower. Sometimes I visit my aunt who lives right next door. I spend the whole day there. Sometimes when my mom gets home from work, we'll go to the store. We go to Walmart to buy stuff or to Ross and then we come home.

Dulce is not allowed to go out with her friends other than to the park with Olivia because her parents do not want her out too late. She would like to go out, especially to dances. On rare occasions, she is allowed to go with her aunt who is forty years old. Things may change soon for Dulce, however, as her sister who has been living in New York and is only a couple of years older will be moving to Napa. I assume that, once her sister arrives, they may discuss the contrast between the hustle and bustle of New York and the calmness of Napa. Perhaps Dulce will be allowed to go out more when her sister arrives. Amid the mundane details that Dulce provides, examples of her duties and responsibilities are clear. Both her parents work and so she spends very little time with them. Like Olivia, Dulce spends a lot of her time on her own.

Silvia also spends a lot of time on her own. From Monday to Friday, she is at school. When she gets home, her routine is similar to that of Dulce and Olivia.

> S: I get out [of school] at three. We get out and, um, I walk to the bus stop with a friend of mine and catch the bus to get home. I get home and I start cleaning up. No one is usually home. My little brother goes out to play with his friends and I stay home alone. I clean up and start cooking. I clean the big house, sweep and mop. When I'm alone, I usually do my homework. Before six, I go into the house and take a shower. By the time I get out, my dad's home. My mom's the last one to get home, usually between eight and nine at night. We eat and that's about it.
>
> LS: What do you do on weekends?
>
> S: I stay home . . . like, on Saturdays, no one is home because everyone works. I stay home alone. There's a girl who lives here too and we chat sometimes. Sometimes we go shopping or window-shopping!
>
> LS: Where do you go?
>
> S: She has a truck and we go to Mervyn's or Ross.
>
> LS: Do you go to the flea market?
>
> S: I hardly ever go to the flea market because they never take us, but I'd like to go more because you run into people from your hometown, you smile at them and remember La Estancia. Or, when you run into them, it brings back memories and I like that. It keeps the memories alive. Every time I go there, I smell perfumes I used to smell at the

tianguis [Mexican Flea Market] in La Estancia . . . I like going, but we
just don't go that often.

The pattern continues with Silvia's narrative. She describes coming
home from school to her household obligations. Her parents are usually
at work, so she spends a lot of time on her own. Because her family rents
a room in the back of the house, Silvia has to go into the main house to
cook and to use the bathroom. She showers early so as to not be in the
way when the family, who live in the main house, returns. When she
lived in Mexico, she used to spend a lot of time with her mother. Now,
her mother is hardly home. This is an adjustment she was not quite prepared for.

Leti describes a similar routine:

Sometimes we have a lot of homework. I do my homework but, at times,
my little brother wants me to take him to the park. He's still little, well,
he's almost ten years old, but still likes to run around, like, he's very active
and he tells me, "Leti, let's go to the park!" and I say, "All right! Let's go!"
And that's what we do. Sometimes he'll ask how to do things [homework]
and I tell him but I get frustrated when he does not get it so I stop and
think about how I was when I was his age and so I find other ways to
explain things to him. But, usually, as soon as I get home from school,
I clean up and cook. On weekends, I clean a lady's house. Sometimes,
when there are parties, we go and, if not, we're home . . . it really varies.
We don't do the same things every Saturday. But, on Sundays, we usually
go to church. Sometimes we go to Yountville or to the store with friends,
to Mervyn's, Ross, Walmart . . . Sometimes we go to the mall in Fairfield.

Leti has lived in the U.S. longer than the other girls, which perhaps
explains why she seems to have a more active social life. In her answers,
Leti actually mentions friends, whereas the other girls mention mainly
family members or immediate neighbors. Yet again, a predictable pattern appears: cooking, cleaning, and looking after younger siblings. Leti
is the one in charge of raising her little brother because her parents are
always at work.

After school, Lucy stays home and does her homework. She likes to
do the extra credit worksheets on her English Language Development

workbook. When she is finished, she watches *telenovelas* for three hours. Sometimes, she strolls to a nearby park or joins her sister Eliza and her older sister on an outing to Walmart. When I asked her about the wineries, she told me that she had been there once. Shortly after her arrival in Napa, she said, "we were just there, looking at the grapes, like, there are different types of grapes." I asked her if she ever thought about working in the wineries and she said no. Her father, she says, did not bring them to the U.S. just so they could work in the fields. For Lucy, a winery means fields and fieldwork. What her father does not want is for her to be "killing [herself] all day." Instead of visiting wineries, Lucy spends her time with her family. On Saturdays, they usually stay at home. On Sundays, they first go to mass and then to *el remate*: "we go to the flea market. And then my sister has to go to work. Then, from three on, um, we just stay home. Then my aunt calls to, like, they make something like *carne asada*, so then we go over to my aunt's." Thus, Lucy's family also joins the Sunday pilgrimage to *el remate*. The rest of the time, when not at school, Lucy stays home reading and practicing her English.

The majority of the girls interviewed mentioned Walmart, Ross, Mervyn's, and the flea market as their afterschool or weekend shopping destinations. Other girls shared similar stories. Elena (chapter 5) related that: "[the flea market] was one of the first places we visited." Sixteen-year-old Pati recalls all of the stories she had heard about *el remate*: "when I first got here, I remember my friends would say, 'oh, I went to the flea market, I went to the flea market, I went to the flea market.' They all had gone to the flea market and had seen each other there! I was the only one who had gone to the mall. I'd tell my mom, 'I want to go to the flea market, I want to go to the flea market.'" So they went to *el remate*. None of the other girls had much knowledge of or experience at the tourists' shopping destinations. Only Leti said the following about the Up Valley wineries: "well, at times we'd go to the wineries without really wanting to because my mom used to work there and, like, she worked at the wineries, well, we'd go pick her up. At times we'd go in and see all, all that was there, the machines and all." For her and her family, these were not tourist destinations, but places of work.

These girls spend the majority of their time at home. As studies of immigrant communities have shown, including Nora Hamilton and Norma Stoltz Chinchilla's (2001) *Seeking Community in a Global City*, over time immigrants begin to settle down and become familiar with the spaces they inhabit. However, no amount of settling transforms the girls' perceptions of their town's major industry. The girls' stories confirm the shared experience of the highway 29 journey that sends tourists north to wineries and Mexican immigrants south to *el remate* on a weekly basis. Their only personal connection to the wine industry emerged when they or a family member worked at the wineries or vineyards.

Once the girls arrive in Napa they also begin to experience the limitations placed on their movement based on the assumed dangers of U.S. society. Suddenly they have to ask permission from both parents before they can go out. For many, this necessity is completely startling. They also find that their gender determines this necessity. Their families suddenly begin treating girls differently. They become in charge of the household labor and childcare. Fathers who had not previously been consistently present in their lives become in charge of the household. Their mothers, many of whom had held the family together in Mexico while the men worked abroad, now allow the men to take full control of their daughters and their whereabouts. In Mexico, Dulce had heard that Napa was a "pretty" place where she could go anywhere she pleased. Instead, she found the opposite to be true. Her father hardly ever allows her to go anywhere outside the home where she and the majority of the other girls are stuck looking after their younger brothers and sisters. Only when an older sibling or a parent returns can they go out. No longer can the girls casually hang out after school with their friends as they had in Mexico.

Conclusion

The girls arrived in Napa at a time when the wine and tourist industry was at its peak, and the city of Napa was undergoing major transformations. This historical temporality created tourist spaces that they did not visit, but also a new migrant underscape composed of parks, the church, the flea market, and discount stores in shopping malls.[88] Migrant time transformed the spaces of their households through new gendered and age-related obligations and responsibilities. They also found that they spend a lot of time on their own.

Migrant imaginaries emerge from, and speak back to, new temporalities and spatialities. The girls arrive in Napa at a historical time of an economic boom based on tourism and wine-making, which is also the time of an economic crisis in Mexico orchestrated by neoliberal patterns of investment, austerity, and labor control. These factors make them move across specific spaces, from Mexico to Napa most obviously, but also south on highway 29 on Sundays rather than north, and to the church, the flea market, and the discount store rather than to the upscale restaurant or winery. The long hours that their parents work, coupled with their gendered household responsibilities, shape the temporality of their daily round. The personal freedom and consumer-centered modernity that they envisioned has not yet arrived.

Conclusion

This book examines the lived experiences of Mexican teenage girls raised in transnational families and the varied ways they make meaning of their lives. Interviews with some sixty girls conducted over a six-year period in Napa, California, and Zinapécuaro, Michoacán, reveal the ways in which gender and generation shape perceptions of place and time. There is no uniform, universal, and undifferentiated migrant experience. Migrants do not so much move transnationally from Mexico to the U.S., but rather travel translocally from Zinapécuaro, Atacheo, and Morelia to Napa, Chicago, and Portland. The traditional distinction in migration scholarship between countries of origin and countries of arrival becomes complicated when girls in Mexico grow up as migrants in waiting exposed to many aspects of modern life in the U.S. via images and products present in global commercial culture, as well as from return migration, circular migration, temporary visits, and texts, phone calls, and letters from family members across the border. Even when they live in the same geographic locality, access to and control over space differ for men and women or for girls and boys.

Movement across space influences the experience of time. Within transnational families, it is often the father who migrates first, creating a time lag that is lived in the mode of seemingly endless waiting: waiting for remittances sent home, waiting for the return of absent family members, waiting to migrate sequentially. Adolescence is generally a time of waiting, expectation, and anticipation, but the life course of migrant girls entails additional dimensions of uncertainty and interruption. Just as migration shapes the chronology of individual life courses, it also produces distinct temporalities in the daily round of migrant girls. As the global economy outsources the burdens of neoliberal economics onto individual migrant workers, those workers expect their wives to take on new public and private roles, which they can only do by outsourcing cleaning, cooking, and childcare to their daughters. Thus, the sense of suspended animation and living in a time lag that permeated their lives as migrants in waiting endures at the place of arrival as girls wait for their school day to end, for their parents to return from long hours at work, for the brief opportunities they have to socialize or go shopping with each other.

The temporality of migration is not only personal and private, but also public and political. Centuries of theory and practice organized around the idea that Mexico needs to enter modernity configures the nation's economy and political system as suspended in time, as not yet fully what it wishes to be. Transnational living is similar. It is about short-term sacrifices for long-term benefits. Girls are raised in transnational families that are fractured by migratory practices. Assurance that their future will be better is always present. This, too, has to do with the temporality of transnational families. It resonates with the sacrifices that the Mexican nation-state implemented during *la crisis*. This is a lesson that I argue the girls and their fathers learned well.

Yet the ideal of and imperative for linear chronological progress in time conflicts radically with the actual changes over time that the economy and the political system perpetually produce. For the girls interviewed in this study, their fathers' migration did not take place because of a general upward movement toward modernity, but rather due to the failures of the modern system in the form of the peso devaluations and economic crises of the 1980s, and the devastating effects of free trade policies in the 1990s. Migrant girls in Napa in 2006 did not experience a smoothly functioning modern society, but rather faced a vicious and vile nativism legitimized by H.R. 4437, which threatened to criminalize their very existence.

The promises of modernity proffer an ideal of fulfillment, completion, and wholeness. Yet it works to produce vulnerability, powerlessness, unpredictability, and fragmentation. Migrant girls experience their lives betwixt and between nations, languages, locations, and different forms of family life.

Despite being victimized by patriarchal power, economic exploitation, and anti-immigrant suppression and oppression, migrant girls are not victims. They develop migrant imaginaries that empower a fragile agency that enables them to see themselves as active subjects rather than passive objects, to feel at home from afar, and to forge new forms of family affection and affiliation despite fragmentation.

Levitt and Glick Schiller illuminate an important dimension of temporality within transnational migration.[1] They explain that simultaneity, rather than sequentiality, now defines the migrant experience. The phone call, the text message, the online posting, and the satellite transmission of news and entertainment all rely on a simultaneity that blurs the borders that demarcate nations. They produce discursive spaces that transcend the borders of physical places and bounded territories. Within transnational migration, the concept of simultaneity pervades intimate and personal events and experiences: a celebration, the birth of a child, a school graduation, and other emotional occurrences and occasions that allow families separated by borders to participate in the same event. Yet as Nowotny reminds us, the mere existence of simultaneity "does not automatically become translatable to equality."[2] Differently positioned people receiving the same message remain differently situated. In this book I look at the unequal aspects of simultaneity by adding the temporal and spatial imaginaries of Mexican teenage girls to the study of the migrant experience.

The family experiences of migrant girls differ from those prescribed by the dominant culture through its idealization of the heterosexual, heteronormative nuclear family. They often experience this difference as an injury needing repair. They long for the sense of wholeness and fulfillment that family reunification seems to promise. Yet their fragmented family form also enables the emergence of improvisation and adaptation, of the development of new gender roles, new patterns of connection and care, new hybrid literacies and epistemologies.

I argue that, in some ways, Mexican teenage girls inhabit a borderlands: a place where cultures meet.[3] Girls occupy spaces of movement and migration where different ideas are circulated that produce multiple desires. Their experience suggests some generalizable hypotheses about the migration process itself—about its multiplicity, plurality, and diversity, its differentiations across genders and generations, and also its seemingly unexpected opportunities. My interviews conducted in California in 2006 and in Michoacán in 2010 with some sixty girls do not provide a basis for statistic generalizability. The particularities of these girls' places of residence in Mexico and the U.S. inhibit generalizations about migration in other locations. The historical background of longstanding migration patterns and systems of labor control link-ing the U.S. and Mexico and the particular consequences of economic crises, free trade agreements, abandonment of the social wage by governments, and virulent anti-Mexican nativism inflect the testimonies I elicited with specific and particular dimensions that cannot necessarily be generalized or easily transformed into law-like generalizations. Yet the very specificity of these aspects of the interviews underscores the importance of the particularities of place and the constraints of time. Moreover, within the times and place central to this study, some generalizations about gender, generation, and migration may well be warranted.

My aim in coupling these two sets of interviews is to highlight both the ruptures and continuities, the similarities and the differences attendant to girls growing up in transnational families. The two sets of interviews allow for a connective comparison of commonalities among both groups of girls. These commonalities include fathers' departures and commutes to the U.S. since the 1980s and 1990s, and external conditions—historic, structural, and economic—that led to their movement. These are tied to the ways U.S. immigration policies dictate the migrant experience of fathers. The "structure of feeling" that the girls from Zinapécuaro and Napa share is one that marks, inhabits, and processes the affective consequences of growing up in transnational families and within transnational social fields.

Yet even these commonalities are experienced differently. The Zinapécuaro interviews feature girls who are not necessarily saddened by their fathers' commutes. This differs from the affect permeating the Napa interviews. The girls in Napa describe growing up without a father in terms of injury and loss. This was less often the case for the Zinapécuaro girls whose absorption into life in Mexico seems to make them less concerned with their fathers' absences. Perhaps the physical act of migration and its subsequent consequences take a greater toll than researchers and even migrants themselves have realized. Upon migration, the Napa girls had to adjust to a new place, to a new racial order, to a new class configuration in a very different economy, and to new metrics of gender propriety and sexual respectability. In Napa, they reassess the father-daughter relationship. The girls from Zinapécuaro who have yet to experience migration live among the familiar and have yet to feel the full burdens of the family fragmentation dictated by the burdens of new economic and political practices. In the act of crossing, as De La Garza argues, migrant girls can annul a big part of who they were and be overwhelmed by the challenges of who they are becoming.[4]

Napa girls remembered having desires for migration ever since they could recall. A version of Napa already existed in their lives before they left Mexico. Some resented having their desires to migrate thwarted by their fathers. They saw their brothers get special consideration and treatment in the migration process. As I describe in chapter 4, some fathers expressly tell their daughters they do not want to share their social capital with them and therefore do not want to bring them to the U.S. As the interviews reveal again and again, though, the girls are not simply passive victims bereft of agency. They create new forms of affiliation and activity on both sides of the border in response to the disruptions and fragmentations they encounter. They learn to live without wholeness, closure, and finality, to adjust and improvise in the face of new challenges, to forge an understanding of home that does not require a heteronormative nuclear household living without interruption in a single location.

Placing Mexican teenage girls at the center of the study of migration shows how migration shapes and reflects new experiences of gender within the life course. An ethos of patriarchal protection relegates some girls to remaining in Mexico longer than they would like. An economic and political system that lures fathers away from home to work in a country with higher wages can leave wives and daughters feeling abandoned. A descending spiral of gendered power compels women to make up for the wages and reproductive household labor lost when men leave, which they accomplish by recruiting their daughters into premature roles doing childcare for siblings and work outside the home while also finishing school. The effects of these gendered practices do not preclude agency, per se; instead, they can sometimes provoke it. Mothers with partners away take on new roles in the economy and the household that become models for their daughters. The daughters learn that their city in Mexico is connected to a broader field of action that traverses borders. They forge new identities from engaging with more than one space, more than one language, more than one consumer economy, and more than one kind of family network of affection and connection. Mexican girls negotiate complex tensions and contradictions in a world shaped by migrant practices and imaginaries.

Migrant imaginaries help us understand how families can function differently, how idealized constructions always bend to objective needs. In the context of a migration economy, it is difficult to accept the nuclear heteronormative family as either natural or necessary. Migration does not destroy the wholeness of such families, because centuries of father-away labor have impeded their formation and impelled the creation of different kinds of households characterized by different relations between genders and generations. We need to move beyond the romantic myth of one kind of family as natural, necessary, and inevitable, and recognize the plurality and diversity of networks of affiliation and affection made necessary by systematic inequality and exploitation.

When teenage girls are also placed at the center of the immigration story, age, gender, and sex come into clear relief as modalities in which migration is experienced. Teenage girls live in the same chronological time as the rest of their families, but the waiting that they constantly practice promotes a different understanding of temporality. Migrant teenage girls live within the same geographic and juridical boundaries as all of the other residents of Napa and Zinapécuaro, but living in transnational families creates for them cognitive mappings that make each locality a part of the other.

The testimonies presented and analyzed in this book are stories of young women trying to make sense of their lives, of their present and possible future in a world that they did not make and do not control—they are stories of affect and injury, but also of agency and improvisation. They have much to teach us, as they contain intimate and powerful understandings of the complex processes put in play by movement and migration.

ACKNOWLEDGMENTS

As George Lipsitz always says, "writing and research are often conducted in solitude, but never in isolation." I would like to thank those who have been present, in my life, during this writing process. Thank you for allowing me to be and to think.

I was lucky to attend the University of California, Berkeley, where I was part of the Ethnic Studies PhD program. I knew I wanted to write about the experiences of young Mexican teenage girls. The courses, conversations, faculty, staff, classmates, and friends there shaped my methodological, theoretical, and epistemological approach while providing support and good laughs. As a student, I had the privilege of taking courses and working with some of the best faculty at Berkeley: Patricia Penn Hilden, José David Saldívar, Barrie Thorne, Victoria Robinson, Carlos Muñoz, Jr., Mario Barrera, Nelson Maldonado-Torres, and Ruth Wilson Gilmore. The staff—including Lourdes Franco Martínez, Dewey St. Germaine, Laura Jimenez-Olvera, Francisca Cazares, and Jahleezah Eskew—was always supportive and kind. Special thanks to Dulcinea Lara, Gerardo Arellano, Martin Olea, Jordan Gonzales, Clement Lai, John Torok, Mercy Romero, Agustin Palacios, and Julian Ledesma for the conversations, writing groups, comradery and friendship.

I would like to give thanks for the support I received from U.C. Berkeley, including the Graduate Opportunity Grant, the Mentored Research Award, The Bancroft Library Study Award, and several Block Grants. Laura Perez and Nelson Maldonado-Torres awarded me a Block Grant so that I could focus on my writing for the last few months.

I began my research by conducting interviews at Napa High School in Napa, California. I thank principal Barbara Franco and counselor Guadalupe Martinez Ramirez for assisting in the recruitment process. I would also like to thank Angelica Celis for allowing me to sit in on a program of young Latinas, which allowed me to work with her students.

One of my most productive periods was during the 2006–2007 academic year when I was a writing fellow at the Department of Feminist Studies at U.C. Santa Barbara. I would like to thank Barbara Tomlinson, Eileen Boris, Mireille Miller-Young, Leila J. Rupp, Siobhan Brooks-King, and Lou Anne Lockwood for their warmth and support during my stay.

I was awarded the University of California President's Postdoctoral Fellowship at U.C. Los Angeles where I immediately joined a writing group with other fellows in the Chicana/o Studies Department. It was during this time that I began to publish. I thank Ofelia Ortiz Cuevas, Leisy J. Abrego, and Sylvanna M. Falcón for sharing their work and writing tips with me.

While at UCLA, I traveled to Zinapécuaro, Michoacán, to conduct research. I thank my cousins Chilo and Chole for helping me with recruiting teenage girls from their local neighborhood. My tía Lucina, who was still alive then, made sure I completed the number of interviews I said I would do. Whenever I would go to her house, she would ask me how the interviews were going and if I needed more girls to interview. It has been so special to me to know that part of this project is homegrown. I thank my cousins and my tía for allowing me to feel that family can also be part of research.

The University of Wyoming has provided tremendous assistance— both personal and professional—that has facilitated the completion of this project. I would like thank Vanessa Fonseca, Irlanda Jacinto, Margarita Pignataro, Eric Sandeen, Frieda Knobloch, Andrea Graham, Jo-Anna Poblete, Nicole Choi, and the amazing Sophia Beck. UW has also provided funding from the International Programs Office, the Caitlin Long Excellence Fund, the Social Justice Research Center, and the Basic Research Grant. The American Studies program has been nothing but supportive of my research and I thank both Eric and Frieda for being so willing to help in any way they could. Frieda Knobloch has been one of the biggest cheerleaders I have encountered at UW. I especially thank Frieda for believing in me and my work. I also feel lucky that I get to see Sophie every day at UW. Her words and blessings brighten my day. I also thank my students Alin Badillo Carrillo, Norma Lira-Pérez, Bianca Infante, Jordan Norviel, Josh Sainz, Mike Morrow, Jose Rivas, and Sandra Loza. They make me a better teacher, researcher, and overall a much more grounded human being. My time at UW is all the better because I get to work with such a wonderful group of students.

I would also like to thank the Ford Foundation for awarding me a Postdoctoral Fellowship for the 2012–2013 academic year. My mentor Leo R. Chavez at U.C. Irvine has been one of the best mentors I have ever had. He read my work, offered critical feedback, and shared readings that made me a better scholar. During my time there, I began to meet weekly with my dear friend Gerardo Arellano. We shared our writing and exchanged ideas. There are no words to describe how much I benefitted from Gerardo's keen insight. I thank Gerardo for taking the time to read my work, ask questions, and offer suggestions. I could not have finished this project without his assistance.

The last part of the writing benefitted from my participation in The Bancroft Seminar on Latina/o History at U.C. Berkeley. I thank David Montejano for the invitation. The brilliant Pablo Gonzalez offered thorough feedback. Pablo's comments made me feel like my work mattered. My participation in the National Endowment for the Humanities (NEH) summer seminar "The Cross-Border Connection: Immigrants, Emigrants, and their Homelands" under the directorship of Roger Waldinger in 2015 could not have come at a better time. The six weeks we spent reading and discussing transnational migration strengthened my understanding of migration. I thank all of the participants for sharing their work and ideas. Finally, George Lipsitz organized a School Of Unlimited Learning writing workshop where I had the opportunity to share (and finish) the manuscript. I thank Jason Ferreira, Melissa Guzman, Patrick Lopez-Aguado, Manuel Callahan, Jodi Rios, Yoel Haile, Sunny Lim, and Orlando Carreon for taking the time to read the manuscript and offer valuable feedback.

I thank my dear friends who are very close to my heart. I do not see them enough, but I have felt their love and support for many, many years. I thank my amigas Dulcinea Lara, Mary Claire Gatmaitan, Elizabeth Romero, and Hermelinda Gonzalez.

Mentorship has been key for me. I have been blessed to encounter Patricia Penn Hilden and George Lipsitz, and to have them in my life. I do not know how I got so lucky. During my first semester at Berkeley, I was trying to figure out which classes to take. I was debating between two classes and Jahleezah Eskew recommended Pat's class. This was back in 2001. I remember that, early on in the semester, Pat asked us to email her ideas for the research paper we would turn in at the end of the term. I sent her some random notes on wanting to write about Mexican immigrant girls, to hear and give voice to their stories. During the following class, we shared our ideas with our classmates. Pat made me feel like I had something smart to say and write about. That year, she took about eight students under her wing. I was one of them and have not let go. She has been so encouraging since. I thank Pat for her continued guidance and friendship.

I remember stumbling into George Lipsitz's office for office hours back in 1995 while I was an undergraduate at U.C. San Diego. I had received a low grade on a midterm and wanted to know how I could improve my grade. That has turned into at 20+-year mentor/mentee relationship. I write what I write and do what I do because I have benefitted from his guidance. I cannot thank him enough for all of his help with this project. I could not have finished it without his endless assistance. His mentorship and trust have meant the world to me.

To my *familia*: I come from a family of *campesinos* with very limited schooling. My father Matias taught himself how to read and write when he was eight years old by copying the shapes of letters from magazines and newspapers he found. So he learned the alphabet. My mother Maria Elena has a sixth-grade education. Somehow their love and curiosity for knowledge allowed them to raise six daughters—four of us have varied kinds of college degrees. I do not know what they did or how they did it, *pero no me va a alcanzar la vida para agradecerles. Gracias por hacerme y dejarme ser. Hermanas*, I hope to continue to lean on you for love, support, and encouragement. We are *las chiquillas*. To the next generation— Jiulian, Sofia, my beloved Eztli, and Jay Jay—let's continue to grow and to be. Thank you for showing me patience and unconditional love.

Finally, I thank all of the girls who trusted me with their stories. I am deeply sorry that I cannot name them. I hope that those who read their stories will find power and strength in them as I have. I wrote the book hoping to share the stories of migration that are rarely heard. These girls' stories are painful testimonies of the consequences of migration and transnational familial formations, but also of imagining a different future. During these very tough times filled with hate and anti-immigrant sentiment, we have to continue to talk about people's lives in humanizing ways and to imagine a different present and future. I hope that this book contributes, even if only a little, to changing the conversation of how we view peoples' movement across international borders.

NOTES

INTRODUCTION

1 I then traveled to Mexico to conduct interviews there. For analytical purposes, and as will be examined further in this chapter, I invert time periods and I begin with Mexico, as accounts of migration usually do.

2 I actually interviewed twenty girls: nineteen Mexican and one Guatemalan. I chose to omit the story of sixteen-year-old Erika because the context of Guatemala shapes her migratory journey before, during, and after migration. I felt I could not do her story justice by overlooking her Guatemalan background and context the way I write about Mexico, as it is beyond the scope of this project.

3 This speaks to a trend within migration studies whereby new areas of focus seem to replace and move away from earlier findings. For example, the late 1990s and early 2000s witnessed a wide range of studies on transnational motherhood that replaced dated frames of study pointing to varied definitions and forms of mothering. From roughly 2005 to the present, the frame has turned to the deportation of families on the U.S. side of the border. During the Obama administration, we witnessed a high increase in deportation practices and the breakup of families. The focus has turned to the detention of Central American children traveling by themselves to the U.S. This book brings the focus back to the initial formation of a transnational family, because one trend does not replace another. For a partial literature list on transnational motherhood, see: Dreby 2006; Parreñas 2005; Schmalzbauer 2004; Levitt 2001; Michele Ruth Gamburd 2000; Pierrette Hondagneu-Sotelo and Avila 1997. For transnational families, see: Abrego 2014; Dreby 2010; and Hondagneu-Sotelo 1994. For President Barack Obama's deportation practices, see: Dickson 2014. For recent stories of the detention of children, see: Dart 2014.

4 "Commute" here simply means the pattern of comings and goings fathers established as they traveled between Mexico and the U.S. for work. It is similar to what Roger Rouse (1989) calls "shuttling," which he explains as the movement between Aguililla, Michoacán, and Redwood City, California. Those who "shuttled" between these two locations were unable to stay connected and informed of matters that happened in either place. In the *Crucible of Struggle*, Zaragosa Vargas (2010) also refers to these types of migrants as commuters. I opt to use the word "commute" because it gives a sense of where the girls think their father lives and works. Fathers, according to the girls, only go to the U.S. for work—they engage in long

commutes to return home after their labor journey is completed. See: Rouse 1989 and Vargas 2010.

5 Patricia Zavella documents how Mexican men suspend familial formations when they travel to the U.S. for work. See: Zavella 2011.

6 In the next pages, I explain why I selected Napa and Zinapécuaro.

7 Gordon 1997.

8 Salazar 2010.

9 Jessica finally moved to the U.S. on January 28, 2013. Her journey will be discussed in chapter 4.

10 Camila was not accepted into the Military Medical School. By 2014, she was in her last year of college completing a bachelor's degree in nursing.

11 By spring of 2014, Toñita was in her third year of high school.

12 As will be examined in chapters 5 and 6, what this tells me is that a change unfolds when migration actually happens and girls reassess their pre-migration lives.

13 Levitt and Glick Schiller 2004, 1009.

14 Zavella (2011, 8) defines peripheral vision as "based on frequent reminders that one's situation is unstable in comparison to those on the other side."

15 Massey 1999.

16 Abrego 2014, 59.

17 Hondagneu-Sotelo (1994) says women had to develop their own social networks as the husbands sometimes did not want to bring them.

18 Unlike the current crisis of Central American children migrating by themselves, and as I will explain in the latter part of the chapter, girls in this study are not likely to migrate on their own.

19 Schmidt Camacho 2008.

20 Dalsgård and Frederiksen 2014, 9.

21 Salazar 2010, 56.

22 Schmidt Camacho 2008, 5.

23 Salazar 2010, 56.

24 Schmidt Camacho 2008, 4.

25 Ibid, 5.

26 Dalsgård and Frederiksen 2014, 10.

27 I borrow the phrases "separated by borders" or "divided by borders" from Dreby (2010).

28 Ngai 2005.

29 Hall 1987, 4.

30 Williams 2001, 64.

31 Storey 2006, 35.

32 See: Lowe 2002, 3; and Gilmore 2016.

33 Zavella 2011, 10.

34 In the section on transnationalism, I qualify my use of the term diaspora.

35 Appadurai 1996, 4. See also: Martínez 2001.

36 Pitti 2003.

37 Levitt and Glick Schiller 2004.

38 Schmidt Camacho 2008, 1.

39 Glick Schiller, Basch, and Blanc-Szanton 1992, 1.

40 Levitt 2001, 11; Perez 2004; Stephen 2007; Zavella 2011.

41 Levitt and Glick Schiller 2004, 1004.

42 Tsuda 2012, 632.

43 Waldinger and Fitzgerald 2004.

44 Anderson 1992, 2.

45 Glick Schiller 2005, 290.

46 Levitt and Glick Schiller 2004, 1022.

47 Hondagneu-Sotelo and Avila state that a transnational approach to migration may lead to an "understate [of] the permanency of Latino/a immigrant settlement." See: Hondagneu-Sotelo and Avila 1997, 6.

48 See for example: Stephen 2007.

49 Waldinger and Fitzgerald 2004, 1193.

50 See: Demmers 2002.

51 Hall 1987.

52 Quijano (2007) examines the idea of "better" being somewhere else. He explores the transformation of Western ways as an aspiration for citizens of non-Western spheres as "a way of participating and later to reach the same material benefits and the same power as Europeans." I explore this in latter chapters. See: Quijano 2007, 169.

53 Bonfil Batalla 1996 and García Canclini 1995.

54 Fabian 1983.

55 See also: Quijano 2007 and 2000.

56 In *Against War*, Maldonado-Torres (2008) cites Sylvia Wynter who says that it constitutes not only a denial of coevalness but a denial of humanness—meaning, "the discourse and practices of racialization and their many contributions with other forms of difference" (xii).

57 García Canclini 1995, 2.

58 Amuchástegui 1998, 107.

59 I borrow this observation from Martínez (2001).

60 Appadurai 1996, 2.

61 Nowotny 1994, 33.

62 Cole 2008, 102.

63 Bauman 2003.

64 Flaherty 2014, 178.

65 Honwana 2012, 4.

66 Cole and Durham 2008, 10.

67 Flanagan 2008, 126.

68 Jeffrey 2010, 12.

69 Honwana 2012.

70 Weinbaum et al., 2008, 9.

71 See for example: Valenzuela 1999; Bettie 2003; Mendoza-Denton 2008; García 2012.

72 This is not the case in novels and memoirs. See for example: Santiago 1993; Pérez 1999; Danticat 2007; Grande 2006 and *2012*.

73 Hall 1987, 4.

74 Martínez 2001, 66.

75 Espiritu 2003, 179.

76 Like Marcelo and Carola Suárez-Orozco (2001), Abel Valenzuela Jr. (1999) examines how immigrant boys and girls are gendered differently in the U.S. For children, gender differences also take place before migration. When we account for age, gender, and sex before migration, patriarchal and sexist narratives evolve.

77 Hondagneu-Sotelo 1994, 3.

78 Chavez 1992, 4; Martínez 2001; Massey, Durand, and Malone 2002.

79 Hondagneu-Sotelo 2003, 5.

80 Ibid, 7.

81 Ibid, 9.

82 See for example: Segura and Zavella 2007; González-López 2005.

83 Cantú 2009, 132; Carrillo 2004; González-López 2005.

84 Minian 2012.

85 Thorne 2004, 404.

86 Flaherty 2014, 187.

87 Weinbaum et al. 2008, 3.

88 Marcus 1995, 96.

89 Rosaldo 1993, 17.

90 As will be discussed in chapter one, *Televisa* also aired similar commercials in the 1980s.

91 "Elas [sic] Son" 2010.

92 Kilkenny 2012.

93 Reyes 2012.

94 Azul 2012.

95 I keep thinking of the different experiences between the girls in this study and the Central American children traveling on their own.

96 "Is Mexico 'under siege'?" 2011.

97 Pallares and Flores-Gonzalez 2010.

98 Glaister and MacAskill 2006.

99 Napa High School: A California Distinguished School, *"Focus on Learning WASC Self Study~*2009–2010," n.d., www.nvusd.granicus.com.

100 Napa High School 2016.

101 Massey and Malone 2002; Massey, Alarcon, Durand, and Gonzalez 1990.

102 Appadurai 1996, 2.

103 Salazar 2010, 56.

104 See: De Genova 2002, 424, and Sassen 1998, 56. The latter citation comes from De Genova's article.

CHAPTER 1. THE WHY OF TRANSNATIONAL FAMILIAL FORMATIONS

1 Zavella 2011, 135.
2 *La Michoacana* is Morelia's main public university, the Universidad Michoacana de San Nicolas de Hidalgo. It is commonly known as *La Michoacana*. *La Normal* is short for La Escuela Normal Superior de Michoacán. *La Normal* is the school where students who hope to become teachers enroll. I discuss this more thoroughly in chapter 3.
3 Parreñas 2005.
4 Massey, Durand, and Malone 2002.
5 Still, by 1924, Mexicans were racialized as white, and therefore considered citizens. See: Ngai 2005, 50–52; Lopez 2006; Gómez 2007; Zavella 2011, 28; Molina 2013, 2 and 16.
6 This citation and reference comes from De Genova's article. See: De Genova, 424; Sassen, 56. Please note that this is mentioned in the introduction.
7 Massey et al. 2002, 25.
8 Pitti 2003.
9 Massey et al. 2002, 25.
10 As I write this chapter, at least two different migratory patterns have unfolded. First, a decrease in U.S.-bound Mexican migration. Passel et al. attribute the decrease to the U.S. economy, border enforcement, increase in deportations during the Obama administration, dangers in border crossing, and a decline in Mexico's birthrates (6). See: Passel, Gonzalez-Barrera, and Cohn 2012. Second, there has been an increase of women and children from Mexico and Central America who have arrived to the border and have been placed in detention centers. See: Preston 2014 and Belson 2014.
11 Rosas 2014.
12 De Genova 2002.
13 Massey et al. 2002.
14 Ngai 2005, 18.
15 Ibid, 20.
16 Ibid. 68; Lytle Hernández 2010, 2.
17 Stephen (2007) cites Carey McWilliams who stated that, during the period of repatriation, Mexicans continued to be recruited for work in Southern California. See Stephen 2007, 71.
18 See: Calavita 1992; David Gutiérrez 1995; Sanchez 1995; Ngai 2005, 129.
19 Ngai 2004, 139.
20 Rosas 2014, 6.
21 Massey 2002.
22 Ibid.
23 Parreñas 2005.
24 Hondagneu-Sotelo 2003.
25 González-López 2005.

26 Hondagneu-Sotelo 1994.
27 Stephen 2007, 124.
28 Ibid, 131.
29 Ibid.
30 Ibid, 134.
31 Please see note three in the introductory chapter.
32 Parreñas 2005.
33 Abrego 2014.
34 Anzaldúa 1987, 7.
35 Nevins 2002.
36 Ngai 2005.
37 Lytle-Hernández 2010, 1.
38 Ngai 2005, 61.
39 There are, of course, debates surrounding the cyclical—and thus temporary—
    nature of migration, which ignores its permanency.
40 Vargas 2010, 369–370.
41 Zavella 2011, 12.
42 See: Andreas 2000, 228, and Nevins 2002.
43 Andreas 2000.
44 Ibid.
45 Ibid, 7.
46 Alvarez Jr. 2005.
47 Abrego (2014) makes a similar observation.
48 Stephen 2007, 123–124.
49 Adler Hellman 1994, 224.
50 See: Escobar Lapatí and González de la Rocha 1995, 58; Lustig 1998, 17.
51 Stephen 2007, 123.
52 Castañeda notes the following: "In many cases, their ancestors began this rite of
    passage nearly a century ago." See: Castañeda 2009, 44.
53 Roger Rouse notes these satellite communities. See: Rouse 1991.
54 Lustig 1998, 17.
55 Grayson 1980, 142.
56 Hellman 1994, 6.
57 See: Paoli Bolio 1982, 70; Martínez Laguna 2004; Skidmore and Smith 1997, 252.
58 Skidmore and Smith 1997, 252.
59 Adler Hellman 1983.
60 Hellman 1983, 220.
61 Ibid, 220.
62 Hellman 1983, 224; 1994, 6.
63 Hellman 1983, 222.
64 Lomnitz-Adler 2003, 130.
65 Ibid, 133–134.
66 Ibid, 132.

67 Ibid, 134.

68 Ibid.

69 Haber et al. 2008, 1.

70 Escobar Lapatí and González de la Rocha 1995, 61.

71 Ibid, 63.

72 Ibid.

73 I remember growing up in Mexico in the early 1980s. My mother used to shop at the Conasupo in Morelia and purchase Aladino Peanut Butter. Our many visits to California made my sisters and me addicted to peanut butter and jelly sandwiches. Once GATT forced Mexico to open its markets, Skippy Peanut Butter replaced Aladino. Please note that Hellman also argues that Mexico's industry never produced enough to feed its citizens.

74 Debt negotiations offered little relief to Mexico, a pattern familiar elsewhere. When countries experience an economic crisis and turn to the International Monetary Fund (IMF) or the World Bank (WB) for loan relief, they are required to make structural adjustments. These include easing trade barriers, which then lead to foreign products flooding into local markets often sold at prices so low that local products cannot compete. Once the local economy is in shambles, a price increase on foreign products is made.

75 Escobar Lapatí and González de la Rocha 1995, 64.

76 Martínez Laguna 2004, 2036.

77 Ibid, 132.

78 The account of the chief of police known as El Negro Durazo serves as an example of how the narratives of sacrifice were only for the middle class and the working class. See: González González 1983.

79 Adam McKeown makes a similar argument about Chinese migrant networks and migrants. See: McKeown 2001.

80 Massey and Singer 1995.

81 Bacon 2004, 44.

82 Castañeda 1995, 26.

83 Bonfil Batalla 1996.

84 Bacon 2004, 46.

85 Ibid, 48.

86 Pacheco-López 2005, 1169.

87 Castañeda 2009, 30.

88 Zavella 2011.

89 Smith 2002, 435.

90 Lomnitz-Adler 2003.

91 Ibid, 132.

92 Appadurai 1996, 153.

93 Cole and Durham 2008.

94 Schmidt Camacho 2008, 5.

95 Salazar 2011, 577.

96 Appadurai 1996, 1.
97 Dussel 2016.
98 Appadurai 1996, 1.
99 Quijano 2007.
100 Hall 1996, 1.
101 Rogers 2016.
102 Massey, Arango, Hugo, Kouaouci, Pellegrino, and Taylor 1993, 451.

CHAPTER 2. GROWING UP TRANSNATIONAL

1 These were 2010 prices.
2 Marisela was actually born in Los Angeles, California, to Mexican parents. She migrated to Mexico for her singing career. During the 1980s, her music was heard all over Mexico as one of the country's main producers was supporting her. Marisela was the Selena of the 1980s, pre-Selena.
3 Anzaldúa 1987, preface.
4 Cuéntame. "Informacion por entidad." http://cuentame.inegi.org.mx/.
5 Rouse 1992.
6 López Lara 1977, 209.
7 Because the cross is made out of cornhusks, the box where El Señor is carried is not supposed to be heavy. However, according to those who have carried him, its weight depends on the carrier's sins. If a man with too many sins carries El Señor, it will feel very heavy. If a man has no sins, he will feel light.
8 The aquatic park of La Atzimba is named after the legend of Purépecha Princess. According to the legend, Princess Atzimba used to bathe in what are now swimming facilities after falling ill. After her tragic death, the town adopted her story and established a resort to attract visitors and its local and diasporic citizens. See: López Lara 1977, 39.
9 Gamboa 2013.
10 Jameson 1988, 347–357.
11 In their book, Weinbaum et al. look for the modern girl around the world during the first half of the twentieth century and examine what allowed for her to appear at a global level in various contexts. They examine sameness and difference of the modern girl and the uniqueness of each place in which she appeared. See: Weinbaum et al. 2008, 3.
12 Ibid.
13 Dreby 2006, 46.
14 Abrego 2014.
15 Zavella 2011.
16 Dreby 2006.
17 Gordon 1997.
18 Yola and Sara have an older sister who was born in Zinapécuaro. She cannot travel to the U.S. as she does not have legal documents, and therefore has even

less contact with her father. Their household in Mexico includes U.S. citizens—another aspect of mixed-status families common in the U.S.

19 Schooling practices will be explored in chapter 3.
20 Stephen 2007.
21 A discussion of EL CBTIS is included in chapter 3.

CHAPTER 3. *MUCHACHAS MICHOACANAS*

1 Fabian 1983.
2 "Televisa Lanza" 2010.
3 See for example: Galeano 1997.
4 "TV Azteca" 2009.
5 See for example: Paz 1994; Monsiváis 1978; Fuentes 1999.
6 See: Anzaldúa 1987.
7 I will mention a girl's age the first time she is introduced in the chapter.
8 Stephen (2007) makes a similar observation.
9 These were 2010 prices.
10 Salazar 2010, 57.
11 Ibid, 56.
12 Rosaldo 1993, 17.
13 Schmidt Camacho 2008.
14 Rosaldo 1993, 17.
15 Gordon 1997.
16 Although Lorena García's (2012, 5) ethnographic study is based in Chicago, Illinois, I borrow her concept as it is applicable to girls' lives in Mexico.
17 James 2001, 167–179.
18 García 2012, 74.
19 This argument reminds me of Barbara Tomlinson and George Lipsitz's assertion on neoliberalism: "It demands the individuation of collective social process." See: Tomlinson and Lipsitz 2013, 5.
20 García 2012, 74.
21 These were 2010 prices.
22 By 2012, Marbe was nineteen years old.
23 García 2012, 25.
24 González-López 2005, 5.
25 Directed by Juan Carlos Rulfo and Carlos Loret de Mola 2012.
26 These statistics are similar to those of U.S. Latinos. See: Yosso and Solórzano 2006.
27 García 2012, 5.
28 González-López 2005, 5.
29 The documentary *Los Que Se Quedan*—directed by Juan Carlos Rulfo and Carlos Hagerman (2010)—presents a visual representation of teenage girls and soccer teams as part of the afterschool and weekend activities.
30 García 2012.

CHAPTER 4. MIGRATION MARKS

1 Even before migrating to the U.S., Jessica is already treated as a second-class citizen.

2 As discussed in the introduction, Ngai (2005, 58) also discusses time lag in the migrant experience.

3 As discussed in the introduction, this type of suspension of the present is explored by Lomnitz-Adler. See: Lomnitz-Adler 2003.

4 Levitt 2001, 11; Perez 2004; Stephen 2007; Zavella 2011. Please note that this is also mentioned in earlier chapters.

5 Soja 1989, 10, citing Michel Foucault.

6 Soja 1989.

7 Pitti (2003, 18) says: "As in other parts of Alta California, bells rang throughout the day to mark the rhythms of daily life at Santa Clara and San Jose missions and to remind residents of the developing economic system."

8 Fabian 1983.

9 Original italics. See: Fabian 1983, 31.

10 In quoting Sylvia Wynter, Maldonado-Torres (2008) argues that it is not only the denial of coevalness but the denial of humanness—meaning, "the discourse and practices of racialization and their many contributions with other forms of difference." (xii). Please note that this is also discussed in the introduction.

11 Bonfil Batalla 1996.

12 Recent struggles in Chiapas demonstrate the continuity of much more ancient Mesoamerica than many Western observers have noted.

13 Lomnitz-Adler 2003, 127.

14 Fuentes 1999, 16.

15 García Canclini 1995, 47.

16 Amuchástegui Herrera 1998, 107. Please note that I say this in the introduction.

17 Hondagneu-Sotelo 1994.

18 Martínez 2001, 25.

19 Among others, see: Levitt 2001 and Farr 2005.

20 See: Martínez 2001; Stephen 2007; Flores 2007.

21 Levitt and Glick Schiller 2004, 1009.

22 Nowotny 1994, 27.

23 Ibid, 33.

24 Laguerre 2003.

25 Ibid, 2003, 2.

26 Dreby 2010, 33.

27 Ibid, 37.

28 Castañeda 2009, 16.

29 Manuel Gamio noted their economic contributions back in 1930 and 1931.

30 This rhetoric full of praises is also found among Filipino migrants who return to the Philippines. See: the documentary *Chain of Love* (Icarus Films, 2002).

31 Castañeda 2009, 5.

32 Martínez 2001, 25.

33 *La Fuerza del Destino*, n.d. www.imdb.com.

34 Directed by Gregory Nava and Anna Thomas. *El Norte*. Script City, 1983.

35 *La Academia*, n.d. www.imdb.com.

36 Pitti (2003) found that, as early as the 1860s, Mexican migration to the U.S. became common.

37 Paz 1994.

38 At the Immigration Symposium sponsored by the University of Wyoming on September 18, 2014, retired Wyoming Senator Alan K. Simpson spoke of the time he met Mexican president José López Portillo. This was a time when Simpson was trying to work on what became the Immigration Reform and Control Act of 1986. Simpson said that President López Portillo told him: "please treat them [Mexican immigrants] well."

39 Espiritu (2003) also argues that, by the time Filipino migrants arrive in the U.S., they are already racialized.

40 Zavella 2011.

41 Hall 1987.

42 Boehm et al. 2011, 17.

43 Please note that this is mentioned in earlier chapters.

44 Please note that Carmen's experiences are also discussed in chapters 2 and 3.

45 Both González-López 2005 and Zavella 2011 found experiences of men who drink in the U.S. to deal with family separation and melancholia.

46 Please note that Paloma is also discussed in earlier chapters.

47 Schmidt Camacho 2008.

48 Toñita and Emilia are her younger siblings. They were also interviewed.

49 Most recently, González-López (2005) has tackled one-dimensional portrayals of Mexican men as *machistas* and of patriarchy as these have led to stereotypes and generalizations. As mentioned in earlier chapters, González-López examines various forms of patriarchy that range from urban to rural. In some ways, González-López is in conversations with both Hondagneu-Sotelo (1994) and Gutmann (1996). See: Gutmann, 1996.

50 Again, this resonates with González-López's analysis of girls having limited options for economic stability, as discussed in earlier chapters.

51 Schmidt Camacho 2008.

52 See: Dominguez Villegas. For a visual representation, see: *La Vida Precoz Y Breve de Sabina Rivas*, directed by Luis Mandoki (2012).

53 In a similar context, Espiritu (2001, 415) examines how racialized immigrants use gender and sexuality as a way to "assert cultural superiority over the dominant group." See also: González-López 2004, 1127.

54 González-López 2004, 1119.

55 Ibid, 1128.

56 Amuchástegui Herrera 1998.

57 Gordon 1997, 4.

58 This interview took place in 2012. By then, Toñita was fifteen years old.

59 Jeffrey 2010.

60 Lomnitz-Adler 2003.

CHAPTER 5. THE TELLING MOMENT

1 In relying on oral sources and memory, Alessandro Portelli posits that what becomes important are not necessarily the actual facts of the event. See: Portelli 1991, 26.

2 In *Sacrificing Families*, Abrego (2014) found that many Salvadoran families had already experienced separation within El Salvador prior to migration and family reunification.

3 Tyrrell 2011, 28.

4 Yarris 2014, 284–309.

5 Tyrrell 2011, 28.

6 Ibid, 31.

7 See for example: Chavez 1992, 4; Martínez 2001; Massey, Durand, and Malone 2002.

8 Coutin 2005, 196.

9 For further analysis on the marches, see: Pallares and Flores-Gonzalez 2010.

10 National Council of La Raza, n.d., "Sensenbrenner Bill—H.R. 4437," www.nclr.org. Accessed May 19, 2008.

11 See: Muñoz Jr. 1989.

12 Chavez 2013.

13 Ibid, 53.

14 McKinnon 2006.

15 Chavez 2013, 6.

16 Elena's story is also discussed in the introduction and in chapter 1.

17 Levitt 2001, 11; Perez 2004; Stephen 2007; Zavella 2011.

18 See for example: Castañeda, Manz, and Davenport 2002, 103–123.

19 Alexander 2005, 8.

20 Ibid, 8.

21 Anzaldúa 1987, 3.

22 Chavez 1992, 4.

23 Ibid, 4–5.

24 Levitt 2001.

25 This is mentioned in an earlier note.

26 Stephen 2007, 155.

27 Zavella 2011, 57.

28 Zavella 2011, 57, citing Maria Luisa De La Garza.

29 Coutin 2005, 196.

30 Santiago 1993, 206.

31 Red and blue are gang-affiliated colors that were prohibited at middle schools and high schools in Napa. The Napa Valley Unified School District no longer has this rule.

32 Stephen 2007.

33 Chavez 1992, 4.

34 Alexander 2005, 8.

35 Zavella 2011, 57.

36 Coutin 2005, 197.

37 Zavella 2011, 57, citing Maria Luisa De La Garza.

38 Schmidt Camacho 2008.

CHAPTER 6. IMAGINARIES AND REALITIES

1 This quote comes from Salazar (2011, 58), who cites similar observations made by Jónsson (2008) and Ferguson (2006).

2 Salazar 2010, 58.

3 Ibid, 58.

4 Ibid, 57.

5 Cresswell 2004, 11.

6 In chapter 4, I discuss González-López's (2005) concept of *capital femenino*.

7 Nichols 2002.

8 See: Weber 1998, 17; Dillon 2004, 41.

9 Weber 1998, 17; Lukacs 2000, 60.

10 Lukacs 2000, 60.

11 Weber 1998, 27; Dillon 2004, 4.

12 Dillon 2004, 4.

13 Siler 2008, 2.

14 Nichols 2002, 67.

15 Lukacs 2000, 4.

16 On tourists, see: Conaway 2002, 7. On Napa as the Disneyland for adults, see: Martin 2004, 6.

17 Moskin and Severson 2008.

18 Elsewhere, popular historians have attributed the commercialization of the wine and tourism industry to Robert Mondavi. Deutschman (2003, 96) says: "[t]he Napa Valley was invented by Robert Mondavi."

19 Calavita 1992, 23.

20 Castañeda 2009, 20.

21 Since 1862, there have been twenty-one serious floods recorded. Napa County 2004.

22 Ibid.

23 Jameson 1988.

24 Salazar (2010) also makes this observation. See: p. 57. Please note that I use the same quote in a latter part of the chapter.

25 Salazar 2010, 55.

26 Schmidt Camacho 2008, 5.

27 Quijano 2007, 169.

28 Eliza's story is examined in chapter 5.

29 Zavella 2011.

30 Martin 2004.

31 Skinner, "Napa Valley, California: A Model of Wine Region Development," 293.

32 Mitchell 2002, 102.

33 Lukacs makes the following statement: "It contends, however, that wine histori-cally has been Western's culture's beverage of moderation, a mark of civilization because [it is] itself a civilized thing." This quote is also used in chapter two. See: Lukacs 2000, 14.

34 This was at the Napa Valley Wine Auction back in 2000. See: Deutschman 2003, 84.

35 Ibid, 82.

36 Ibid, 78.

37 The Silverado Trail is called the "Napa Valley's road less traveled" because it has much smaller wineries than those found on Highway 29. See: www.silveradotrail.com/splash.

38 Coodley 2003, 144.

39 The Napa River Flood Protection Project (2004).

40 Moskin and Severson 2008.

41 "Visionary Statement" on www.copia.org (no longer extant), accessed on May 19, 2008.

42 Franson 2003.

43 Ibid.

44 "About Us." www.oxbowpublicmarket.com. Accessed on May 19, 2008.

45 Hoge 2007.

46 Courtney 2007.

47 Coodley 2003,147.

48 Ibid, 144.

49 Swinchatt and Howell 2004, 171.

50 Heyhoe and Hock 2004, 153.

51 At the Napa Valley Wine Auction 2000, a bottle of wine was auctioned for $5,000,000 to Chase Bailey. See Deutschman 2003, 82.

52 Ibid, 86.

53 Lukacs contends that "wine historically has been Western's culture's beverage of moderation, a mark of civilization because [it is] itself a civilized thing." The logic here is that wine is a civilizing drink, and therefore those who drink it and write about it must also be civilized—a problematic statement. See Lukacs 2000, 14.

54 See reviews of her book on Amazon, accessed via amazon.com on May 30, 2008.

55 Barron 1995, 135.

56 Ibid, 26.

57 Chavez 2013.

58 Sullivan 1994, 323.

59 Bonné 2007.

60 Coodley 2003, 204.

61 Conaway 1990, 222.

62 Inglenook is one of the original wineries that was "making good wine" during the late 1800s. See: Conaway 1990,107.

63 Ibid, 220.

64 Many of the "original" families of the Valley in the late 1800s include those of Georges de Latour, Jacob Beringer, Gustave Niebaum, and Charles Krug himself. Some of these lost their wineries during Prohibition, while others were forced to sell in the 1960s and 1970s to corporations. See: Conaway 1990, 139.

65 Ibid, 389.

66 Coodley 2003, 144.

67 Hall 2003.

68 Murphy 2006.

69 Siler 2008.

70 Bonné 2007.

71 Elkjer 2005.

72 Murphy 2005.

73 Coodley 2003; Heidenreich 2007.

74 Coodley 2003, 7.

75 Ibid, 7.

76 Heidenreich 2007, 1.

77 Pitti (2003, 79) says the following about the people he writes: "Rewriting the California past requires listening to residents long ignored by official state chroniclers."

78 Martin 2004.

79 Nichols 2002.

80 Ibid, 22.

81 Ibid, 67.

82 Ibid, 68.

83 The census makes no distinction among the various Latino immigrant groups that live in Napa County. Over the years, the census has listed Latinos as: "Persons of Spanish Origin or Descent" (1970s); "Spanish Origin" (1980s); "Hispanic" (1990s); "Hispanic or Latino" (2000). See: "Bay Area Census, Napa County." www.bayareacensus.ca.gov. However, the majority of the Latino population living in Napa is of Mexican decent.

84 Chicanos and Whites also visit the flea market, but the majority of the patrons are Mexican immigrants.

85 As Napa's Spanish-speaking Catholic population increases, St. John the Baptist has increased its number of Spanish masses. By 2014, there were three Spanish masses offered: Saturday at seven p.m., and Sundays at eight a.m. and noon.

86 I recall being at church the day the announcement was made and I was in disbelief upon hearing the reasons as to why mass was moved to noon.

87 Valenzuela Jr. 1999, 728.

88 By underscapes, George Lipsitz (2018) means the spaces where "poverty, political powerlessnesss, and racism" are present, which are then transformed by artists and activist to produce "sacred spaces." Here the connection that I am making is how new migrants transform the spaces they occupy away from the tourist spaces that are produced in the Napa Valley. See Lipsitz 2018.

CONCLUSION

1 Levitt and Glick Schiller 2004.

2 Nowotny 1994, 33.

3 Anzaldúa 1987, 19.

4 Zavella 2011, 57, citing Maria Luisa De La Garza.

BIBLIOGRAPHY

Abrego, Leisy J. 2014. *Sacrificing Families: Navigating Laws, Labor, and Love Across Borders*. Stanford: Stanford University Press.

Alexander, M. Jacqui. 2005. *Pedagogies of Crossing: Meditations on Feminism, Sexual Politics, Memory, and the Sacred*. Durham: Duke University Press.

Alvarez Jr, Robert. 2005. *Mangos, Chiles, and Truckers: The Business of Transnationalism*. Minneapolis: University of Minnesota Press.

Amuchástegui Herrera, Ana. 1998. "Virginity in Mexico: the Role of Competing Discourses of Sexuality in Personal Experience." *Reproductive Health Matters* 6.12: 105–115.

Anderson, Benedict. 1992. "Long-Distance Nationalism: World Capitalism and the Rise of Identity Politics." *Centre for Asian Studies Amsterdam (Wertheim Lecture): University of Amsterdam.*

Andreas, Peter. 2000. *Border Games: Policing the U.S.-Mexico Divide*. Ithaca: Cornell University Press.

Anzaldúa, Gloria. 1987. *Borderlands/La Frontera: The New Mestiza*. San Francisco: Aunt Lute Books.

Appadurai, Arjun. 1996. *Modernity at Large: Cultural Dimensions of Globalization*. Minneapolis: University of Minnesota Press.

Azul, Rafael. 2012. "Police assault protesting students in Mexico." World Socialist Website (May 1). www.wsws.org.

Bacon, David. 2004. *The Children of NAFTA: Labor Wars on the U.S./Mexico Border*. Berkeley: University of California Press.

Barron, Cheryll Aimeé. 1995. *Dreamers of the Valley of Plenty: A Portrait of the Napa Valley*. New York: Scribner.

Bauman, Zygmunt. 2003. *Wasted Lives: Modernity and Its Outcasts*. London: Polity.

Belson, Ken. 2014. "Child Migrants Strain Makeshift Arizona Shelter." *New York Times* (June 7). www.nytimes.com.

Bettie, Julie. 2003. *Women Without Class: Girls, Race, and Identity*. Berkeley: University of California Press.

Boehm, Deborah A., et al. 2011. "Introduction: Children, Youth, and the Everyday Ruptures of Migration." *Everyday Ruptures: Children, Youth, and Migration in Global Perspective*, 1–19. Tennessee: Vanderbilt University Press.

Bonfil Batalla, Guillermo. 1996. *México Profundo: Reclaiming a Civilization*. Translated by Philip A. Dennis. Texas: University of Texas Press.

Bonné, Jon. 2007. "Napa Valley Stunner - Famed Winery Sold." *San Francisco Chronicle* (August 1).

———. 2007. "Sour Grapes: Napa Valley Abuzz Over a Tell-All Book About How Modavi Family Lost Empire." *San Francisco Chronicle* (June 19): Section A.

Calavita, Kitty. 1992. *Inside the State: The Bracero Program, Immigration, and the INS.* Louisiana: Quid Pro Books.

Cantú, Lionel. 2009. *The Sexuality of Migration: Border Crossings and Mexican Immigrant Men,* eds. Nancy A. Naples and Salvador Vidal-Ortiz. New York: New York University Press.

Carrillo, Hector. 2004. "Sexual Migration, Cross-Cultural Sexual Encounters, and Sexual Health." *Journal of NSRC* 1(3) (September): 58–70.

Castañeda, Jorge G. 2009. *Ex Mex: From Migrants to Immigrants.* New York: New Press.

———. 1995. *Sorpresas Te Da la Vida . . . : México, Fin de Siglo.* Mexico: Aguilar Nuevo Siglo.

Castañeda, Xóchitl, Beatriz Manz, and Allison Davenport. 2002. "Mexicanization: A Survival Strategy for Guatemalan Mayas in the San Francisco Bay Area." *Migraciones Internacionales* 1(3) (July-Dec): 103–123.

Chavez, Leo R. 1992. *Shadowed Lives: Undocumented Immigrants in American Society.* Massachusetts: Cengage Learning.

———. 2013. *The Latino Threat: Constructing Immigrants, Citizens, and the Nation,* 2nd Edition. Stanford: Stanford University Press.

Coe, Cati, Rachel R. Reynolds, Deborah A. Boehm, Julia Meredith Hess, and Heather Rae-Espinoza, eds. 2011. *Everyday Ruptures: Children, Youth, and Migration in Global Perspective.* Tennessee: Vanderbilt University Press.

Cole, Jennifer. 2008. "Fashioning Distinction: Youth and Consumerism in Urban Madagascar." *Figuring the Future: Globalization and the Temporalities of Children and Youth,* eds. Jennifer Cole and Deborah Durham, 99–124. Santa Fe: School for Advanced Research Press.

Cole, Jennifer, and Deborah Durham. 2008. *Figuring the Future: Globalization and the Temporalities of Children and Youth.* Santa Fe: School for Advanced Research.

Conaway, James. 1990. *Napa: The Story of An American Eden.* Boston: Houghton Mifflin.

———. 2003. *The Far Side of Eden: New Money, Old Land and the Battle for Napa Valley.* New York: Houghton Mifflin.

Coodley, Lauren. 2003. *Napa: The Transformation of an American Town.* Charleston: Arcadia.

Courtney, Kevin. 2007. "Putting on the Ritz? High-End Hotel Chain Rumored for Napa, But No One Can Say for Sure," *Napa Register* (April 13).

Coutin, Susan Bibler. 2005. "Being En Route." *American Anthropologist* 107.2 (June): 195–206.

Cresswell, Tim. 2004. *Place: A Short Introduction* (Malden, MA: Blackwell Publishing).

Dalsgård, Anne Line, and Martin Demant Frederiksen. 2014. "Introduction: Time Objectified." *Ethnographies of Youth and Temporality: Time Objectified*, eds. Anne Line Dalsgård, Martin Demant Frederiksen, Susan Højlund, and Lotte Meinert. Philadelphia: Temple University Press, 1–22.

Danticat, Edwidge. 2007. *Brother, I'm Dying*. New York: Alfred A. Knopf.

Dart, Tom. 2014. "Child Migrants at Texas Border: an Immigration Crisis That's Hardly New." *The Guardian* (July 9). www.theguardian.com.

De Genova, Nicholas. 2002. "Migrant 'Illegality' and Deportability in Everyday Life." *Annual Review of Anthropology*: 419–447.

Demmers, Jolle. 2002. "Diaspora and Conflict: Locality, Long-Distance Nationalism, and Delocalization of Conflict Dynamics." *Javnost–The Public* 9.1: 85–96.

Deutschman, Alan. 2003. *A Tale of Two Valleys: Wine, Wealth, and the Battle for the Good Life in Napa and Sonoma*. New York: Broadway Books.

Dickson, Caitlin. 2014. "Is Obama Really the Deporter-in-Chief? Yes and No." *Daily Beast* (April 30).

Dillon, Richard H. 2004. *Napa Valley Heyday*. San Francisco: The Book Club of California.

Dominguez Villegas, Rodrigo. "Central American Migrants and 'La Bestia': The Route, Dangers, and Government Responses." *Migration Information Source* (September 10). www.migrationpolicy.org.

Dreby, Joanna. 2006. "Honor and Virtue: Mexican Parenting in the Transnational Context." *Gender and Society* 20.1: 32–59.

———. 2009. "Gender and Transnational Gossip." *Qualitative Sociology* 32.1: 33–52.

———. 2010. *Divided by Borders: Mexican Migrants and their Children*. Berkeley: University of California Press.

Dussel, Enrique. 2016. Lectures at Decolonizing Knowledge and Power Summer School (July 18–July 21). UAB-Universidad Autónoma de Barcelona, Casa de la Convalescencia, Barcelona, Spain.

"Elas [*sic*] son 'Estrellas del Bicentenario.'" 2010. Agencias. www.zocalo.com.mx.

Elkjer, Thom. 2005. "Loveable Rouge: Carl Doumani Has an Uncanny Knack for Getting Into Just the Right Amount of Trouble." *San Francisco Chronicle* (April 7): Section F, 7.

Escobar Lapatí, Agustín, and Mercedes González de la Rocha. 1995. "Crisis, Restructuring and Urban Poverty in Mexico." *Environment and Urbanization* 7.1: 57–76.

Espiritu, Yen Le. 2001. "'We Don't Sleep Around Like White Girls Do': Family, Culture, and Gender in Filipina American Lives." *Signs* 26.2: 415–440.

———. 2003. *Home Bound: Filipino American Lives Across Cultures, Communities, and Countries*. Berkeley: University of California Press.

Fabian, Johannes. 1983. *Time and the Other: How Anthropology Makes Its Object*. New York: Columbia University Press.

Farr, Marcia. 2005. *Rancheros in Chicagoacán: Language and Identity in a Transnational Community*. Austin: University of Texas Press.

Ferguson, James. 2006. *Global Shadows: Africa in the Neoliberal World Order.* Durham: Duke University Press.

Flaherty, Michael G. 2014. "Afterword" in *Ethnographies of Youth and Temporality,* eds. Anne Line Dalsgård, Martin Demant Frederiksen, Susanne Højlund, and Lotte Meinert, 175–190. Philadelphia: Temple University Press.

Flanagan, Constance. 2008. "Private Anxieties and Public Hopes: The Perils and Promise of Youth in the Context of Globalization." *Figuring the Future: Globalization and the Temporalities of Children and Youth,* eds. Jennifer Cole and Deborah Durham, 125–150. Santa Fe: School for Advanced Research Press.

Flores, Juan. 2007. *The Diaspora Strikes Back: Caribeño Tales of Learning and Turning.* New York: Routledge.

Franson, Paul. 2003. "Boomtown: City of Napa No Longer a Tasting Room Wasteland." *San Francisco Chronicle* (February): Section D, 27.

Fuentes, Carlos. 1997. *A New Time for México.* Translated by Marina Gutman Castañeda and Carlos Fuentes. Berkeley: University of California Press.

———. 1999. *The Buried Mirror: Reflections on Spain and the New World.* New York: Mariner Books.

Galeano, Eduardo. 1997. *Open Veins of Latin America: Five Centuries of the Pillage of a Continent.* Translated by Cedric Belfrage. New York: Monthly Review Press.

Gamboa, Luz. 2013. "Receta de Corundas: Tamalito Michoacano." Museo de Arte Popular (February 8). amigosmap.org.mx.

Gamburd, Michele Ruth. 2000. *The Kitchen Spoon's Handle: Transnationalism and Sri Lanka Migrant Housemaids.* Ithaca: Cornell University Press.

Gamio, Manuel. 1930. *Mexican Immigration to the United States: A Study of Human Migration and Adjustment.* Chicago: University of Chicago Press.

———. 1931. *The Mexican Immigrant, His Life-Story: Autobiographic Documents.* Chicago: University of Chicago Press.

García, Lorena. 2012. *Respect Yourself, Protect Yourself: Latina Girls and Sexual Identity.* New York: New York University Press.

García Canclini, Nestor. 1995. *Hybrid Cultures: Strategies for Entering and Leaving Modernity.* Translated by Christopher L. Chiappari and Silvia L. López. Minneapolis: University of Minnesota Press.

Gilmore, Ruth Wilson. 2016. Lectures at Decolonizing Knowledge and Power Summer School (July 18–July 21): Universitat Autónoma de Barcelona.

Glaister, Dan, and Ewen MacAskill. 2006. "US Counts Cost of Day Without Immigrants." *Guardian* (May 1). www.theguardian.com.

Glick Schiller, Nina. 2005. "Blood and Belonging: Long-Distance Nationalism and the World Beyond." *Complexities: Beyond Nature and Nurture:* 289–312.

Glick Schiller, Nina, Linda Basch, and Cristina Blanc-Szanton. 1992. "Transnationalism: A New Analytic Framework for Understanding Migration." *Annals of the New York Academy of Sciences* 645.1: 1–24.

Gómez, Laura E. 2007. *Manifest Destinies: The Making of the Mexican American Race.* New York: New York University Press.

González González, José. 1983. *Lo Negro del Negro Durazo*. Mexico City: Editorial Posada.

González-López, Gloria. 2004. "Fathering Latina Sexualities: Mexican Men and the Virginity of Their Daughters." *Journal of Marriage and Family* 66.5: 1118–1130.

———. 2005. *Erotic Journeys: Mexican Immigrants and Their Sex Lives*. Berkeley: University of California Press.

Gordon, Avery F. 1997. *Ghostly Matters: Haunting and the Sociological Imagination*. Minneapolis: University of Minnesota Press.

Grande, Reyna. 2006. *Across a Hundred Mountains: A Novel*. New York: Simon and Schuster.

———. 2012. *The Distance Between Us: A Memoir*. New York: Simon and Schuster.

Grayson, George W. 1980. *The Politics of Mexican Oil*. Pittsburgh: University of Pittsburgh Press.

Gutiérrez, David Gregory. 1995. *Walls and Mirrors: Mexican Americans, Mexican Immigrants, and the Politics of Ethnicity*. Berkeley: University of California Press.

Gutmann, Matthew. 1996. *The Meanings of Macho: Being a Man in Mexico City*. Berkeley: University of California Press.

Haber, Stephen H. 2008. *Mexico Since 1980*. New York: Cambridge University Press.

Hall, Christopher. 2003. "What's Doing in the Napa Valley." *New York Times* (January 19).

Hall, Stuart. 1987. "Minimal Selves." *Identity: The Real Me*, ed. Homi Bhabha. ICA Documents 6. London: Institute of Contemporary Arts.

———. 1996. "Introduction" in *Modernity: An Introduction to Modern Societies*, eds. Stuart Hall, David Held, Don Hubert, and Kenneth Thompson, 3–18. Oxford: Blackwell Publishing.

Hamilton, Nora and Norma Stoltz Chinchilla. 2001. *Seeking Community in a Global City: Guatemalans and Salvadorans in Los Angeles*. Philadelphia: Temple University Press.

Heidenreich, Linda. 2007. *"This Land Was Mexican Once:" Histories of Resistance from Northern California*. Austin: University of Texas Press.

Hellman, Judith Adler. 1983. *Mexico in Crisis*, 2nd Edition. New York: Holmes & Meier Publishers.

———. 1994. *Mexican Lives*. New York: The New Press.

Heyhoe, Kate, and Stanley Hock. 2004. *Harvesting the Dream: The Rags-to-Riches Tale of the Sutter Home Winery*. New York: John Wiley & Sons.

Hoge, Patrick. 2007. "Napa: Long-Awaited Luxury in the Works for City / Time Has Come: Developers Plan High-End Properties." *San Francisco Chronicle* (May): 27.

Hondagneu-Sotelo, Pierrette. 1994. *Gendered Transitions: Mexican Experiences of Migration*. Berkeley: University of California Press.

———, ed. 2003. *Gender and U.S. Immigration: Contemporary Trends*. Berkeley: University of California Press.

Hondagneu-Sotelo, Pierrette, and Ernestive Avila. 1997. "'I'm Here, but I'm There:' The Meanings of Latina Transnational Motherhood." *Gender and Society* 11.5: 548–571.

Honwana, Alcinda Manuel. 2012. *The Time of Youth: Work, Social Change, and Politics in Africa*. Sterling, VA: Kumarian Press.

"Is Mexico 'under siege'?" 2011. *New York Times* (October 22). www.nytimes.com.

James, Allison. 2001. "To Be (Come) or Not to Be (Come): Understanding Children's Citizenship." *Annals of the American Academy of Political Science* 633.1: 167–179.

Jameson, Fredric. 1988. "Cognitive Mapping." *Marxism and the Interpretation of Culture*, 347–357. Macmillan Education UK.

Jeffrey, Craig. 2010. *Timepass: Youth, Class, and the Politics of Waiting in India*. Stanford: Stanford University Press.

Jónsson, Gunvor. 2008. *Migration Aspirations and Immobility in a Malian Soninke Village*. Oxford: International Migration Institute.

Joseph, Gilbert M., and Timothy J. Henderson, eds. 2002. *The Mexico Reader: History, Culture, Politics*. Durham, NC: Duke University Press.

Kilkenny, Allison. 2012. "Student Movement Dubbed the 'Mexican Spring.'" *The Nation* (May 29). www.thenation.com.

Laguerre, Michel S. 2003. *Urban Multiculturalism and Globalization in New York City: An Analysis of Diasporic Temporalities*. New York: Palgrave Macmillan.

Levitt, Peggy. 2001. *The Transnational Villagers*. Berkeley: University of California Press.

Levitt, Peggy, and Nina Glick Schiller. 2004. "Conceptualizing Simultaneity: A Transnational Social Field Perspective on Society." *International Migration Review* 38.3: 1002–1039.

Lipsitz, George. 2018, forthcoming. "Conjuring Sacred Space in the Gulf Coast Cities." *Journal of the American Academy of Religion*.

Lomnitz-Adler, Claudio. 2003. "Time in Crisis: Historicity, Sacrifice, and the Spectacle of Debacle in Mexico City." *Public Culture* 15.1 (Winter): 127–147.

Lopez, Ian Haney. 2006. *White by Law: The Legal Construction of Race*. New York: New York University Press.

López Lara, Ramon. 1977. Zinapécuaro: *Monografías Municipales del Estado de Michoacán*. Mexico: Imprenta Madero.

Lowe, Lisa. 2002. "Immigrant Literatures: A Modern Structure of Feeling." *Literature on the Move: Comparing Diasporic Ethnicities in Europe and the Americas*, eds. Dominique Marçais, Mark Niemeyer, Bernard Vincent, and Cathy Waegner, 1–14. Heidelberg, Germany: Universitätsverlag Winter.

Lukacs, Paul. 2000. *American Vintage: The Rise of American Wine*. Boston: Houghton Mifflin.

Lustig, Nora. 1998. *Mexico: The Remaking of an Economy*, 2nd Edition. Washington, D.C.: Brookings Institute Press.

Lytle Hernández, Kelly. 2010. *Migra!: A History of the U.S. Border Patrol*. Berkeley: University of California Press.

Maldonado-Torres, Nelson. 2008. *Against War: Views from the Underside of Modernity*. Durham: Duke University Press Books.

Marcus, George E. 1995. "Ethnography in/of the World System: the Emergence of Multi-Sited Ethnography." *Annual Review of Anthropology*: 95–117.

Martin, Glen. 2004. "Grapes of Wrath, Revisited." *San Francisco Chronicle Magazine* (December 19): 6–14.

Martínez, Rubén. 2001. *Crossing Over: A Mexican Family on the Migrant Trail*. New York: Picador USA.

Martínez Laguna, Norma. 2004. "Oil Politics and Privatization Strategies in México: Implications for the Petrochemical Sector and its Production Spaces." *Energy Policy* 32.18 (December: 2035–2047.

Massey, Douglas S. 1999. "Why Does Immigration Occur? A Theoretical Synthesis." *The Handbook of International Migration: The American Experience, eds.* Charles Hirschman, Philip Kasinitz, and Josh Dewind, 34–52. New York: Russell Sage Foundation.

Massey, Douglas S., and Audrey Singer. 1995. "New Estimates of Undocumented Mexican Migration and the Probability of Apprehension." *Demography* 32. 2 (May): 203–213.

Massey, Douglas S., Joaquin Arango, Graeme Hugo, Ali Kouaouci, Adela Pellegrino, and J. Edward Taylor. 1993. "Theories of International Migration: A Review and Appraisal." *Population and Development Review* 19. 3 (September.): 431–466.

Massey, Douglas S., Jorge Durand, and Nolan J. Malone. 2002. *Beyond Smoke and Mirrors: Mexican Immigration in an Era of Economic Integration*. New York: Russell Sage Foundation.

Massey, Douglas S., Rafael Alarcon, Jorge Durand, and Humberto Gonzalez. 1990. *Return to Aztlan: The Social Process of International Migration from Western Mexico*. Berkeley: University of California Press.

McKeown, Adam. 2001. *Chinese Migrant Networks and Cultural Change: Peru, Chicago, and Hawaii 1900–1936*. Chicago: University of Chicago Press.

McKinnon, Julissa. 2006. "Labor Day Immigration March Planned." *Napa Register* (September 3).

Mendoza-Denton, Norma. 2008. *Homegirls: Language and Cultural Practice among Latina Youth Gangs*. New York: John Wiley & Sons.

Minian, Ana. 2012. "Queer Ideologies, Straight Migrations: The Role of Sexuality in Mexican Undocumented Migration, 1965–1986." *Tepoztlán Institute for the Transnational History of the Americas* (August 3).

Mitchell Don. 2000. *Cultural Geography: A Critical Introduction*. Malden, MA: Blackwell Publishing.

Molina, Natalia. 2013. *How Race Is Made in America: Immigration, Citizenship, and the Historical Power of Racial Scripts*. Berkeley: University of California Press.

Monsiváis, Carlos. 1978. "Notas Sobre Cultura Popular en México." *Latin American Perspectives* 5.1: 98–118.

Moskin, Julia, and Kim Severson. 2008. "Copia, a Food and Wine Center, Files for Bankruptcy." *New York Times* (December 2). www.nytimes.com.

Muñoz Jr., Carlos. 1989. *Youth, Identity, Power: The Chicano Movement*. New York: Verso.

Murphy, Linda. 2005. "Napa Valley's Grande Dame Schrambergs' Jamie Davies Coaxes Champagne Quality from California Grapes." *San Francisco Chronicle* (December 22): Section F.

———. 2006. "Judgement Day: Part Deux: What the 2006 Showdown Between California and France Really Proves." *San Francisco Chronicle* (June 1): Section F.

Napa County Flood Control and Water Conservation District. 2004. "Napa River Flood Protection Project: Progress and Plan Summary 2004." www.napaflooddistrict.org.

Napa High School. 2016. "Napa High School Profile, 2015–2016." www.napahigh.org.

Napa Valley Unified School District. 2010. "*Napa High School: A California Distinguished School: Focus on Learning WASC Self Study 2009 –2010*." www.nvusd.granicus.com.

Nevins, Joseph. 2002. *Operation Gatekeeper: The Rise of the "Illegal Alien" and the Making of the U.S.-Mexico Boundary*. New York: Routledge.

Ngai, Mae M. 2005. *Impossible Subjects: Illegal Aliens and the Making of Modern America*. Princeton, NJ: Princeton University Press.

Nichols, Sandra. 2002. *Saints, Peaches and Wine: Mexican Migrants and the Transformation of Los Haro, Zacatecas and Napa, California*. PhD diss., University of California, Berkeley. Ann Arbor: UMI, 3063502.

Nowotny, Helga. 1994. *Time: Modern and Postmodern Experience*. United Kingdom: Polity.

Pacheco-López, Penélope. 2005. "Foreign Direct Investment, Exports, and Imports in México." *World Economy* 28.8 (August): 1157–1172.

Pallares, Amalia, and Nilda Flores-Gonzalez, eds. 2010. *Marcha: Latino Chicago and the Immigrant Rights Movement*. Chicago: University of Illinois Press.

Paoli Bolio, Francisco José. 1982. "Petroleum and Political Change in México." *Latin American Perspectives* 9.1 (Winter): 65–77.

Parreñas, Rhacel Salazar. 2001. *Servants of Globalization: Women, Migration, and Domestic Work*. Stanford: Stanford University Press.

———. 2005. *Children of Global Migration: Transnational Families and Gendered Woes*. Stanford: Stanford University Press.

Passel, Jeffrey S., D'Vera Cohn, and Ana Gonzalez-Barrera. 2012. *Net Migration from Mexico Falls to Zero—and Perhaps Less*. Washington, D.C.: Pew Research Center.

Paz, Octavio. 1994. *The Labyrinth of Solitude: The Other Mexico, Return to the Labyrinth of Solitude, Mexico and the United States, The Philanthropic Ogre*. New York: Grove Press.

Perez, Gina. 2004. *The Near Northwest Side Story: Migration, Displacement, and Puerto Rican Families*. Berkeley: University of California Press.

Pérez, Loida Maritza. 1999. *Geographies of home: A Novel*. New York: Viking.

Pitti, Stephen J. 2003. *The Devil in Silicon Valley: Northern California, Race, and Mexican Americans*. Princeton, NJ: Princeton University Press.

Portelli, Alessandro. 1991. *The Death of Luigi Trastulli and Other Stories: Form and Meaning in Oral History*. Albany: State University of New York Press.

Preston, Julia. 2014. "Migrants Flow in South Texas, as Do Rumors." *New York Times* (June 16). www.nytimes.com.

Quijano, Anibal. 2000. "Coloniality of Power, Eurocentrism, and Latin America." *International Sociology* 15.2: 215–232.

———. 2007. "Coloniality and Modernity/Rationality." *Cultural Studies* 21.2–3 (March/May): 168–178.

Reyes, Laura. 2012. "Los Maestros Se Resisten a Que Evalúen la Calidad de la Educación." *Expansión* (March 15). www.expansion.mx.

Rogers, Tim. 2016. "Supreme Court Tie is a 'Huge Blow' to Immigrant Rights." *Fusion* (June 23). www.fusion.net.

Rosaldo, Renato. 1993. *Culture & Truth: The Remaking of Social Analysis*. Boston: Beacon Press.

Rosas, Ana Elizabeth. 2014. *Abrazando el Espíritu: Bracero Families Confront the U.S.-Mexico Border*. Berkeley: University of California Press.

Rouse, Roger. 1989. "Mexican Migration to the United States: Family Relations in the Development of a Transnational Migrant Circuit." PhD diss., Stanford University.

———. 1991. "Mexican Migration and the Social Space of Postmodernism." *Diaspora* 1.1: 8–23.

———. 1992. "Making Sense of Settlement: Class Transformation, Cultural Struggle, and Transnationalism Among Mexican Migrants in the United States." *Annals of the New York Academy of Sciences* 645.1: 25–52.

Salazar, Noel. 2010. "Towards an Anthropology of Cultural Mobilities." *Crossings: Journal of Migration and Culture* 1.1: 53–68.

———. 2011. "The Power of Imagination in Transnational Mobilities." *Identities: Global Studies in Culture and Power* 18: 576–598.

Sanchez, George. 1995. *Becoming Mexican American: Ethnicity, Culture, and Identity in Chicano Los Angeles, 1900–1945*. New York: Oxford University Press.

Santiago, Esmeralda. 1993. *When I Was Puerto Rican*. New York: Vintage Books.

Sassen, Saskia. 1998. *Globalization and Its Discontents: Essays on the New Mobility of People and Money*. New York: New Press.

Schmalzbauer, Leah. 2004. "Searching for Wages and Mothering from Afar: The Case of Honduran Transnational Families." *Journal of Marriage and Family* 66.5: 1317–1331.

Schmidt Camacho, Alicia. 2008. *Migrant Imaginaries: Latino Cultural Politics in the U.S.-Mexico Borderlands*. New York: NYU Press.

Segura, Denise A., and Patricia Zavella, eds. 2007. *Women and Migration in the U.S.-Mexico Borderlands: A Reader*. Durham, NC: Duke University Press Books.

Siler, Julia Flynn. 2008. *The House of Mondavi: The Rise and Fall of an American Wine Dynasty*. New York: Gotham.

Skidmore, Thomas E., and Peter H. Smith. 1997. *Modern Latin America*, 4th Edition. New York: Oxford University Press.

Skinner, Angela M. 2000. "Napa Valley, California: A Model of Wine Region Development." *Wine Tourism Around the World: Development, Management, and Markets,* eds. Michael C. Hall, Liz Sharples, Brock Cambourne, and Niki Macionis. Oxford: Butterworth Heinemann.

Smith, Neil. 2002. "New Globalism, New Urbanism: Gentrification as a Global Urban Strategy." *Antipode* 34.3 (June): 427–450.

Soja, Edward. 1989. *Postmodern Geographies: The Reassertion of Space in Critical Social Theory.* New York: Verso.

Stephen, Lynn. 2007. *Transborder Lives: Indigenous Oaxacans in Mexico, California, and Oregon.* Durham, NC: Duke University Press.

Storey, John. 2006. *Cultural Theory and Popular Culture: a Reader.* Upper Saddle River, NJ: Pearson Prentice Hall.

Suárez-Orozco, Carola, and Marcelo M. Suárez-Orozco. 2001. *Children of Immigration.* Cambridge, MA: Harvard University Press.

Sullivan, Charles L. 1994. *Napa Wine: A History from Mission Days to the Present.* San Francisco: The Wine Appreciation Guild.

Swinchatt, Jonathan, and David G. Howell. 2004. *The Winemaker's Dance: Exploring Terroir in the Napa Valley.* Berkeley: University of California Press.

"Televisa Lanza la Campaña Estrellas del Bicentenario." 2010. Merca2.0 (January 13). www.merca2o.com.

Thorne, Barrie. 2004. "Theorizing Age and Other Differences." *Childhood: A Global Journal of Child Research* 11.4 (November): 403–408.

Tomlinson, Barbara, and George Lipsitz. 2013. "American Studies as Accompaniment." *American Quarterly* 65.1 (March): 1–30.

Tsuda, Takeyuki. 2012. "Whatever Happened to Simultaneity? Transnational Migration Theory and Dual Engagement in Sending and Receiving Countries." *Journal of Ethnic and Migration Studies* 38.4: 631–649.

"TV Azteca Presentó Oficialmente las Actividades Para el Bicentenario." 2009. Organización Editorial Mexicana (November 7). www.oem.com.mx.

Tyrrell, Naomi. 2011. "Children's Agency in Family Migration Decision Making in Britain." *Everyday Ruptures: Children, Youth, and Migration in Global Perspective,* eds. Cati Coe, Rachel R. Reynolds, Deborah A. Boehm, Julia Meredith Hess, and Heather Rae-Espinoza, 23–38. Tennessee: Vanderbilt University Press.

Urrea, Luis Alberto. 2005. *The Devil's Highway: A True Story.* New York: Back Bay Books.

Valenzuela Jr., Abel. 1999. "Gender Roles and Settlement Activities Among Children and Their Immigrant Families." *American Behavioral Scientist* 42.4: 720–742.

Valenzuela, Angela. 1999. *Subtractive Schooling: U.S.-Mexican Youth and the Politics of Caring.* New York: State University of New York Press.

Vargas, Zaragosa. 2010. *Crucible of Struggle: A History of Mexican Americans from Colonial Period to the Present Era.* Oxford: Oxford University Press.

Waldinger, Roger, and David Fitzgerald. 2004. "Transnationalism in Question." *American Journal of Sociology* 109. 5 (March): 1177–1195.

Weber, Lin. 1998. *Old Napa Valley: The History to 1900*. St. Helena: Wine Ventures Publishing.

Weinbaum, Alys Eve et al., eds. 2008. *The Modern Girl Around the World: Consumption, Modernity, and Globalization*. Durham: Duke University Press Books.

Williams, Raymond. 2001. *The Long Revolution*. Canada: Broadview Press.

Yarris, Kristin Elizabeth. 2014. "'Quiero Ir y No Quiero Ir' (I Want to Go and I Don't Want to Go): Nicaraguan Children's Ambivalent Experiences of Transnational Family Life." *Journal of American and Caribbean Anthropology* 19.2: 284–309.

Yosso, Tara J., and Daniel G. Solórzano. 2006. "Leaks in the Chicana and Chicano Educational Pipeline." Latino Policy and Issues Brief 13 (March):. UCLA Chicano Studies Research Center.

Zavella, Patricia. 2011. *I'm Neither Here nor There: Mexicans' Quotidian Struggles with Migration and Poverty*. Durham, NC: Duke University Press.

INDEX

Abrego, Leisy J., 9, 44, 56, 66

Age: category, 24; decision-making, 5, 7, 24–28; as factor, 141; and gender, 130, 159, 170; and gender and sex, 208; as identity, 22, 24; intersections of, 22–23, 33, 87, 133; and obligations, 201; and sex, 126; 128; social capital/networks, 24; and waiting, 18

Agency: display, 70, 101, 123; fragile, 6–13, 59, 130, 164–165, 170, 178, 204; gendered practices and, 207; girls and, 6; hierarchy of, 5; improvisation, of, 208; locating, 10, 20; temporal, 25; transitioning, 23, 25

Alexander, Jaqui M., 151

Altamira, José, 174

Alvarez, Robert Jr., 46

Ambiguity. *See* Temporality

Amuchástegui Herrera, Ana, 19, 113, 116, 132. *See also* Temporality

Andreas, Peter, 46

Anzaldúa, Gloria, 151. *See also* Borderlands

Anxiety. *See* Temporality

Appadurai, Arjun, 14, 20, 26, 52, 54

Arrival: diaspora, 19, 62; immigrants, 174, 177; migration, 121, 117; place, 10, 110

Barron, Cheryll, 191

Basch, Linda, 16

Bauman, Zygmunt, 21

Boehm, Deborah, 120

Bonfill Batalla, Guillermo, 18, 55, 113

Border, 5, 10, 12, 14, 16, 20, 37, 46; border patrol, 41, 45–46, 165; Chiapas-

Guatemala, 130; control, 42, 45–47, 149, 156, 194; crossing, 12, 17, 45–46, 150–152, 164–166, 169, 203; divides families, 12, 20, 36, 53, 115, 141, 205; elasticity, 47, 138, 151–152, 162, 164, 169; militarization of, 17, 39, 45–46; national politics, 12; operation gatekeeper, 46; operation hold the line, 46; production of illegality, 5, 13; transcending, 16, 20, 62, 205; U.S.-Mexico 8, 24, 41, 43, 46, 130, 169, 181. *See also* Immigration policy

Borderlands, 62, 82; inhabiting, 59, 82, 205; living within, 62; policing, 45. *See also* Identity

Boys: migration as rite of passage for, 130, 142; shared experience, 23–25; social capital/networks, 23, 130

Bracero program, 41–43; descendants, 36, 69; guest-worker program, 40; migration, 47, 175, 193; termination of, 41–42; wives of, 42. *See also* Immigration policy

Bush, George H. W., 50

Calderón, Felipe, 29, 116

California: anti-immigrant sentiment, 31, 50, 144, 183, 190; commutes to, 15, 40; missions, 174; Proposition 187, 50; receiving state, 19, 41, 59, 62; wine, 175. *See also* Napa

Camacho, Alicia Schmidt, 9, 10–11, 15–54, 177, 178

Cantú, Lionel, 24

Carillo, Hector, 24

ABOUT THE AUTHOR

Lilia Soto is Associate Professor of American Studies and Latina/o Studies at the University of Wyoming. From a historical and ethnographic position, her research focuses on comparative/relational race and ethnic studies, transnational migration, identity formation, and the interconnectedness of time, place, age, gender, and sexuality.